fixed it

Jane Gilmore was the founding editor of *The King's Tribune*. She is now a freelance journalist and a regular columnist for *The Age* and *Sydney Morning Herald*. Jane holds a Master of Journalism at the University of Melbourne and has a particular interest in feminism, media and data journalism.

fixed it

VIOLENCE AND THE REPRESENTATION OF WOMEN IN THE MEDIA

Jane Gilmore

VIKING
an imprint of
PENGUIN BOOKS

VIKING

UK | USA | Canada | Ireland | Australia
India | New Zealand | South Africa | China

Penguin
Random House
Australia

Viking is part of the Penguin Random House group of companies
whose addresses can be found at global.penguinrandomhouse.com.

First published by Viking, an imprint of Penguin Random House Australia Pty Ltd 2019

Cover design by Adam Laszczuk © Penguin Random House Australia Pty Ltd
Typeset by Midland Typesetters, Australia
Printed and bound in Australia by Griffin Press, part of Ovato, an accredited ISO AS/NZS 14001
Environmental Management Systems printer.

A catalogue record for this
book is available from the
National Library of Australia

ISBN 978 0 14379 550 6

penguin.com.au

MIX
Paper from
responsible sources
FSC® C009448

To my mother, who taught me how to think,
and Margaret Simons, who taught me how to write

Contents

Introduction

I slid into journalism sideways on a banana skin. When I was in Year Eleven I was offered a cadetship at *The Age*. After many arguments with my mother, and some adolescent door-slamming, I finally agreed to finish school first and apply for the cadetship again after I graduated. I did finish school but didn't get the cadetship. It was fifteen years before I came back to journalism. In those fifteen years I travelled a bit, had children a bit, worked a bit, got an undergrad in accounting and finally came back to journalism one night in a pub after an air guitar competition.

Our local wine bar, The King of Tonga, used to run trivia nights and talent competitions, as well as the aforementioned air guitar competition. After we'd finished applying all the neck braces to the heavy metal fans, and downed more than a few drinks, someone suggested the bar needed its own newspaper to report on vital issues such as who won the air guitar competition, who should have won the air guitar competition and who had been bribing the judges with free pints during the air guitar competition. Thus, *The King's Tribune* was born.

The first issue was a double-sided A4 page, full of typos, with an amateur layout and genuinely terrible writing. It slowly got bigger and better, but no less full of typos. After six months, we took it out of the bar, picked up some local advertising and turned it into a small local newspaper. A year later we were distributing it across Melbourne as a snappy little zine that covered politics, current affairs and social commentary. Three years later it was a full-size glossy magazine with a national subscriber base. By this stage advertising and subscriptions were very nearly covering our costs. My accounting degree had helped me land a boring but well-paid job playing with spreadsheets, so I was able to afford a media hobby. *The King's Tribune* went online in 2008 and continued until 2014 as a semi-successful independent publication. We published some amazing writers – some of whom had never been published before and are now writing professionally – and I am still proud of the journalism we did. We were heavily critical of mainstream media and had all the arrogance of ignorance and passion. After seven years of barely staying afloat, *The King's Tribune* was hit by the same financial challenges that were facing all media outlets at the time. The changing digital landscape meant advertisers no longer needed us, and subscribers weren't enough to keep us going. I fought it longer than I should have, and finally, in September 2014 I killed my darling. But I wasn't done with writing news. I packed in the safe and boring spreadsheet job and started a career as a freelance journalist.

I'd been skating around the edge of mainstream journalism long enough to know how difficult it can be. But I was also far enough from the traditions of media to see the problems bias and sexism created, especially when they were reporting on men's violence against women.

In July 2013 a woman called Tracy Connelly was murdered in Melbourne. It made headlines in most of the national newspapers, all of which used some variation of the phrase 'St Kilda Prostitute Killed'. The story dropped off the front page of every website within a day.

Less than a year before Tracy's murder, another woman, Jill Meagher, was murdered. Remember Jill? How could we forget her? So young, so beautiful, so beloved, so normal. The reporting reached saturation with a gorgeous photo of her happy, smiling face. We saw footage of her poor, heartbroken husband and heard the shocked and trembling voices of her colleagues at the ABC. The coverage went on for weeks. It made her a real person to everyone who read about her murder.

But what about the 'St Kilda Prostitute'? Was she not just as much a person as Jill? Tracy Connelly was forty years old when she was murdered. She lived just a few streets from my house. Tracy was real; she was a person, she had a community who valued her and a boyfriend who loved her. Why was she so dehumanised in the coverage of her murder?

The answer is, of course, all too obvious. She wasn't a person, she was a 'prostitute'. The news stories sensationalised some aspects of her life – her line of work – and ignored all the parts of her life that made her a person, the things the coverage of Jill Meagher's included that humanised her so thoroughly.

The way the media chose to frame Tracy's story, by constantly referring to her as a 'prostitute', suggested that in some way she deserved what happened to her. That she should have known better, and that she was asking for trouble by doing the work she did.

The opening lines of a story about her murder in *The Age* in July 2013 read:

Tracy Connelly had walked St Kilda's red light district for at least a decade and knew her work was dangerous. In 2005, her minder was run over by a man who was angry that she refused to get in his car, Ms Connelly once told a court.

What if, instead of 'St Kilda Prostitute Brutally Murdered', the headline had been: 'Tracy Connelly Brutally Murdered in Her Home Yesterday'?

What if they'd led with a photogenic image of Tracy's beautiful, pale, smiling face and this paragraph:

> Tracy Connelly's traumatised boyfriend discovered her body in their home yesterday afternoon. There was no sign of forced entry and police believe she may have been killed by someone she knew. Tearful friends talked about what a caring, loving person Tracy was, and how devastated their community is by this horrible crime.

Would Tracy be a person to us then? Would she be so easily forgotten? Or would we have to wait until her killer, like Adrian Bayley, attacked a white, middle-class woman for the world to remember that a murdered woman is a person? That no person asks for or deserves murder, or any other form of attack. That blaming the victim is never acceptable, regardless of their profession, clothing, activities or housing circumstances.

Being a sex worker is dangerous. But it's not as though sex workers are surrounded by dangerous chemicals or heavy machinery or wild animals. It's dangerous because they are working with men. Their work makes them vulnerable to the sort of men who want to be violent to women who have little means of defending themselves. It's not the people who do sex work who cause the danger. It's the men who take advantage of their circumstances to commit violence. But the underlying assumption, that sex workers are responsible for the violence done to them, is reproduced and exacerbated by news media reports.

The media (both mainstream and social) are easy to blame because they are our only source of information about what happens in the wider world, beyond our immediate circle. The way they frame that information – the words they use, the level of coverage and importance given to a story, the type of details that might be emphasised or omitted – influences how we think of it. Jill Meagher, ABC staffer, was one of their own. They reported her death as the tragic event it was. Tracy was not one of their own – her life was very different from the vast majority of mainstream journalists' lives – so she was reduced to a stereotype.

The simplicity of the Fixed It project, where I take a red pen to headlines, hadn't occurred to me back then, but I wrote about Tracy and how her murder had been portrayed in the media. The response was overwhelming. People in her community got in touch to tell me about the rage they felt seeing Tracy dehumanised by every newspaper in the country. Women from all over the world sent me headlines from their local news outlets, saying journalists turned murdered women into salacious, sensationalised clickbait. The most heartbreaking were the people who knew and loved a murdered woman, and had to watch as the media blamed her for her own murder and made excuses for the man who killed her.

'Why don't journalists think women are people?' read the subject line of one email.

After Tracy's murder, and the contemptible way it was reported in the press, I started seeing it everywhere. Not just in crime reports but also in political reporting, sports reporting, even articles about musicians and artists. Women are not people in the eyes of the news, at least not the way men are. Women are tits and arse, they're glamorous or fat, they're wives or mothers or stupid or demanding or nagging or annoying or sweet or pretty. Men, on the other hand, are fully-rounded, complex people – as long as they're not too 'womanlike'.

After responding to the treatment of Tracy in the media, I continued writing articles and blog posts about it, but nothing ever really cut through. Then, in September 2015, one of the major news sites in Australia published an article about a man who murdered his ex-girlfriend under the headline: 'Townsville police say selfie could have led to alleged stabbing murder'. I pulled out my phone, fixed the headline and snapped it back on Twitter. Fixed It was born.

Townsville police say ~~selfie could have led to~~ man's decision to stab a woman caused **alleged stabbing murder**

After that first fix, which got a huge response on social media, I started noticing terrible headlines more and more. I tried a few different ways of calling attention to them but nothing was as effective as the simple red-pen rewrite. A picture was quite literally worth a thousand words. Within a few months I was regularly scanning news sites and by the beginning of 2016 I had set up daily Google alerts for any news story about men's violence against women. I was making the fixes on a daily basis and posting them on a website I had originally set up as a focal point for my freelance writing. Over the next two years Fixed It gained a strong social media following and I found myself regularly speaking at public events and writing articles about the way the media reports men's violence against women. I incorporated it into my Master's degree and spent hundreds of hours researching the cause and effect of this kind of reporting. This book is the culmination of all that work.

There have been hundreds of headlines in Fixed It over that time. Drunk teenagers getting themselves raped, lying sex workers, houses committing rape, brooms beating women, loving fathers killing their children, Susan Sarandon being old in public, broken hearts causing murder, women too stupid to understand superannuation, Bill Clinton's wife running for president, forty-year-old men in 'sexual relationships' with twelve-year-old girls, the prime minister of England's legs, women too old to be hot while playing football, domestic violence 'stunts', 'sex romps' killing MPs, countless invisible murderers and endless victim blaming.

In all that time, only one editor has ever got in touch to ask how they could write stories about women differently. Otherwise, journalists and editors don't engage. And I understand. No one likes to be publicly smacked down, and it can be frustrating and humiliating to be accused of sexism or victim blaming – particularly if the journalists involved think I don't understand the pressures they're under or the legal restraints they must work within. This was certainly true in the early days of Fixed It. But now I have a much better understanding of and more sympathy for court reporters and editors of online news who have to do far too much with far too little. I also recognise the limitations of reporting on crimes that have not been through the court. You can't call someone a rapist if he has not been convicted of rape. But even taking into account these limitations, there are ways to rethink how we report such crimes. For example, you can (and should) call it an alleged rape instead of 'sex'. The presumption of innocence does not prevent someone describing an alleged crime. No reporter would ever write that an accused car thief was driving their own car home because it hadn't yet been proven in court that he stole it. You would probably see headlines along the lines of: 'Kris Kafoops has been charged with theft after a car disappeared from High Street last week'; 'Police allege Kris Kafoops stole a car from High Street'; 'Alleged car thief Kris Kafoops appeared in court today'. Bog standard reporting like this wouldn't raise an eyebrow anywhere. Sexual violence, however, appears to present reporters and editors with difficulties that don't occur in any other criminal act. Far too often, alleged rape is reported as 'sex', which is not a crime. Rape is not sex and no one has ever been charged with having consensual sex. 'Kris Kafoops faces court over sex claim' is as inaccurate in reporting on an alleged rape as 'Kris Kafoops faces court over driving a car claim' would be in reporting on an alleged car theft.

The rules of sub judice contempt require that journalists cannot report someone is guilty of a crime before they are convicted, which is why the word 'alleged' is so ubiquitous in crime reporting. This does not explain or excuse the way rape is so often described as sex, as if the words are interchangeable. They're not. It happens because all the myths about violence are so deeply embedded in our culture, and further entrenched by journalism. There was a vast difference in how Tracy Connelly and Jill Meagher were each treated by media in their respective murders. Tracy was dehumanised, Jill was not, and this is not unique to Australia or even to modern reporting. For millennia, women have been divided into 'good women' – wives and mothers, sweetly pretty, conservatively dressed nice girls, and 'bad women' – sirens and sex workers, drug addicts, page three girls and drunken, promiscuous sluts. Good women are help-less victims, but bad women ask for trouble. The reality is that there is no type of woman who could conceivably deserve violence, but this entrenched division of good and bad women still strongly influences how traditional media report on complex issues, and reduces women to these arbitrary categories.

For this reason, the main focus of this book is on the violence men commit against women and children. But before we get under way, there are a few standard assumptions and responses to address.

MAN-HATING FEMINISTS

Feminists are often perceived as ball-breaking, man-hating hysterics, who think every man is a rapist and a wife beater. In fact, feminists argue the opposite: that men are not inherently violent simply because they are men, and they are not helpless children incapable of questioning and rejecting an idea of masculinity that endorses violence. Rather, femi-nists argue, violence is a choice made by individuals, and any person who makes that choice is responsible for it. Men don't rape and mur-der just because they are men or because they habitually lose control of themselves. They are adults and are fully able to make choices and manage their emotions. The way the media reports on sexual violence often implies that if a woman rejects or otherwise upsets a man, she is to blame for his violent reaction. I believe men are better than that. Adult men do not deserve to be treated like children and one of the most important aspects of being an adult is taking responsibility for the consequences of the choices we make.

NOT ALL MEN

No, not all men. Of course not all men. The idea that all men are rapists or violent is demonstrably false. And yet the endless cry of 'Not all men' echoes around the internet every time a woman writes about men's violence against women. What they really mean when they say not all men is, 'Specifically not *me*! I am not violent.' It's a defensive reaction to a perceived personal attack.

Men are so used to being the hero and the focus of every story that it can be difficult for them to understand that stories about women's experiences are about women, not men. The defensiveness occurs because men think those stories *are* about them.

When I am writing about violent men I am writing specifically and only about the men who commit violence. If you are not a violent man, then I'm not writing about you. If you are the kind of man who is disgusted by the idea of committing violence against the women and children in your life, then I am clearly not writing about you. Men are not all the same any more than women are all the same. Not all men are violent, but the overwhelming majority of the perpetrators of violence are men. It is a logical fallacy to conflate this with 'therefore all men are violent'.

WHAT ABOUT MALE VICTIMS AND FEMALE PERPETRATORS?

Statistically, men are more likely than women to be the victims of violence. Men are more than twice as likely to be assaulted as women, three times as likely to be murdered and six times as likely to die by suicide. The tragedy for everyone is that it is almost always men who are the perpetrators of violence, whether it's against women, children, other men or themselves. An in-depth study of crime statistics collected by Victoria Police in 2014 showed that 87 per cent of homicides, 98 per cent of sexual assaults, 83 per cent of non-sexual assaults, 90 per cent of robberies and 92 per cent of abductions were committed by men. While most of the sexual assault victims were women, the majority of victims of all other crimes were men.

There's a mass of complex interweaving reasons for the disproportionate levels of violence committed by men. The stereotype of the Aussie male – stoic, strong and unsentimental – can force men into silence, fear and isolation. Traditional gender roles that require men to be in charge and women to be submissive can make equal, loving shared relationships seem threatening to outdated concepts of masculinity. Men who feel afraid, powerless or vulnerable can feel lost in waves of frustration, fear and rage. They take that out on themselves and each other at frightening rates. While this book is not specifically about the reasons for male violence, we cannot ignore the way the media reporting can reinforce the perceptions of manliness that locks some men into a cycle of violence they don't know how to escape.

Crime reporting is not the only area of journalism where gendered treatment of news reflects a negative view of women. Politics and sport have long been the province of men and reporting on it has primarily been by and about men, despite women being active in these areas for many years. Women's professional presence in sport and politics has grown over the past few decades, but this is rarely met with comfortable acceptance in news media. Journalism has remained a conservative profession in many ways. There are longstanding traditions that haven't changed much since the 1950s. Hard news and deep investigative styles of reporting are still viewed as serious journalism and these topics are still mostly covered by men. Only experienced journalists with years in the press pack have earned the right to be taken seriously in political commentary. Female journalists in this group are still in the minority and while there are some very good female journalists in this space, they stand out precisely because they are so unusual.

The conservative male-dominated political press demonstrates a persistent discomfort with women in power, as the constant gendered badgering of Hillary Clinton and Julia Gillard so clearly showed. Who is looking after their husbands and children? Or, if they have no husband and children, what is wrong with them? Why couldn't they find a man? Why are they so emotional? Why are they so cold? Why are they so ambitious? Why are they so bossy? These sorts of questions pop up constantly, mostly implicitly but sometimes explicitly, in coverage of female politicians.

Almost all the sports pages in print and online media are devoted to men's sport. Until the last few years women weren't considered strong enough, interesting enough, tough enough or good enough to warrant mainstream coverage. While this is beginning to change, men's sport remains the focus of most sports reporting. There's sport and then there's women's sport. Sport is played by big strong men. It's also reported on by mostly men. The Mates Over Merit report conducted by Women in Media and iSentia in 2015 found that less than 10 per cent of sports reporting in print, television and radio was done by female reporters.

The only area of journalism where women dominate is in what is referred to as 'lifestyle' sections. The Mates Over Merit report showed the only topics where female reporters managed to get over the 50 per cent line (and then only just) were retail, social issues, health, lifestyle and celebrity gossip.

Lifestyle sections are an unwieldy amalgamation of feminist writing, celebrity news, social commentary, fashion and personal essays. All the things traditional newshounds dismiss as not 'real' journalism. They're rarely given any attention or credibility by male editors. It's all vaginas and cupcakes and nothing that would be relevant to 'real' news. As with sports reporting, there's news and then there's women's news.

Women make up half the population, but only about a third of the consumers of hard news. Media outlets desperate for audience share and subscribers might, in the interest of increasing their reach, pay attention to the reasons women feel excluded from journalism, both as participants and consumers. The changes in media brought about by the digital revolution demand a different approach. One of the major changes journalism is going to have to face is that the middle-class white man's point of view is not the baseline any more. Where newspapers, radio and television used to be the only source of news and thereby maintained a stranglehold on what and how news was reported, the internet gave space and voice to a huge range of different perspectives. Blogs and start-up news sites had little or no cost other than time, social media provided a connection to audiences and many people were (and still are) able to bypass the mainstream news organisations and go directly to a growing readership.

Journalism needs more voices and more faces. It needs to widen its perception of the world and understand that women, people of colour, people with disabilities and people of different genders and sexualities are all news consumers. And they are not interested in news that ignores their existence or dismisses them as archaic stereotypes.

MAKING CHANGE

There are two things I want to achieve with Fixed It. One is to push back against the conscious and subconscious language decisions made by news directors, editors and journalists. To ask them to think about the words they're using and how this shapes readers' perceptions of the world around them. The other, which may be the more important one, is to remind media consumers that journalism is no longer one-way communication and editors cannot dictate the tone and style of news without accountability to their audience.

Digital publishing and social media have given audiences enormous power. At the same time, they have soaked up the advertising revenue and barriers to entry that protected former media fiefdoms. Media outlets might not be forced to change because of one annoying feminist, but they have to listen to their audience. The only way they can stay in business is if readers trust them. They need their audiences far more than their audiences need them. The result is that by mobilising consumers to put pressure on news publications, we can collectively effect change in the language and manner of news reporting.

ABC: ~~CHILD ABUSE LINKED TO ARTS SCHOOL INCLUDED FORCING 4YO BOY TO HAVE SEX, POLICE ALLEGE~~
FIX: *CHILD ABUSE LINKED TO ARTS SCHOOL INCLUDED RAPE OF 4YO BOY, POLICE ALLEGE*
This headline relates to a horrific series of revelations of child abuse at an arts school in New South Wales between 2014 and 2016. Seven adults (four women, two men and a seventeen-year-old girl) were charged over the alleged rape and sexual abuse of three little boys. The details are graphic and devastating, even for me, and I spend too much time every day reading about abhorrent crimes.

Our publicly funded national broadcaster ran the story under a headline that described a four-year-old boy as 'having sex'. This book has an entire chapter devoted to the damage done to victims and public perception by describing rape and child abuse as 'sex'. In the few years of the Fixed It project this was, tragically, a regular theme.

Towards the end of 2017, after six months of regular posts on this specific wording, I noticed that where it used to come up almost daily it had dropped to less than one a week. The ABC headline about the child abuse at the NSW arts school appeared in February 2018. It was all the more shocking because many news outlets had retreated from misnaming abuse in this manner, but the way it played out that day proved how much things had changed.

I posted the fix on my website at 9.30 a.m. on 8 February, 2018. By 3.30 that afternoon dozens of people had made formal complaints to the ABC and the headline was changed to 'Child abuse linked to arts school included raping 4yo boy, police allege'.

People who had made complaints to the ABC forwarded to me replies from the news director apologising for the initial headline and thanking them for their intervention. All this took less than a day.

This is just one of many examples I've seen through the Fixed It project. Sometimes headlines were changed within hours of a Fixed It post going out, but the text of the article, which still included terms like 'child sex', remained, as was the case with this ABC article. Other times, editors didn't change their headlines but when I skimmed through their websites a week or so later, I'd see a change in the style of reporting similar crimes.

When readers express their anger over sexist or victim-blaming headlines, publications have to pay attention. They might not like it, they may not even truly understand it, but they don't want to be publicly shamed for doing a disservice to victims of violence. And they certainly don't like being told they are not doing their jobs properly. A journalist from News Corp told me recently that an editor she worked with wrote a headline that contained undertones of victim blaming. Before she had a chance to ask him to change it he started muttering, 'Bloody internet feminist will start yelling,' and changed it himself. In a perfect world he would have changed the headline because he understood that blaming victims for crimes committed against them is vile, but while the world is still imperfect, fear of pushback is good enough.

I love journalism and, although it might be an odd thing to say in a book all about how the media can get things so wrong, I love journalists. As a group they're passionate, smart, demanding, determined and endlessly curious. They can also be imperfect, arrogant, mired in outdated traditions and contemptuous of their audience. It's a frustrating and fascinating business but change is always possible. When enough people demand it, change is inevitable. You don't even need to be an annoying feminist to change the world, but it certainly helps.

Part I
Journalism
and Gender

Chapter 1
Why we have news

Journalism is the conduit between the power structures of society and the people who live in that society. Without journalism it would be difficult for many of us to know what goes on in our parliaments, crime, the justice system, academic and scientific research, global politics, international affairs, social justice issues and so many other things we understand more of when we consume news. It's not a perfect system. If journalists are the conduit of this information, they are also the gatekeepers. Decisions about what to report, when to report it and how to explain it are all made by people with their own biases, sympathies and gaps in knowledge. These are often subconsciously spread and reinforced. Most journalists want to do the best job they can; they work hard and with the best of intentions. When they fail it is almost always due to ignorance rather than ill intent. The effects of this are dangerous, but lack of knowledge is far easier to address than malice, and audiences are no longer the silent masses who just pay and cannot respond. They have a great deal of power and can therefore be a major part of the push for change.

WHAT IS JOURNALISM?

News, in some form, has been part of human society since we came down from the trees. It is not solely contained in the earnest reporting of Serious Investigative Reporters. Journalism is simply telling stories about ourselves and the world we live in. And we've always done that.

Town criers and court circulars existed hundreds of years before the printing press because we have always been curious about the activities of the people we know and the people we don't. What did the King wear to his coronation? Where is the wool we shear from our sheep being sold? Who committed the gruesome murder in the village two days' ride from here? How tight are our breeches now and what colour should they be? What laws exist in our society and who is breaking them? What wars are being fought and who is winning? How is crime punished and how are great achievements recognised? Who has power and what are they doing with it?

People have always wanted to know the answer to these questions and consuming journalism is how they find those answers. And of course, it has always had its dark side. Spreading propaganda and fear to maintain existing power structures is the flip side of the revolutionary press. Tension between the status quo and the need for change are entwined in the history of journalism.

One of the first newspapers ever issued was a monthly handwritten paper published by the government of Venice in 1556. It cost one gazetta (thus the word 'gazette' that so frequently appears in the titles of newspapers) and was used to give information about political, military and economic news in Europe to the merchant class.

Gutenberg's printing press in 1440 had been the beginning of mass media and by the 1600s most major cities in Europe were producing an early form of newspapers. Monarchies all over Europe attempted some method of censorship but it worked no better then than it does now. Angry young revolutionaries have never been easily silenced, and mass production of revolutionary screeds has been an effective way of inciting outrage since Gutenberg and the industrial age combined to give us easily produced writing for the newly literate masses.

Over the centuries journalism developed from a trade to a craft and then into a profession. But the beginnings of journalism are still reflected in the modern era. Some publications pride themselves on producing impartial balanced reporting. Others are wildly partisan and exist to push a political or social agenda. Some are global conglomerates that cover all forms of news; others run on a shoestring and focus solely on one specific issue. The digital age has given people unprecedented access to skip across all these publications without requiring that we pick one masthead and stick to it.

WHAT IS NEWS?

It is part of the business of a newspaper to get news and to print it; it is part of the business of a politician to prevent certain news being printed.

Journalism as a Profession, Lord Northcliffe, 1903

News used to be whatever editors decided it would be. They were the gatekeepers and the agenda setters. To some degree they were anticipating an audience response, but it was difficult to measure how much engagement each story had with readers and there was very little data to put against an editor's personal biases. Now, when every website can find granular details on who is reading each story, how long they spend reading it and how often they share it, audiences have far more influence on the subject and style of news.

In May 2017 Carter Wilkerson, a sixteen-year-old from Nevada, tweeted at Wendy's, a fast-food outlet, to ask how many retweets he'd need to get a year of free chicken nuggets. Whoever was managing the

Wendy's Twitter account came back with what was almost certainly a throwaway line and told him he'd need 18 million. He's now got nearly 4 million retweets. How do we know this? It's been reported in hundreds of outlets around the world and a Google search of his name brings up over 400 000 results.

A teenage boy wants free chicken nuggets. Is that news? Pretty much every major news outlet in the world thought it was. *The New York Times*, CBS, *USA Today*, *Time*, *Forbes*, *The Daily Mail*, the BBC and *The Guardian* published articles about chicken nugget kid, but what exactly makes it newsworthy news? And does being newsworthy make something journalism?

These are perennial questions, inextricably linked, and there are no definitive answers. But it might help to have a clear understanding of what journalism is and what purpose it is supposed to serve.

One of the best definitions of journalism, which appears in the MEAA code of ethics for journalists, is that it describes society to itself. News (reporting on events that happen day to day) is part of journalism. Analysis, commentary, opinion, rants and even cartoons are also part of journalism, even if they're not news. Comment and opinion pieces are telling society about the ideas present within itself. Analysis pulls apart those ideas and examines their viability. Cartoons and satire can help us question unexamined preconceptions and thereby recognise the issues that are part of our society.

So if we return to the story of the chicken nuggets teen, we see an example of both news and journalism. *The Guardian* didn't only report to its readers that a sixteen-year-old boy wanted free chicken nuggets, they also investigated and reported on how corporations are using social media as a marketing tool. The Wendy's Twitter account kept the tweet going with retweets, jokes and celebrity endorsements. Other brands, including Google, Amazon and Microsoft, got involved too. A mattress company offered Wilkerson a free mattress if he got the 18 million retweets and United Airlines promised a free flight to any Wendy's outlet in the world.

Take another example of news versus 'newsworthy'. In 2017, *The Sun* reported a story with the headline, 'RUDEY DENCH: Dame Judi Dench says she still has sexual desires at 82 – and still loves naughty knickers'.

A woman in her eighties has an active sex life and doesn't get about in voluminous granny pants. It was reported by most of the media outlets in the U.K. as well as *The New York Post, The Jakarta Post, The New York Times* and CBS, among many others. It also generated dozens of comment pieces discussing whether it is okay for older women to display sexuality and why the very notion of it is so bewildering, or even threatening. The extent of the reporting and comment pieces shows how newsworthy it was deemed to be. But it also proves the disparity in how journalism, and society, view men as opposed to women. Imagine Rupert Murdoch declaring in an interview that he still enjoys an active sex life and likes to wear silk boxer shorts (apologies to my readers for the imagery; this book does not always make for comfortable reading). Would it elicit such patronising delight as with Dame Judi? Rupert Murdoch hasn't in fact declared such a thing in an interview, but it's also very possible that no interviewer would think to ask a man whether he still has a sex life in his later years. They just assume he does. If a man in his eighties confessed to losing his sexual desire or ability, the implication might be that he'd lost something of his manhood. Women on the other hand lose all sexuality by that age, in the eyes of society. Even Judi Dench, one of the most beautiful and talented women in the world.

News, therefore, is a lot more than just what happens in police stations and parliaments. All the events of society are news, even if they are not always reported. Journalism is how we understand the events that are reported and fit them into our understanding of the world. The role of journalists in this process is to choose what events to report and the context we give them.

Who chooses the stories?

There has always been tension between editors and journalists on what is deemed newsworthy enough for a story. Journalists will go to editors with something they are convinced is a story. They might be given grudging permission to follow it up. The editor might bin it immediately. Or they might spend months working together on it. A lot depends on the editor, the journalists, the relationship between them, and their abilities to find and recognise news.

Editors also commission stories. A journalist once told me about the time her editor sent her off to investigate because someone on Twitter had mentioned a weird smell in north-east Melbourne. She spent a couple of hours driving around the area with her head out the car window trying to sniff it out. She asked dog walkers and busy shopkeepers if they'd noticed any unusual smells, even stopped at the police station to ask if anyone had reported a smell. All she found out was that people get offended when you ask if they've noticed any bad smells, and most cops find fart jokes hilarious. And sure, it sounds like a farce, but it could very easily have been news. What if the smell was caused by a gas leak, illegally dumped waste or toxic pollution? Journalists often do not know whether something is news until they've spent a fair bit of time investigating.

But budget cuts and limited resources in the modern newsroom probably mean that weird smells in Eltham don't get investigated any more. A gas leak or illegal waste would only become news if the authorities got involved and even then, only if someone cared enough to tip off a journalist.

News about crime is suffering the same restraints. Courts and police stations used to be regular beats for journalists. And they were training grounds for young reporters learning the basics of accurate, relevant and legal journalism. Report on a thief being convicted in court and get his name wrong and suddenly you're on the wrong end of a defamation suit. And rightly so, if you've told the world that an innocent man was stealing from his workplace. Try to publish five stories on a guy who got done for stealing stationery from his office and not only will no one read your stories, they might stop reading all the stories in your publication because they don't think it has anything interesting to tell them.

In 2013 the Los Angeles Superior Court shaved $10 million off its budget by getting rid of more than sixty official court reporters. One court, one city, one budget cut. That decision has been repeated countless times around the world and most of the lower courts now operate without any scrutiny. High profile or particularly shocking cases might still make the news but the day-to-day operations of the lower courts and magistrates are rarely seen in the news cycle.

In some cases there is no one at all standing between a reporter and the outside world and this can have disastrous consequences.

In 2015 Yahoo7 journalist Krystal Johnson published an article about a murder trial in Melbourne. Johnson, who had not been in court to report on the case, copied details from an accurate article about an earlier hearing, including some material from Facebook, to use in her piece. What she didn't know was that the details she'd included had been declared inadmissible by the judge and were therefore not supposed to be available to the jury. Because of her article, the judge declared a mistrial. It was a terrible outcome for everyone involved, and although the accused was eventually convicted of beating his girlfriend to death, her family had to suffer through two trials and more delays before they could put the trauma of the trial behind them.

Johnson was eventually found guilty of contempt of court and Yahoo7 was fined and convicted. Justice John Dixon found the company had had 'primary responsibility for the contempt'. He also found that Yahoo7 had failed to ensure its systems for supervising journalists and controlling the publication of information 'were sufficient to prevent prejudicial material from being aired'.

He recognised the reasons for this, stating that commercial and time pressures were understandably at the forefront of Yahoo7's considerations, and that 'in view of the kind of high-volume, time-pressured work Yahoo7 expected of its journalists, Johnson's mistake was readily foreseeable'.

In the digital age, we have a much wider scope for finding news ourselves. The prominence of social media timelines and sharing means that audiences are leading the news cycle. Journalists find themselves glued to their phones, searching for snippets they can pick up from the zeitgeist. Picking up on an off-colour tweet or a hilarious photo is quick, easy and cheap. If you can get people angry or make them laugh, a piece that took ten minutes to write can suddenly be shared widely and prominently. It's entirely understandable that media outlets prefer to spend their limited resources on churning out shareable audience-building pieces than devoting days or even weeks to a single story that will disappear within hours. *Buzzfeed* built a global business on exactly that premise. And if you respect the audience, you have to respect the content they choose.

Increasingly, it is the audience who chooses the news, within the confines of the material served to them by Google and Facebook. They choose with their clicks and shares and email sign-ups and subscriptions. If journalism is failing in its duty to describe what is happening in society, at least part of the reason for that is the audiences who don't want or think they don't need to know about more complex (or boring) stories.

Journalism, however, is not an innocent victim here. The rivers of gold might have dried up but publications like *The Guardian* and *The New York Times* are expanding their operations and subscriber lists on the basis of producing quality journalism. And there are thousands of smaller magazines and online publications still putting out intelligent, useful and original reporting to an engaged readership who are only too willing to pay for it. It is disingenuous for publications to chase the lowest common denominator down the drain and then blame their audience for not leading them out of the sewage. The variety of news available is a reflection of the variety of audience interests.

Journalism is going through a seismic change and how we define news and journalism will be shaken even more before it's over. Whatever definition we end up with will be an unprecedented collaboration between the producers and consumers of news and it is vitally important that readers understand the power they have in changing the way journalists understand the purpose of their profession.

VIOLENCE IN THE NEWS

Violence has always sold newspapers. Monstrous criminals make the best headlines. Jack the Ripper, the Boston Strangler, Mr Cruel.

But, until very recently, the everyday violence of ordinary people was rarely the subject of journalism. Before the early 2000s, the newsroom never screamed to a halt when the police scanner reported that a plumber in the suburbs beat his wife. It's 'just a domestic', a 'private matter', not news a real newsman would waste his time on.

If it was a particularly weird or gruesome murder, or if the circumstances were salacious enough, the gutter press might come out with screaming headlines like 'Axe Murder in the Leafy Suburbs', 'Jealous Wife Stabs Husband and His Lover' or 'Unfaithful Wife Buried Under Potting Shed'. Otherwise, such things were not the subject of Serious News.

Most of us have heard the term domestic violence, but it's relatively new to the mainstream media. And because it covers a range of behaviours and scenarios, its meaning can seem vague. Too often it is taken to mean purely physical violence rather than a pattern of behaviour designed to exert power and control over the victims. The cold rage of a successful man in an expensive suit interrogating his wife about where she was at lunchtime is domestic violence. As is a young man intimidating his brothers and sisters into silence and fear, or a middle-aged woman keeping her aged and infirm parent imprisoned in their home, sick and underfed. Domestic violence, when it is not properly understood, appears simple; physical, definable, visible and escapable. The truth is that it is none of these things. Journalists who write about domestic violence have a responsibility to explain that.

JOURNALISM JARGON

Journalism, like any profession, has its own jargon and customs. Even people who consume a lot of journalism don't necessarily know the ins and outs of what makes up a news story. On the other hand, some readers may be familiar with these terms. If so, think of the following pages as a refresher.

Ledes, hard news, op eds and features

The lede refers to the first paragraph of a news story, which sometimes appears in bold at the top of the article. Traditionally it is no longer than thirty words, and summarises the most important points the reader needs to know first. Reporters might write their own ledes but they're frequently rewritten by editors or subeditors.

Hard news stories are usually around 600 words and typically conform to the inverted pyramid style, where the most important information comes at the top of the story and background details are at the bottom. Hard news is supposed to be just the facts: it provides new information and answers only the basic questions of who, what, when, where, why and how. For example, when the terrorist shootings at the Christchurch mosques occurred, hard news stories reported information on the shooter, the number of victims and whether he had been caught.

Opinion pieces can be news, but they include the one element that is not supposed to exist in hard news – personal opinions of the writer. It's the difference between reporting that a terrorist had attacked Muslims in Christchurch and discussing the reasons the terrorist had become radicalised to the point of committing mass murder.

Feature pieces sit somewhere between hard news and op eds. They're typically longer than other forms of journalism and give a lot more context and background to their subjects. A feature piece on the Christchurch shootings might give more details about the victims' lives, stories about individual acts of heroism or grief and background on how they came to join that particular mosque and what they did for the community there. A slightly different feature piece, more correctly labelled analysis, would be something like Jessie Smith's article for the *Sydney Morning Herald* called 'Christchurch: Why avoiding terror laws might be best for victims'. Smith is a former Melbourne criminal defence lawyer currently studying for her PhD at Cambridge in counter-terror law and is thus qualified to examine the relevant laws and analyse the pros and cons of applying the legislation to specific acts.

Who writes the headlines?

Journalists never used to write the headlines for their own articles. Newspaper headlines were written by subeditors and approved by editors. Subeditors would also check every word in an article before it was published. They'd correct grammar, spelling and punctuation, check facts, make sure the writing was clear and readable, and sometimes cut text to fit into a defined space on the printed page.

While that is still the case with some print media, in most digital publications the lines between editor, subeditor and journalist are blurring. Many news outlets will still have subeditors for the print edition but rely on editors only for the online version. They essentially do a job that was once shared by two or three people. Editors assign stories to staff reporters and commission the growing number of freelancers; they proof, sub and edit articles, write the headlines, choose the images and send the finished piece online, often with little or no assistance. Editors do the best they can, but when you have one person working across a number of roles, each requiring different skill sets, it becomes near impossible to maintain an expert level of quality and accuracy.

SEO vs clickbait

SEO stands for search engine optimisation. In the simplest terms, it's about getting links to a specific website as close to the top of the Google search as possible.

A Google search on Donald Trump brings up about 265 million results. The first entry that comes up is a link to his Twitter account, the second is a link to his Wikipedia page. Links under that move around a lot depending on where he's making news on any given day. On 16 September, 2017, the third link was a CNN story titled 'The Volcanic Temper of Donald Trump'. It was about Trump's latest tantrum over investigations into Russian involvement in the 2016 election. So how did the CNN story beat out so many millions of others to get into the top five?

Search engines like Google and Bing work like sophisticated library catalogues. Programs called crawlers scan every page on the internet and use complex algorithms to determine what the page is about and the search words that should bring it up. The crawlers look at the title, text and images, but they also note and count all the links to and from the individual page and the site more generally. Google keeps track of high traffic and reputable sites. CNN will always sit higher on Google search results than a news site dedicated to a small country town because it has millions of people clicking in and out each day, plus millions of tweets, Facebook posts, blogs and other media outlets linking to thousands of stories across the CNN site.

SEO is a lot more complex than I can go into here, but it is relevant when we talk about the language of headlines.

The Google crawlers look at the entire text of an article, but the title of the article has more impact on where the piece ends up in the search results than the text. For a news story to have strong SEO potential, it needs key search terms as near the beginning of the headline as possible. The CNN article on Trump would also have had keywords hidden in the website's code for the Google crawlers that would probably focus on words like 'angry', 'temper', 'Russia' and 'election'. But the article title has more impact on the Google algorithm than the hidden keywords, so Trump's name and 'temper' are words an editor has probably seen coming up in a lot of recent Google searches.

Clickbait is different. It is geared towards making readers curious or angry or amused enough to click on a link, and can be quite misleading. Clickbait headlines often look like this: 'One Simple Change to My Diet and You'll Never Believe What Happened Next!', 'Headless Body in Topless Bar', 'Welfare Queen "Too Beautiful" to Get a Job', '19 Quokka Photos So Cute They'll Make You Scream at Your Phone in Delight'. Even when we recognise these headlines as clickbait, they can still draw us in. Besides, who wouldn't want to share adorable photos of a quokka with all their friends on Facebook?

Hard news stories are an uneasy combination of SEO and clickbait. If it is breaking news, people aren't necessarily searching for it, so hitting high search results is less of a priority at this point. But as the story spreads across the internet, people start using search engines to find out more. The first few stories break the news, while follow-up articles provide more detail and analysis. The breaking story needs as much detail in as few words as possible, but the follow-up articles must be attractive to those Google crawlers, putting out the right data so this particular news organisation's articles come up first in searches.

All these factors contribute to the decisions editors make about the headlines they write. There are others, such as time and resource pressures and subconscious biases, but we'll come to those later.

Chapter 2
Male-dominated newsrooms and why it matters

Women have had a presence in journalism for hundreds of years, but they've traditionally been limited to women's magazines or lifestyle sections in newspapers, while male journalists have tended to dominate the 'hard news' sections. Though this has slowly changed over the past forty years – some truly exceptional women have built strong careers as journalists – modern newsrooms still tend to be male-skewed, and most senior positions in mainstream journalism are held by men.

Feminists, and those often rendered invisible by society, such as people of colour, single mothers, children and young people, the LGBTQIA+ community, people with disabilities and other minority groups, have always tried to combat the way words are used in the media to maintain the status quo. Social media opened a space for conversations and transmission, so these groups were able to reframe conversations and offer an easily accessible alternative to the messages of mainstream media. They remain, however, on the fringe. The majority of news consumed by the public still comes from mainstream sources, made up of those newsrooms I described earlier – with straight white men very much at the helm of the hard news cycle. The problem becomes apparent: how can journalism 'describe society to itself' when those doing the describing are so homogenous in a diverse society? The values and assumptions and the structural, hidden biases inform how men in the newsroom 'choose the news' and unintentionally distort the description, rendering it unrecognisable to the majority of people living in it.

'REAL JOURNALISM'

Scholars and industry bodies have studied the changes in the field, as a result of technology, in particular, in how journalism is defined. While almost all definitions agree that the purpose of journalism is to provide information to the general public, there is some disagreement over the methods and elements of journalism, as opposed to mere publication. One of the main points of difference is whether 'real' journalism must fulfil the traditional requirements of being objective, independent and verifiable. In other words, the industry disagrees over whether any writing about opinion or personal experience can still count as journalism.

Bill Kovach and Tom Rosenstiel are among the leading academics of modern journalism. Their 2007 in-depth consultation with journalists and academics concluded that journalism's primary obligation is to the truth. It must be independent, proportional, comprehensive and seek verification. The journalists surveyed believed journalism's first loyalty is to citizens, and that one of its main purposes is to provide them with the information they need to function in a free and self-governing democracy. The American Press Institute specifically excludes opinion and assertion from journalism and stresses the importance of verification. The Australian Code of Ethics, on the other hand, includes providing opinion and ideas as well as verified information in its list of recognisable forms of journalism.

Through the late 90s and early 2000s, the digital age crashed through all the high-cost barriers to entry that had kept mainstream news unassailable for so long. Niche publications and websites run by and for minority groups rose all over the world, finding large and loyal audiences who were delighted to finally see their views and voices represented. But the problem remained: how to pay for the effort that goes into producing free content? Mainstream digital news faced the same problem. Some of the independent news sites, such as *Mamamia*, *Crikey* and *New Matilda*, were able to convert their specific market into advertising income, while others scrape by on subscriber revenues. *Mamamia* and *Crikey* have both gone beyond mere survival and expanded far beyond their one-person-and-a-keyboard start.

This concept of 'serious' journalism, that is, impersonal, verifiable and independent truth, is based on gendered standards. Journalism was historically almost entirely the domain of men. Thus the ethics and definition of journalism are embedded with values traditionally ascribed to male intelligence, such as logic and objectivity. Traditionally feminine values, such as empathy and community, are not highly regarded in journalism. Their feminised nature is set against and below the masculine ones. Obviously, these notions are firmly based in outdated concepts that assign personal characteristics to gender rather than personality, environment or learned behaviour, but at the time they were entrenched in journalistic values they were seen as essential to the concept of the strong (male) reporter. Because of this, one of the concepts of journalism raised by noted journalism scholar Michael Schudson is frequently ignored by journalists who grew up inculcated with the old-school ideas of objectivity and verification. Schudson said 'social empathy' is a basic requirement of journalism. Social empathy encourages compassion for people whose lives are unexplored in public debate and often means using personal stories to illustrate larger themes. This is something he advocated as being particularly beneficial in male-dominated topics such as political journalism and war and conflict reporting, where the human cost is often discounted.

There is, of course, the exception that proves the rule, where a tough, cynical newspaperman can write an emotive, personal piece about a particular experience as a journalist in terrible circumstances. War zones, disaster reporting or bereavement are particular favourites in this genre, and men who do it are almost always lauded for their brave step outside the traditions of journalism. Books by male journalists, such as Anderson Cooper's *Dispatches from the Edge: A Memoir of War, Disasters, and Survival*, Seymour Hersh's *Reporter: A Memoir* and Alan Rusbridger's memoir, *Breaking News: The Remaking of Journalism and Why It Matters Now*, are often described as compelling, or noted as being remarkable in their self-reflection. Chris Ayres's *War Reporting for Cowards* was described as entertaining and unconventional. Reviews of memoir by female journalists, however, can be highly gendered. Kim Barker's *Taliban Shuffle: Strange Days in Afghanistan and Pakistan* was met with some praise but equal amounts of derision, where she was dismissed as an ingénue (a word that does not have a male equivalent) and castigated for being impolite, overly sentimental, self-obsessed, lacking politesse, and shallow. Likewise, *Every Man in This Village is a Liar: An Education in War* by Megan Stack was praised for its journalism but also criticised for writing described as melodramatic, compassionate, moving, beautiful, intimate, ornate, flowery, intimate and emotional. Such differences in language demonstrate the usually subconscious bias deeply embedded in expectations of men's and women's writing. Kim Barker noted this in a 2016 interview with *The Guardian* after her memoir was adapted into a feature film:

Why are women only allowed one narrative? We have one overseas adventure and that's supposed to be *Eat, Pray, Love*. It's supposed to end in a man. And this is not that . . . It just goes to show the limited span that we've got for women and adventure stories.

As Kim Barker noted, women's journalism is not given the same freedom of movement as men's journalism. Women are expected to either play by the rules of 'serious' journalism and write in the traditional format, or write about emotions, meaning they get siloed off to women's writing, intended only for a female audience.

MALE-DOMINATED NEWSROOMS

Gender skews in journalism have been the subject of research and analysis for years. Almost every study in the U.K., U.S., Australia, Canada and New Zealand has come up with depressingly similar results. Not only are around 70 per cent of news articles written by men, but also most of them are also about men. They quote men at a higher rate, show predominantly photos of men and feature men's achievements.

Women are seen, heard or read about in less than one quarter of stories produced and they make up less than 15 per cent of quoted experts. The 2015 Women in Media Report showed that although women appear to make up half the reporting workforce in Australia, female journalists are the named producers of only 30 per cent of content. Where women were named as producers of content, they tended to dominate only in the traditional women's content of celebrity news (65 per cent), health and lifestyle (57 per cent) and social issues (55 per cent). Male journalists are significantly overrepresented in sport (90 per cent), politics (74 per cent) and finance (70 per cent). It's worth pointing out the report showed that crime, which covers court reporting as well as wider law and order, is equally reported by male and female journalists, but the news editors who direct style and subject, as well as writing the headlines, are predominantly men. So the area of news where most reporting of men's violence

is done is not necessarily covered by a male-dominated news team. This
would suggest that the overall culture of the newsrooms is what leads to
problematic crime reporting.

Dr Louise North is one of the leading Australian academic researchers on gendered newsrooms. Her research has found a range of indicators
that gender plays a role in the workplace, including masculine organisa-
tional cultures, high levels of sexual harassment, an under-representation
of women in decision-making roles, antagonism to feminist viewpoints,
lack of flexibility regarding staff members' parenting responsibilities and
a persistent gender pay gap.

Australia doesn't collect information on the race or ethnicity of
reporters, so it's difficult to prove the dominance of white Australia
in journalism, although a stroll through most big metro newsrooms
reveals a distinct difference there from the mix of people walking past
the front door. This data is collected in America, however, where African
Americans make up around 5 per cent of journalists and 13 per cent
of the population, and Hispanics make up 5 per cent of journalists and
18 per cent of the population. Australian researchers, however, have
found that, apart from being predominantly men, 84 per cent of journalists are university-educated and, as with any profession, tend to skew
older the more senior they get.

The perception that middle-aged white men rule the world is
based in fact. According to the 2016 census, there are around 24 million people in Australia. Around 11 per cent of them are men between
the ages of forty and sixty. There's no data on white men, but if we
take the percentages of people with a U.K. background and third-
generation Australians as a very rough guide, somewhere between 8 and
10 per cent of the Australian population are middle-aged white men.
Assuming that not all male journalists are middle aged, and taking
into account that they're mostly university graduates, it's reasonable to

assume the vast majority of journalists are between the ages of twenty-five and sixty. Men in that age group are still only 24 per cent of the population and white men of that age are around 18 per cent. Which demonstrates exactly how disproportionate that 70 per cent of credited content in the media really is.

Research I conducted for the University of Melbourne in 2018 showed results strikingly similar to Dr North's findings from 2012 and the Women in Media report in 2015. Women writers were disproportionately assigned to the lifestyle section and soft news topics, while men were overrepresented in opinion and analysis sections, as well as in traditionally 'male' topics like sport, foreign affairs and business. This data might be skewed by the fact that the publication I reviewed had a specific section for women readers and you would expect articles intended for a female audience would be more likely to be written by women. It was, however, one of the largest publications in Australia and my findings correlated with broader research from all over the world.

In the context of a gendered newsroom, the women's section can be viewed as both a positive and a negative force. It certainly encourages more writing by women and allows women of varied backgrounds to write about a variety of different topics. But, it also contains women's writing in a silo, which could reinforce the idea that women's journalism is only relevant to a female audience and is concentrated on so called 'soft' topics such as relationships and social issues. The idea that these topics are only relevant to women is demonstrably untrue. As well as celebrity and fashion, lifestyle sections include articles about parenting, relationships, food, travel and social issues. Men are just as likely to be in relationships as women, they are also parents, they go on holidays, eat food, wear clothes and are affected by social issues. The assumption that men are not interested in reading about these topics might be true, but it is reinforced by the siloed publication of such articles, which discourages a male audience and reinforces the perception of these topics as women's writing.

Proving that news journalism is still dominated by men is not the same as saying male journalists cannot do well-informed and accurate reporting on issues like men's violence against women. This is clearly not true. The *Herald Sun*'s 'Take A Stand' campaign, which was one of the first cohesive mainstream media campaigns reporting on domestic violence in Australia, was conceived by *Herald Sun* editor Damon Johnston working with then deputy editor Ellen Whinnett. It undoubtedly played a part in moving public perception of domestic violence from a series of isolated incidents where only the individuals involved were responsible to understanding it as a social issue requiring a whole of community response (more on that in Chapter 5). There are many other male journalists who do excellent work reporting on issues outside their lived experience (Eryk Bagshaw at *The Age*, David Marr at *The Guardian*, Waleed Aly at the *Sydney Morning Herald* to name a few), but this is not about the individuals. It's about the perspective and culture of journalism that gets distorted by the dominant privileged white male point of view. It is the culture where nearly half of all women who work in media say they've been subjected to intimidation, abuse or sexual harassment in the workplace. The Women in Media report found the figure to be 48 per cent. My guess is that figure is too low. I've spoken to women in journalism who tell me they've never been sexually harassed but, when I dug a little deeper, they also told me about 'jokes' colleagues have made about their bodies, their sexual preferences and proclivities and the likelihood that they screwed their way into a promotion or a particularly revealing interview. They told me it wasn't sexual harassment, but they also conceded those sorts of 'jokes' aren't made about the men in their office. Even if you take the view that sexual harassment is in the eye of the beholder, nearly half of all women is still horrifically high. To give it some context, the Human Rights Commission reports found around 25 per cent of women in the defence forces and 40 per cent of women in Victoria Police had experienced sexual harassment and bullying. And let me tell you, those reports got a lot more news coverage than the Women in Media report. We don't want to look in our own backyard, and we certainly don't want our audiences doing it.

JOURNALISM IN THE DIGITAL AGE

Thousands of words have been written about the way the internet changed journalism, and it is a subject too complex to detail here, but in summary, we can see that the effect on the media landscape has largely been financial. Sure, journalism has always adapted to different forms as new technology changed the way we reached our audiences; radio and television both had huge impacts on how we delivered and consumed news as they became ubiquitous in the societies we describe. The difference with the internet is that the revenue model was irrevocably changed. Advertising, once the source of the rivers of gold that funded journalism, was equally effective across print, television and radio. The digital age happened quickly, and its impact was vastly underestimated by almost all media outlets in the early days. Content, which readers had always assumed they would pay for, was provided free of charge online. But publishers' digital advertising income did not follow the same path it took in print and television news. There's a famous story (verified by someone who'd been present in the room at the time) about a chairman of a large Australian media outlet slamming a paper copy of his company's newspaper down on the boardroom table, thundering, 'I do not want to hear another word about anyone in this town looking for a job, a house or a car and not finding it in this newspaper.' His wish was granted, and within a few short years entrepreneurs had drained all the revenue from classified ads into online start-ups. In hindsight it looks almost criminally short-sighted, but at the time he was far from being the only media mogul who did not understand the changes rushing at him from the online world. Most of them didn't. They didn't know how targeted ads online could be evaluated and proven to be next to useless. They didn't predict the rise of Google and Facebook as sources of purchasing decisions and news consumption. They had no idea how quickly people would perceive online news as a product they did not have to pay for. They certainly didn't see how this would tear millions of dollars out of journalism and leave publishers struggling to stay afloat, let alone produce the quality content their audiences expected.

Two decades later, thousands of jobs have disappeared forever. Some publications have clawed back classified ad and sponsored content revenue, while many others were unable to make the transition and vanished into history. After years of expecting free content online, audiences are slowly and reluctantly beginning to recognise that they might need to pay for the journalism they consume on their screen. Competition for audiences has become more intelligent, and news organisations are using technology to find and retain their readers. They now look beyond the simple number of clicks and seek engagement with their content. *The Guardian*, for example, published an article about Beyoncé's performance at the 2010 Grammys. The sudden influx of clicks was due to people hearing about the performance and wanting to read more about it, and so searching for articles about 'Beyoncé at the Grammys'. Most of those people were not regular readers or subscribers, and very few of them could be converted by one article about Beyoncé (even her power is not that strong). A *Guardian* article about the efficacy of solar panels and Tesla batteries might get many fewer clicks but readers of this article would find other content of interest to them on *The Guardian* website. It also reinforces the idea for regular readers or subscribers that *The Guardian* is worth supporting.

Publications are now forced to deal with readers responding on social media to news they don't like or believe. Social media itself has become news, with movements such as #MeToo and #CasualSexism entering mainstream discourse. The large public debate surrounding Gillette's ad from January 2019, in which Gillette took their thirty-year-old slogan, 'The Best a Man Can Get', and turned it into a reflection on toxic masculinity and the influence good men can have, made top-of-the-page news around the world.

One of the effects of this is that publications have tried to strengthen their relationship with their readers by sticking to a clearly identifiable 'house style'. This is present not just in the look and colour of a publication's website but also in the ideological bent it gives to the stories it puts out. News publications have been upfront about their political leanings since before the internet, and particular newspapers were identifiably left or right leaning, but an increasingly dire need for audience engagement among the noise of the online news world has polarised this distinction even further. Broadly speaking, in online Australian media, News Corp has strengthened its claim to the conservative, male, right-wing media space. Its approach to news stories shows a refusal to recognise climate change as a global threat caused by human activities, which can be seen in the prominence given to climate change deniers such as columnists Andrew Bolt and Miranda Devine, and their clear disdain for unions, welfare, immigration and feminism. What used to be known as Fairfax Media has tried to stick to the middle ground of political ideology on all these issues by providing more information on facts and expert analysis, while still acknowledging the more reasonable naysayers. *The Guardian* has staked its claim to left-leaning readers who reject and dislike the News Corp stance almost as much as News detests the 'leftist' view. Their opinion, feature and analysis articles are usually written by people who have already accepted the progressive premise and argue on the details of implementing change they understand to be necessary. All of these publications claim they are producing fair, verifiable and objective journalism. The public broadcaster is left swinging unhappily between all points of view and takes a battering from all sides for doing so.

There are all kinds of economic, political, environmental and social rabbit holes to disappear down in this discussion, but this book is about how media reports on and represents (or misrepresents, or fails to represent) women. News Corp's right-wing stance expresses itself in hostility to feminists and feminist principles, as described by prominent writers such as Miranda Devine, Rita Panahi, Tim Blair and Andrew Bolt. While there are many highly professional and skilled women working for News Corp, some who even express feminist points of view and approaches to news, they are the exception. News Corp's editors and senior staff are overwhelmingly white and male. Their approach to news is aimed at a primarily male audience, with a strong focus on men's sport, right-wing politics, sensationalised crime and opinion writing that is deeply hostile to feminist aims. Some women thrive in this environment, such as the aforementioned Miranda Devine and Rita Panahi. Others I've spoken to find it impossible to work with and are forced to seek work outside the News Corp enclosures. This is working (for now) as News Corp slowly raises paywalls around most of its content, but the News Corp audience doesn't only skew male, it also tends to be older than the readership for other publications. So far, they are not doing much to attract a younger market, but it seems likely that demographics might force them to change their approach. It will be interesting to see how they go about wooing the youth market who have grown up with digital content and have far different expectations and attitudes to the people who currently make up most of News Corp's readership. Anti-feminist and conservative approaches to gender roles are not just going to fail to appeal to millennials

Can't get enough of *The Untethered Soul*?

🔊 Hear Michael A. Singer read from *The Untethered Soul* at: **newharbinger.com/tus**

🖱 Find AUDIO TALKS by Michael A. Singer at: **store.untetheredsoul.com**

🎥 Watch the BOOK TRAILER at: **bit.ly/tustrailer**

▶ Watch an in-depth INTERVIEW with Michael A. Singer at: **bit.ly/tusinterview**

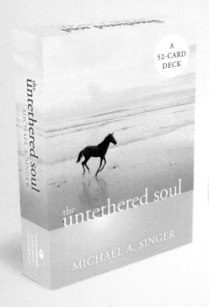

and their younger siblings, they're also going to be almost incomprehensible to them.

It's worth remembering, before we move on, that Fixed It is not about News Corp bashing. With the exception of *The Guardian* in Australia, male-dominated newsrooms exist in almost every mainstream media outlet in Australia and the U.K. As I'll detail in a later chapter, men themselves are not the problem here, but the embedded, self-perpetuating toxic boys' club culture, dominated by a narrow perspective and wary of challenges to its dominance, can skew the what when and how decisions of everyday journalism. The Fixed It project would not have started or continued for so long if these perceptions were not so deeply embedded in traditions of reporting on men's violence against women.

TROLLS, WOMEN AND THE ONLINE WORLD

I hope I get to watch you fucking die in a ditch, you fat ugly cunt.

Anon, 2017

You're nothing but a communist in panties.

Twitter, 2012 (my favourite tweet ever)

The moment you realise you're bored by death threats is an odd one, to say the least. But this is the reality for many women in online journalism. If you are a woman and you have an opinion and you write about it online, handling violence or death threats, along with denigration of your face, body, sexuality, age, hair, clothes, voice and sexual desirability can become part of your job. If your opinion, factual account or analysis is about politics, climate change, the gender pay gap or men's violence, and you are not defending men in the face of facts about the way economic disadvantage and violence are wielded, trolling can become so frequent it ceases to be shocking and just gets annoying until one day you wake up, check your emails and realise you are now bored by death threats.

A 2018 study by the International Federation of Journalists found that two thirds of women in journalism have experienced online abuse and that this abuse is almost always gendered. Men in journalism are told they are idiots, fuckwits, dickheads, clueless, left-/right-wing shills but the focus of the abuse is rarely, if ever, on their appearance. For example, they are never called 'fat' in the course of such messages. On the flipside, a person who is recognisably not white, straight and able-bodied is more likely to receive abuse that targets their appearance if the abuser disagrees with them.

Similarly, age is never a factor for male journalists. They are never too young or too old to do their jobs. Women on the other hand are often told they're either too young or too old to do their job competently. Too good looking or too ugly. Too fat or too skinny. Too fuckable or not fuckable enough. I'll explore this in more detail in later chapters. Some male journalists report receiving threats of violence, but they are many fewer than the female journalists who report this and, while insults can come from both men and women, threats and sexual denigration, in my experience, almost always come from men. Men are not threatened with rape as punishment for daring to state an opinion. It is an extraordinarily common threat against women. The logic, as far as I can tell, is that if a woman suggests that men are primarily responsible for rape you can prove her wrong by threatening to rape her.

Some women are able to ignore this kind of abuse and remain relatively unaffected by it. I am lucky enough to be one of them. It might be because I was a bit older when I started writing about feminist topics and no longer held the sense of vulnerability I had when I was younger. Possibly if I had started writing in my early twenties, I would find trolling more distressing than boring. Whatever the reasons, I know I am fortunate. Many women have reported that they avoid certain topics or even leave journalism altogether because the barrage of threats and abuse they receive in the course of just doing their job and social media is too much to deal with. Staying away from social media is not an option, particularly not for freelance journalists, who are also, according to the International Federation of Journalists study, more commonly subjected to trolling. Social media is crucial to getting and promoting the work that pays their rent and buys their food.

Even when it's not abusive, the social media response to women in journalism can be hugely time-consuming for those women. Most successful freelance journalists need to maintain profiles on Facebook, Instagram and Twitter in order to build their audiences. A freelancer who can create their own readership base becomes quite attractive to a publication. This level of social media maintenance becomes an additional workload for the freelance journalist, and here lies the downside. You can't ignore private messages for too long – it's common to be commissioned or alerted to a story this way. The abusive messages are easy to identify, block and delete, but this takes time and emotional energy that would be better spent on useful social media interactions or finding new and interesting stories to tell.

As well as abuse, there are also all the #NotAllMen and mansplainers and Well Actuallys who know little and care less about the facts you have written about, but they have very strong feelings and they *demand* a response. These people might not start out being abusive, but they often end up that way, especially if you disprove their argument or ignore them. It's easy enough to avoid the comments under an article or video on the masthead's website or social media pages, and most women interested in maintaining their sanity do avoid them. It's a different matter when people are commenting on your own social media pages.

Firstly, there is an ethical responsibility to the people who come to your page to talk about what could easily be traumatic subjects. No one wants to provide an online space for trolls to abuse survivors or enable an entitled keyboard warrior who shores up his ego by denigrating women online. Secondly, it can be off-putting for people who might want to follow your work or even commission work from you if they see trolls running wild through your posts. Delete and block, delete and block, delete and block: the game of whack-a-mole continues ad infinitum. It's irritating and a grotesque waste of time. One well-known feminist columnist in Australia told me she spends up to twenty hours a week on the unpaid labour of managing social media. Emotional labour, unpaid work, violence, personalised and sexualised denigration. We're told this is the price we have to pay for being a woman with a public profile in the digital age. The price is too high.

Social media, despite its pitfalls for women, is also a huge resource for us to gather, find support, network and ask for help if they're struggling with online abuse or sexist treatment at work. Private groups on Facebook offer thousands of women a safe online space to discuss their work and their lives with other women who can give advice, sympathy, acceptance and the occasional dark humour you need to light the way.

And while journalism is undeniably still a male-dominated field, it is slowly changing. Women are becoming more common and less remarkable in reporting on politics, sport and finance. Some of the best political journalists in Australia are women. Katharine Murphy, Lenore Taylor, Laura Tingle, Leigh Sales, Emma Alberici, Gabrielle Chan, Sarah Armstrong, Samantha Maiden, Lee Lin Chin, Margaret Simons, Kate McClymont, Michelle Grattan and Alice Workman, among many others, have proven that women can produce outstanding journalism. Not because they are women or in spite of it, but simply because they are extremely good at their jobs. Caroline Wilson became one of the leading sports journalists in the country by simply refusing to allow anyone to tell her that she couldn't. Michelle Griffin, one of the few women news directors in the country, does an excellent job of leading *The Age*'s newsroom in producing high quality, objective, relevant news.

New players in the market such as *Buzzfeed* and *The Guardian* simply ignore the white male dominance of journalism and put together teams that cover diverse news as news, rather than as tokenistic offerings to minority groups. Start-ups that survived the new media culling of the early 2000s, such as *Crikey* and *New Matilda*, have found readerships that are willing to support outsider journalism that offers smart, agile alternatives to mainstream news. Networking groups such as Women In Media offer mentorship and professional connections to women who need a way around the old boys' network to progress their careers. These are all signs of positive change. It's sometimes too easy to forget how far we've come when all we think about is how far there is to go.

Karen Middleton, a long-time member of the Canberra Press Gallery, wrote an article for the *Saturday Paper* in 2015 about the sexual harassment she and so many of her colleagues experienced. It was a litany of stories that would be familiar to anyone who followed the #MeToo hashtag, all of them, as Middleton pointed out, about abuse of power, not a mutual attraction.

> One evening I was having an after-work drink with a group of slightly older male journalist mates in what was then the Non-Members' Bar at Parliament House. One of them reached across and, in full view of the others, grabbed both of my breasts and squeezed them hard, to bellowing laughter from the group.

A journalist who is quite new to the press gallery told me that she's heard stories like this from many of her older female colleagues but says such things would not happen now. 'It's not perfect by any means, but there's too many women, too many men around now who just wouldn't put up with it. If a man grabbed another journalist like that at work, he'd be hounded out. It's just not like that any more.'

Not perfect, but getting better.

Chapter 3
Women's journalism

No black woman writer in this culture can write 'too much'. Indeed, no woman writer can write 'too much' . . . No woman has ever written enough.

bell hooks, *Remembered Rapture: The Writer at Work*, 1999

Women's journalism is not a new or even recent phenomenon. Women were writing for British publications as early as 1860s. Novelist Eliza Lynn Linton was the first British woman given a salary for journalism. She was a staunch anti-feminist who did not believe women should be given the vote, although she was in favour of education for women and supported law reform that would allow married women to own property. One of her most well-known articles railed against the 'unnatural', 'distasteful' and 'unfeminine' 'wild women' of politics:

This clamour for political rights is women's confession of sexual enmity . . . No woman who loves her husband would wish to usurp his province. It is only those whose instincts are inverted, or whose anti-sexual vanity is insatiable, who would take political reins from the strong hands which have always held them to give to others – weaker, less capable and wholly unaccustomed. To women who love, their desire is their husbands; and the feeling remains as an echo in the soul even when the master voice is silent. Among our most renowned women are some who say with a whole heart, 'I would rather have been the wife of a great man or the mother of a hero than what I am – famous in my own person'. A woman's own fame is barren.

A woman who viewed power in the hands of women as dangerous would have been attractive to the male bastions of journalism during the lead up to the fight for white women's suffrage, so it's not surprising she was the first woman employed by the U.K.'s mainstream media.

In Australia, women's careers in journalism followed closely along the trajectory of feminism's changes to broader society. There were several women working in journalism in the late nineteenth and early twentieth centuries but they were almost exclusively writing for the women's sections of newspapers or for women's magazines. As the suffragette movement gained strength, more white women started writing, and eventually feminist publications started gaining an audience. In mainstream journalism, however, women were almost always published in clearly delineated women's sections.

World Wars One and Two did for women in journalism what they did for women in many other industries – opened up positions previously filled by men – and women started reporting on war, crime and politics. That all ended after World War Two, as the conservatism of the 1950s bound journalism into strict gender roles and uncontentious subjects.

In the 1960s, Charmian Clift began writing an enormously popular weekly column in the *Sydney Morning Herald*. It was intended to be a well-written but unremarkable column for women, but it touched on a huge range of topics, such as war, politics, conscription, advertising, sexuality, complacency, racism, cultural cringe and architecture. Clift had worked as a journalist since World War Two, when she wrote for army magazine *For Your Information*. She later started working for *The Argus* until she was fired for having an affair with George Johnston while he was still married to his first wife. Johnston resigned in protest at her sacking and they moved to London, then to Greece, where they joined a community of writers, poets and artists. Among them was Leonard Cohen, who later said of them, 'The Australians drank more than other people, they wrote more, they got sick more, they got well more, they cursed more, they blessed more, and they helped a great deal more. They were an inspiration.' At times raging, sometimes almost satirical, and with other moments of tenderness or quiet contemplation, Clift was one of the most popular women journalists of her era and her death in 1969 was widely mourned.

Throughout the 1970s, as the second-wave feminist movement brought about social, legal and economic changes in Australia, women in journalism rebelled against being sidelined to women's pages and began to demand the right to cover politics, crime, sport, corruption and for-eign affairs.

The initial movement came from white women, but it was not long before Aboriginal and non-white people's struggles to be repre-sented began to be recognised. In 1974 Helene Chung became the first person of colour to appear as a journalist on Australian television, as well as the first woman posted abroad by the ABC. In 1978 an article published by *Truth* magazine revealed ABC's management had actually tried to prevent her going on air because she looked 'too Chinese'. The article detailed how she fought this with the support of the Australian Journalists' Association and then Commissioner for Community Relations, Al Grassby.

John Newfong was the first Aboriginal journalist to work in mainstream newspapers. He worked at the *Sydney Morning Herald* and was then hired by *The Australian* in 1971. Despite his skills in reporting general news as well as Aboriginal and Torres Strait Islander issues, he was fired after only a few months because senior editors didn't think 'Australians' (a.k.a. white people) wanted to read about black people. Newfong, a descendent of the Ngugi people of Moreton Bay, had a distinguished career as a writer, activist, journalist, academic and brilliantly articulate protester but, being a gay Aboriginal man of his time, he was never considered by the public or his colleagues to be just a journalist.

Aboriginal women in journalism have always been rare, but the new generation of female Indigenous journalists are supporting each other to change that, and find a balance between telling authentic stories outside the stereotypes of reporting on Aboriginal issues and avoiding the pigeonhole effect of readers and editors assuming these are the only stories they can tell.

By the 1990s many women in journalism felt that the war against sexism and misogyny was won. The *Sex Discrimination Act* had passed in 1984, and women were more frequently reporting on mainstream news issues. While lifestyle sections of newspapers still published stories about food, travel, arts and other 'soft' topics, the specific women's pages such as *Accent* at *The Age* had disappeared. Unfortunately, things didn't continue to improve to the degree that women had hoped. While they had broken through barriers and increased their representation in the media, they stalled at around 30 per cent. In some cases, the number of women in journalism even fell backwards.

In the early 2010s, women's sections started to reappear in mainstream media. What was then known as Fairfax Media (*The Age*, the *Sydney Morning Herald*, the *Brisbane Times*, *The Canberra Times* and a collection of rural papers) launched 'Daily Life' in 2012, which started with an uncompromisingly feminist approach and covered a wide range of topics, stepping on the toes of politics, sport, finance and foreign affairs, as well as social issues such as racism, sexism, welfare inadequacies and crime. News Corp followed with 'Rendezview' and 'Whimn'. Mia Freedman's website *Mamamia* transitioned from personal blog to a wide-ranging women's news site, employing dozens of writers (along with unpaid 'interns') and proving that women's writing was a viable news venture in a still-changing media landscape.

THE POWER OF WOMEN'S WRITING

> When I learnt, however, that in 1911 there had been twenty-one regular feminist periodicals in Britain, that there was a feminist book shop, a woman's press, and a woman's bank run by and for women, I could no longer accept that the reason I knew almost nothing about women of the past was because there were so few of them, and they had done so little.
>
> *Women of Ideas and What Men Have Done to Them,*
> Dale Spender, 1982

In her seminal book, *Man Made Language*, (still stunningly relevant nearly forty years since it was first published) Dale Spender argued that men do 'public' writing and women do 'private writing'. Although male politicians and others in positions of power publish private writing in the form of diaries and letters, this is seen as legitimate public publication because the audience is the general public. Writing that is in the same genre but by a woman in a position of power is often deemed to be personal writing rather than public. In other words, Spender was saying that women's diaries and letters are only relevant to other women, they are not useful or interesting to the general public. Women's journalism therefore, is often perceived as the women's alternative to men's journalism, which is for everyone. So, there's news and then there's women's news.

White men's experiences are taken to be the baseline for knowledge, truth and reality because they are considered 'default human', whereas women have, and continue to be, considered a subset of humanity, with white women as the primary subset and all other women relegated to even smaller niche audiences. Men assume gender is irrelevant (because it is to them) and women who write about gender are only writing for other women. It's a perspective that needs to be disrupted and having women write or speak publicly about personal experiences is an effective way to do that. Humans are and always have been storytellers. It's how we understand lives and experiences unlike our own. I can give you endless data about being a white female journalist in Australia, but that only gives you information, not understanding. If I tell you stories of my experiences in newsrooms and dealing with editors and publishers, for example, having a (older, male) publisher say to me, 'I think you need to stop writing so much about domestic violence; our audience are professional working women, it's not really relevant to them,' this tells you a lot more than a list of statistics about perceptions of domestic violence among male publishers.

This is particularly true for women from oppressed groups. They break the silence of oppression by speaking about their lives and force change just by this powerful act. The more honest women are about their experiences the more they challenge the norms that have been reinforced by the silencing of marginalised voices. It is even more important to hear about experiences that are shocking to men or other women outside the writer's demographic. That it is shocking is proof of the silence imposed upon women previously unable to speak.

By sharing personal information and stories about their lives, women are able to express the truth of female experience and explain the forces that silence women or cause them to fear for their safety, whether it be personal, professional, financial or sexual. Those forces are often unrecognised because they have been normalised. Memoir exposes them from the side of the oppressed rather than reinforcing them from the side of the oppressors. One of the ways oppression works is by silencing. Speaking about personal experiences of oppression is therefore a revolutionary political act.

bell hooks' and Maya Angelou's writing about their experiences as black women in the American South during the civil rights era are essential for understanding the modern experience of African American women, but hooks also makes the point 'there is no one story of black girlhood'. Many voices are needed to provide a diverse and accurate picture of the variations and diversity of a group's experiences (in this instance, that of black American women, but this is true for other identity groups too). In feminist memoir this usually involves a long process of understanding the oppression and social structure of gender and how they changed the writer's life. Sharing that with other women helps the author understand that what they believed was normal is actually oppressive. The result is that it raises women's consciousness about the structural and personal oppression that might affect their own lives.

This comes back to the point I was making earlier about the problem of women's writing being siloed into a mostly women-only audience. We assume women are writing for other women, and, within the women's writing genre, that each group is writing only for its own niche audience. This does a disservice to the writers and the audience. The simplest way to create empathy for people who seem unfamiliar to us is to share stories about our and their lives. The more we see both similarities and differences, the more able we are to understand complexities and not be tricked into believing the unfamiliar is dangerous.

JOURNALISM, MEMOIR AND GENDER
Journalism and memoir have an uneasy relationship. The male-centric traditions of journalism, which are deemed to be objectivity and

verification, do not sit well with personal writing. Memoir is not an aspect of hard news reporting. It is, however, more common in 'soft' topics and opinion writing, where women are more prevalent.

Part of the reason there is so little respect in memoir journalism is that it is viewed as women's writing. In those early years, women who entered journalism were only allowed to write on certain topics. Still, it shouldn't follow that something deemed to be 'women's news' is inherently unreliable and lower status. This is more a result of unconscious bias than an objective evaluation of the memoir form.

Memoir is not necessarily antithetical to the need for verifications. Journalism encompasses a range of stories. It's not only always about facts, but also about human experiences, though the narrative memoir form of journalism by its nature includes the usual confusion and obscurities of human memory. This is particularly notable in light of Michael Schudson's concept that creating social empathy is a primary objective of journalism. For example we could look at how the refugee crisis is reported. There are over 65 million displaced people in the world in 2018, and it is a global issue that affects almost every country in the world. Making policy and social decisions about how we respond to this requires that we know more than just the simple facts: we need to understand how displaced people feel, what they want, how they would like to live, why they left their homes, what are the variations in their experiences. These are not things we can understand from dry, fact-based reporting. Many social issues, which also impact government policy and community cohesion, benefit significantly when writers include personal stories.

Memoir does not have to be suspect and can be as subject to verification as telling one's own or other people's stories to provide a wider truth to the story. DeNeen L. Brown, an African American journalist, told a story about trying to report on the complexities of life for African American women who have achieved financial independence but often have family still trapped in poverty. Facts alone couldn't convey the real experiences she wanted her audience to understand, especially when so many white people would have little comprehension of the social and emotional complexities involved. She asked other African American women who had lived through this change to explain it for her article, but none of them wanted to put themselves or their families in that public spotlight. In the end, the only way to tell the story with the personal element so necessary for social empathy was to write about herself and her sisters. Lauren Slater's essay 'Three Spheres', which investigated the mental health system in America, used her personal experience of being a patient in a psychiatric hospital to humanise and enhance the verifiable facts uncovered in her investigation.

Memoir should be considered more a tool of journalism than a form of it. Writing that is exclusively memoir, with no additional information or verifiable facts, might share experiences and assist with creating social empathy, but can only be considered reliable when the reader has some basis for believing in the credibility of the writer. This might come from a writer's or masthead's established reputation for truth, but where this does not exist, it must be supported by some inclusion of objective or verifiable information to enhance the integrity of the story. Memoir is a tool that journalists can use to describe society to itself.

The research I conducted at the University of Melbourne shed an interesting light on the relationship between gender, memoir and journalism. It found that women are significantly more likely to use this genre in opinion articles than men, but there was a difference in the way women and men used memoir in their journalism. While men were less likely to use memoir, when they did so, they showed a wider variation in the type they used. They used it to reflect on their feelings about events or experiences, to explain wider social contexts and for nostalgic reminiscing. Women mostly used memoir as an explanatory tool to ground their experience in reality. One suggestion for this is that men do not feel the same need to explain and legitimise their experiences. Straight white men are accustomed to being the focus of every story. Their experiences have been treated as universal ones, so it makes sense that they would not feel a need to explain themselves. Nostalgic memoir, on the other hand, becomes more useful, because it is a means of reflecting how time and experience can alter ideas. Women are more likely to use memoir to explain their experiences or to legitimise them. In other words, women's memoir requires the extra work of convincing the public that theirs is a credible experience.

Memoir can be a powerful tool when it comes to how we report on men's violence against women. As Dale Spender wrote in *Man Made Language*, 'The most constructive thing women can do is to write, for in the act of writing we deny our muteness and begin to eliminate some of the difficulties that have been put upon us.'

There is a risk in using memoir for this purpose. Women writing about men's violence often include their own experiences of it as a tool to 'prove' their understanding and authority on the topic. When this becomes the norm in how such stories are told, it can set up a false requirement that personal experience is a necessary prerequisite for writing on this topic. By this I mean that if memoir becomes the primary requirement for authoritative writing about traumatic experiences, the requirement for verification lessens, and risks losing its value. The result is that the use of memoir risks serving only an emotional need, rather than acting as an informative tool. Memoir could therefore become a means of sensationalising violence, which is one of the faults of media reporting of men's violence against women that is frequently identified in Australian and international research.

If writing about violence was limited only to journalists who could demonstrate a lived experience with the topic, a lot of valuable reporting could be lost or dismissed. This expectation puts pressure on individual journalists to disclose their personal experience in ways they may not wish to do in a public setting.

Nina Funnell is a Walkley Award–winning investigative journalist who was largely responsible for exposing the extent and cover-up of sexual assault and harassment in Australian universities. Her reporting adhered to all the journalistic requirements of verification, objectivity and in-depth investigation of large public institutional governance. She is also a woman who has publicly discussed her experience of being sexually assaulted. Nina's work is viewed by much of the profession as activism rather than journalism. She did not win a Walkley for the twelve months of in-depth investigation of sexual assault in Australian universities she published under her own name; she won it for a report on the same subject, co-published with male journalist Eryk Bagshaw.

Nina's story is a stark depiction of many of the themes explored in this book.

Nina Funnell was sexually assaulted in 2007. She was walking home from a function and she'd had a few drinks. This would be the first of many choices she would later be criticised for.

Nina didn't drive at the time, but taxis were expensive, Uber didn't exist yet and the suburb she was walking through was supposed to be a nice, safe place. She weighed the risks and benefits, made all the calculations men never need to make, and decided public transport and walking were the best way to get home. This would be the second decision that meant she'd be blamed for someone else's choice to hurt her.

A man attacked her from behind as she was walking down a suburban street close to her home in an affluent Sydney suburb. He held a blade to her throat and dragged her into a park opposite a girls' high school.

He threw her to the ground, straddled her and punched her repeatedly in the face as he indecently assaulted her.

No one can predict how they will respond to being attacked. Some people will fight. They will scream, kick, claw, punch. Throw dirt and rocks and anything else that comes to hand. Sometimes fighting will free them. Sometimes they will be killed. Other people will flee. Run farther and faster than they've ever been able to. Adrenaline will flood their system, expanding lungs and making the heart pump at a frantic rate. Sometimes they will outdistance their attackers. Sometimes they are not fast enough. The other response people have to being attacked, the most common in women, is to freeze. They disappear into a small space in their mind, take themselves away from what's happening to their body, and endure. Sometimes they will survive by allowing their attacker to do everything, hoping they will stop short of murder. Sometimes murder is where their attack will stop.

Nina fought. It just happened. Her body started fighting before her mind had time to think about what was going on. She clawed and screamed and eventually fought her attacker off. She had already dropped her bottle of soft drink when he grabbed her and during the attack he snapped her necklace. After she broke free, she fled, running towards home. She didn't know where the attacker was. Had he run off or was he still following her? As she ran towards her home she called the police. The operator took her details, told her a car was on its way and hung up. Bewildered, she called back. 'I thought it must have been a mistake,' she said. 'Surely if a woman calls the police and tells them she's been attacked and she's still running, you don't hang up, you stick with her until she safe?' The operator took her details again and, once more, hung up.

'Maybe I sounded too calm. I wasn't crying or screaming, but I told them what happened and I told them I was still out on the street and I didn't know where he was. I still don't understand it.'

Eventually she got home. Her hands were shaking, and she had trouble getting her key in the door. She didn't know whether the man who attacked her had followed her home and, as she struggled with the door, she was already having flashbacks to the moment he had first snuck up behind her and grabbed her.

When she finally got the door open, she ran inside, slammed it shut and immediately changed her clothes and cleaned her teeth.

She doesn't know how long it took the police to arrive. It might have been minutes, but it felt like hours. She was very calm when they did get there and politely offered them a cup of tea. 'I think I wanted to normalise it. I didn't want them to think of me as a victim.'

She explained what had happened and they drove her back to the place her attacker first grabbed her. She walked them through the entire assault. She showed them where her shoes had come off. They found the soft drink bottle she'd dropped. 'I went to pick it up; it felt like I'd been caught littering. But they told me not to touch it.' More police turned up with sniffer dogs to search the area. They found a notebook she'd dropped and her broken necklace, but they didn't find the man who attacked her.

She sat in the car while they searched the area, then she was driven to Gladesville Police Station so they could collect evidence. Police took photos, swabs of the blood on her hands, scraped under her fingernails and took a preliminary statement. They explained to her that a statement taken after alcohol was consumed could be questioned in court. A friend came to pick her up and stayed with her that night.

A few days later she went back to the police station and gave a full statement. They showed her a book of hundreds of photos of people she was told were sex offenders who lived in the area. She didn't recognise her attacker in any of the photos.

'When I was doing the photo book the cop who was showing it to me said, "You poor girls just don't understand the risks that you take and the dangers out there." I was so angry. Tell me I don't understand the dangers of what can happen to women, and the problem is women, tell me that as I'm still covered in bruises and looking at pictures of perpetrators? Don't tell me what I don't understand. I understand a lot.

'I was the "proper" victim, the one everyone understands, where the man who attacked me literally jumped out at me on the street. And even then, they were still questioning my right to be a victim of the man who decided to assault me. I can't even imagine what it's like for women who don't fit the proper victim stereotype.'

Four months after the attack, Nina was still waiting for the results of the DNA tests. Frustrated, angry and recovering from the horror of it, she went to the media to talk about the slow process of testing, and how such delays posed a danger to the general public. 'I know enough about sex offenders to know it's very unlikely a man who attacked me the way he did only did it once. But the police couldn't tell me anything about the investigation. It was incredibly frustrating, and just made me feel powerless all over again.'

After her story aired on Channel 7 the DNA results for her test came back within days. She knows that most people don't have that option.

'It worked for me, but only because I had contacts in the media. What it meant, of course, was someone else got pushed from the top of the list.'

The results found male DNA, but no match in the New South Wales database. Nina doesn't know if the DNA was ever sent to other states for matching.

Police are restricted in the information they can give to victims during the course of an investigation. Telling them anything that might influence their evidence in court could be grounds for a mistrial. That does not, however, mean they can't explain the process to victims. It doesn't mean they can't treat them with respect and dignity.

'Victims might be traumatised, but that doesn't mean they're stupid. The communication process in my case was terrible. I just felt like they weren't doing anything and didn't care about what happened to me.

'The victim divulges all information, no information comes back, so you feel powerless. I felt like they just didn't care and nothing was being done. I get that they had to ask about how much alcohol I'd had but all they needed to do was say, "We need to ask for legal purposes, not because we're blaming you." They need to explain why they can't give you information about the investigation. They need to understand that victims can understand. I was told after the TV thing that it's not the police's fault: a different department deals with processing DNA. From [the] victim's perspective, that doesn't matter.

'[The] police never returned my clothing or necklace. It was really important to me to get the necklace back, reclaiming the part of me that he took. It was broken – he ripped it from my neck, I wanted to protect it and heal it. I went to them and told them I would withdraw my whole complaint if I could just get the necklace back, that will mean more to me than catching him. They said they couldn't give it to me, but they didn't really explain why.'

The day after Nina's interview was aired on national television, the Premier of New South Wales held a press conference about delays in getting DNA test results in sexual assault cases, and promised a review of testing procedures. That was in 2007. In 2018 *The New Daily* published the findings of their in-depth investigation of sexual assault kits held by police and hospitals in Australia. There were nearly 7000 untested kits in New South Wales, Victoria and Queensland, and minimal or no tracking of kits in South Australia, the Australian Capital Territory and the Northern Territory. These figures only cover the kits taken in the previous six years. No data was available on kits taken before then, which could mean that many thousands of rapists have remained free to continue predatory violence against women.

Worse was to come. Five years later, New South Wales police officer Marc Osbourne was charged with a series of offences in which he had filmed himself having sex with various women and showed the films to other officers at Gladesville Police Station. This was the same station Nina had been taken, where she was told she should be more aware of 'the dangers out there'.

'I just felt violated all over again. I felt like that was the culture there. The people who were meant to be taking my case seriously are laughing at sexual violence against women when I'm not there. I felt really dirty. I'd been so vulnerable and put so much trust in them.'

Despite police eventually processing the DNA evidence from the crime scene, no one has ever been charged with Nina's assault.

'When you don't get an outcome,' she says, 'you feel so powerless, and so much of the trauma of sexual violence is being powerless. It shatters your belief that the world is a safe place and that justice is something you can rely on.'

Ten years later, Nina has moved on. Her journalism work was key in exposing the lack of action by universities to protect their students from sexual assault. She has also been open about her own experiences with sexual violence. In 2017 she told her story to me for an article about the staggeringly low conviction rates for rape and sexual assault in Australia.

Nina's experience of sexual assault had nothing to do with her later university exposés; in fact, she says she received outstanding support from her university at the time, and that without this support she might not have been able to complete the honours degree she was doing at the time the attack occurred. Her issues with the way it was handled were to do with police communication and the investigative process. These are not issues she has addressed a great deal in her journalism. Like many journalists she developed expertise in a specific area of investigation, but it was not directly related to her own life. Despite this, she knows her personal experience is used against her.

Nina's investigation of sexual assault on university campuses was always separate to her own experience. Her understanding of sexual assault as a reporter was a result of her journalistic work, while her understanding of sexual assault as a woman was a result of her personal experience. Despite this, her personal experience was used as a way to delegitimise the investigative work she did: 'I'm not seen as a journalist – I'm still a victim. People think I'm doing what I do because I'm angry about what happened to me. There's this perception that I can't be objective because of what I went through. But I'm a journalist. Do they think anyone who has been through something like that can't ever do their job again? That would be millions of people all over the world and it's bullshit. Of course I can do my job.'

We have seen that journalism remains a male-dominated industry. Parts of it are soaked in toxic masculinity and even the best of men in journalism can still lack perspective when they are writing or editing stories about men's violence against women. Though there are many skilled and successful women working in the field, they are usually limited to one of two options: they can produce journalism that adheres to the traditional masculine journalistic values and be lauded for it, or they can be siloed into the 'soft' topics of lifestyle or social issues and accept that they will not be taken seriously as journalists.

Part II
Fixed It

The next few chapters will not be easy to read. Rape, child abuse and domestic violence are still tragically prevalent in most countries around the world, and it's very likely that some of the people reading this book will have suffered from one or maybe all of these types of violence. This is not a suggestion that people who have survived violence shouldn't read these chapters. The fact you survived and are here wanting to read about it proves your resilience and possibly a desire to better understand how men's violence fits into everyday life, for example, in the way news is reported. You are the only person who can decide what is good for you to read or do. I hope that if it gets too much or starts to hurt, you are able to recognise when you need to walk away, or even skip ahead to a later chapter, such as politics or pop culture, where the topics can be a bit more fun and we can talk more about Judi Dench's knickers.

If you find that reading this work brings up overwhelming feelings, please don't try to cope on your own. Australian helplines for people needing assistance with rape, sexual assault, domestic violence, child abuse, men's services and suicidal thoughts are listed below. Reach out to friends, family, doctors, online communities, pets, children or even a soft couch and Netflix if that will help. I started the Fixed It project because I was frustrated by the contempt I saw some journalists showing for people in trauma; Fixed It was never intended to add to that trauma, so please approach this section with care and look after yourself.

1800 RESPECT – Sexual assault, domestic and family violence counselling and support
24 hours a day, 7 days a week
Ph: 1800 737 732
www.1800respect.org.au

Suicide Call Back Service – for anyone struggling with suicidal thoughts
24 hours a day, 7 days a week
Phone: 1300 659 467
www.suicidecallbackservice.org.au

Kids Helpline – counselling service for anyone between the ages of
5 and 25
24 hours a day, 7 days a week
Phone: 1800 55 1800
www.kidshelp.com.au

Child Wise Redress Helpline – for anyone who experienced child abuse
in an institutional context or who wants information and guidance about
engaging with the National Redress Scheme
Monday–Sunday, 9am–5pm
Phone: 1800 99 10 99
www.childwise.org.au

MensLine Australia – counselling service for men with family and relationship concerns
24 hours a day, 7 days a week
Phone: 1300 78 99 78
www.mensline.org.au

SOME NOTES ON LANGUAGE

Fixed It is all about how language can be used to erase crimes and blame
victims. The significance of language, the subtle meanings and inferences
in the words the media chooses to use about violence, is the basis for
most of the next three chapters, so I want to explain the reason for the
words I use to describe the people who have been subjected to violence.

Violence myths

We have a number of terms to describe the myths about men's violence against women, children and other men that permeate so much of how it is reported in the media and perceived by large sections of the public. These terms are variously referred to as 'rape myths', 'myths about violence against women', 'toxic masculinity', 'rape culture' and 'patriarchal attitudes'. All these terms describe specific aspects of the gender differences in how we think about the stereotypical perpetrators and victims of violence. I use 'violence myths' as a catch-all term that covers how all these specific ideas interact to excuse men's violence and shift responsibility from perpetrators to victims.

Victims and survivors

Most academics and professionals who work with men's violence against women use the combination term 'victim-survivor'. It's clunky, but there is good reason for it. Many people who have survived violence do not want to be referred to as victims. It's a helpless word that denotes powerlessness, and survivors are anything but powerless. There are, however, far too many people who did not survive the violence someone chose to enact against them, and we cannot call them survivors. I use the word 'victim' to describe the person who suffered violence while describing the moment of the violence because at that specific time they *were* victims; they had no choice and played no part in the choices made by their abuser. The word victim is accurate for that time. Afterwards, they are survivors. No matter how much they struggle with the effects of violence and trauma, every moment they keep breathing they are surviving, and only someone who has been through that experience can know the effort just drawing another breath can take. I write about violence knowing how difficult it can be for people to read and I do it with as much care as I can, but I do not pretend to know everyone's experience and reactions. I hope no one is hurt by the language I use in this book, but I acknowledge that sometimes I will get it wrong and for that I am truly sorry.

Domestic and family violence

The terms domestic violence and family violence are often used interchangeably, but technically, they have slightly different meanings. Domestic violence is used to describe violence between partners and immediate family members. Family violence is a wider term that also includes violence from extended family and kin relationships that occurs in family settings but may not always involve parent, partner, or sibling relationships. Another reason 'family violence' is a relevant term is the need to recognise indirect victims of violence in families, where they are not the specific targets of abuse, but they see it, hear it and live with the effects it has on the direct victim. Indirect victims are most commonly the children of a parent abusing another parent, but they could be anyone close to the direct victim. Parents, family members and even friends of the victim can be caught up in the abuse, either to ensure their silence or because the abuser manipulates them into colluding with or at least acquiescing to their efforts to control their partner.

I'm not particularly comfortable with either term. The words 'family' and 'domestic' are both soft, comfortable words that focus on specific families or homes, rather than the larger social issue of devastating violence between family members. They also, in my view, tend to diminish the cause and effect of the violence, playing into the 'it's just a domestic' narrative of the recent past. The term 'intimate terrorism', credited to Dr Michael P. Johnson, Emeritus Professor of Sociology, Women's Studies, and African and African American Studies at Penn State, is often used to describe abusive relationships. It's usually understood to apply to violence between intimate partners, where one person exerts coercive

control and power over the other. Intimate terrorism can involve physical violence, but it also refers to psychological, emotional, financial and
sexual abuse. The nature of the abuse is not as important as the intended
effect, which is that the victim is controlled by the abuser.

Violence within families is extremely complex. Where it is based
on power and control, intimate terrorism is the most accurate term for
it. While this is the basis of most forms of violence in families, it is not
the only possible manifestation. Some adults exist in mutually violent
relationships where each person freely and equally uses violence against
the other(s). This is not the same as victims of intimate terrorism acting in self-defence, but it is often cited by abusers to hide genuine acts
of self-defence. This form of domestic violence is rare, but it does happen and needs to be included in our understanding of family violence
dynamics.

Given all the variations and complexities of domestic violence, family
violence and intimate terrorism, I've used the catch-all term 'domestic
violence', despite my discomfort, because it is the most common and
therefore least likely to cause confusion.

Violence against women

As I will describe in more detail over the following chapters, one of the
most consistent issues the Fixed It project has identified is the media's
failure to depict perpetrators of violence, rendering them invisible.
Briefly, it's the difference between a headline that says, 'Woman found
dead' and the far more accurate headline, 'Man murders woman'. The
first one ignores the presence of the perpetrator and even the fact that a
woman was killed; the second one includes all this information with a
simple change in language.

The same issue of invisible perpetrators and lack of information
exists in the term 'violence against women', which is commonly used to

describe violence committed by men but erases the very people committing the violence. The violence described in this phrase is not being done by invisible beings and it is not caused by women. It is committed by men and caused by their choice to do so. When we exclude men from our descriptions of the violence they are choosing to commit, we subtly shift responsibility for it from perpetrator to victim, and make the cause of the violence – men's choices – invisible. The term 'violence against women' is not meant to include other types of violence, such as the less common violence committed by women or the more common violence men commit against other men. The underlying cause of male-on-male violence may be similar, but the expression and effects are not. When men are violent to other men they are much more likely to direct their violence at a stranger or an acquaintance than at someone close to them. It is also far more likely to be a single event and to occur in a public space than when they are violent to women, where it is more likely to be ongoing and to only occur in private.

Men are also significantly more likely than women to do violence to themselves. In most western countries the male suicide rate is around five times higher than the female suicide rate. The reasons for this are tragic and complex, but I would argue they are still related to violence myths and the shame and isolation that myths about masculinity impose on men.

For these reasons, I've chosen not to use the term 'violence against women' throughout this book. Instead I call it 'men's violence against women'.

Toxic Masculinity

This is a relatively recent term and it's frequently misunderstood as meaning that masculinity (and therefore being a man) is inherently toxic. In fact, it means the exact opposite. The Good Men Project defines toxic masculinity this way:

Toxic masculinity is a narrow and repressive description of manhood, designating manhood as defined by violence, sex, status and aggression. It's the cultural ideal of manliness, where strength is everything while emotions are a weakness; where sex and brutality are yardsticks by which men are measured, while supposedly 'feminine' traits—which can range from emotional vulnerability to simply not being hypersexual—are the means by which your status as 'man' can be taken away.

In other words, men are not inherently aggressive. They are not born believing strength is their only option and that weakness emasculates them. These things are taught to some men from boyhood and trap them in a narrow and toxic definition of masculinity that harms them as much as, if not more than, it harms people around them.

Chapter 4
Rape myths

Rape has always been a crime, but its criminal definition has changed in law (if not in practice) over the last fifty years. Rape in marriage was legal until the 1980s in Australia, and as recently as the early 2000s, judges were still warning juries against accepting the testimony of women and children about rape unless they had corroborating evidence. In other words, a woman was not considered a reliable witness to her own rape. While law reform has changed legal definitions and rules, the myths that gave men tacit permission to rape their wives, women of colour and women without social or economic power are still embedded in many of our legal, media and social institutions. I'll explore the data more later in this chapter, but in summary, rape has the lowest rates of reporting, investigation, charges laid, cases at trial, conviction and custodial sentence of any of the violent crimes. At the heart of this are the persistent myths about rape, including gendered perceptions of who is responsible for rape, what constitutes 'real rape' and whether there is a difference between rape and sex (yes, there most definitely is).

VIOLENCE MYTHS ABOUT RAPE

- Women are either 'good' women or 'bad' women. 'Good' women don't get raped and 'bad' women can't be raped.

- Women frequently lead men on, tease and provoke them into consensual sex and afterwards lie about being raped.
- It is only 'real rape' when committed by a recognisably evil man who attacks a good woman he has never met before. She will fight back and suffer obvious physical injuries. She will immediately report it to the police, complete and correct in every detail, and cry while she does so.
- Rape happens when men can't control their need for sex.
- Good men don't have male friends or family who would rape a woman.

To get some idea of the attrition rate of rape reports in the justice system, (that is, the number of reported rapes that do not continue through to investigations or trial) let's take a look at one year in one state in Australia. Keep in mind that the time delays in going to trial means these numbers do not directly correlate, but the rates haven't changed significantly over the last few years, so these figures still provide a good indication of how attrition works. According to the New South Wales Bureau of Crime Statistics and Research, there were 10 944 reports of sex offences made to New South Wales Police in 2015. The Australian Institute of Criminology estimates that less than 30 per cent of sexual assaults and related offences are reported to the police, which means there were around 36 000 actual cases of sexual violence in New South Wales in 2015. In the same year, 1734 resulted in criminal proceedings and 1603 reported sexual assaults went to court; 932 reports were found guilty and, of those, 523 offenders received a custodial sentence. That means that 3 per cent of sexual offences resulted in guilty verdicts and 1 per cent resulted in jail terms. These numbers have not changed substantially in more than twenty years. This chapter looks at some of the reasons for this and specifically the role the media plays in maintaining this abhorrent status quo.

One of the reasons the Fixed It project started is that the language we use and the subtly different meanings of the words with which we describe events and feelings give shape to how we think about them. When it comes to the word 'rape', I define it as sexual penetration of another person without their consent.

Rape is a forceful word that describes a violent act. While legislation and public debate tend towards the more sanitised phrase 'sexual assault', it is not always the most accurate. Sexual assault can be a useful term to describe sexual violence that does not include penetration (without assuming this is any less traumatic and dehumanising than penetrative violence), but the purpose of using it as a euphemism for rape is to soften the impact and reduce the sense of violence in the act. But rape *should* be shocking. We should be rocked back on our feet when we hear someone has committed such a crime. Softening the language does not alter the effect of rape but it does reduce our ability to recognise what a rapist did to their victim.

One of the reasons for the change in terminology in legislation, as both Queensland and New South Wales Justice Departments have said, was their desire to use a gender-neutral term in the legislation, though I struggle to understand why 'rape' cannot apply equally to male victims. Journalists at the time also reported that the legislators hoped perpetrators would be more likely to plead guilty to sexual assault than rape, precisely because the word rape was so shocking. Sexual assault could be as simple as a slap on the bottom, which perpetrators would find less objectionable, but no one wants to be labelled a rapist. The intention was noble, in that it hoped to free more victims from the trauma of testifying at trial, but the effect has been negligible in achieving more guilty pleas. In fact, it has softened the language we use to describe a deeply injurious crime, and in doing so has softened our perception of its enormity.

The change in legislation has had a flow-on effect in the way journalists report on rape. The news will only mention the word rape when
police or courts are involved. This is partly explained by the fact that
hard news requires verifiable facts, but it also perpetuates the silencing
of victims that is so entangled in how we read about, think about, talk
about and understand rape.

Because legislation varies across states in Australia and around the
world, the exact same set of circumstances can result in a charge of 'rape'
in one state, 'sexual assault' in another and even an 'indecent act' somewhere else. Jason Bosland, Deputy Director of the Centre for Media and
Communications Law at the University of Melbourne, says that if a person has been convicted or charged with a crime the legislation calls sexual
assault but which most people would understand as rape, there is no reason
the word rape could not be used in a headline, but as he says, best practice
would always be to include the exact charges in the body of the article.

Also, police usually cannot release details of a rape before trial, which
means most crime reporting on rape contains very few verifiable facts,
particularly during the early stages of an investigation. This is where we
see such a clash between the need to support rape victims and the need
to uphold the fundamental principles of the justice system. Even though
false rape claims are rare (somewhere between 2 and 8 per cent, depending on the research you read), this does not mean we can ignore two
key foundations that underpin our legal system: that a person is innocent until proven guilty; and that everybody has the right to a fair trial.
Reporting on rape charges has to balance the assumption of innocence
against the assumption the victim is telling the truth. It's a very difficult
line to draw and it's not surprising journalists on tight deadlines sometimes get it wrong.

Journalists also need to be very careful about what they say when
they're reporting court proceedings. They cannot give any opinions on

what they saw or heard in court, and they cannot change the evidence presented to the court because they don't like or agree with the way it was presented. It's the ultimate 'just the facts, ma'am' reporting. A lot of what happens in court hearings is procedural, complex and often quite boring, and it either can't be reported or isn't useful information for the public. This means that it can sometimes be very difficult to tell from the media reports what actually happened in court on any one day. Maybe most of the day was taken up with procedural matters. Or maybe the defence opening statement took up most of the day and the prosecutor didn't have time to say much, or a witness was giving very long detailed forensic evidence that doesn't need to be reported in detail. When this happens, it's a court reporter's job to paraphrase and summarise for their readers. Having said that, there is no reason why they can't provide context. If the only evidence given that day was from the defence, journalists should say so. If prosecution will be making their opening statement the next day, journalists should report that. If defence is attempting to create sympathy for the accused by blaming the victim, journalists cannot make subjective claims about it, but they can report any rebuttal by the prosecutors.

According to the Victorian Solicitor-General's Office, sub judice (meaning 'under a judge') contempt, as it applies to criminal trials, is defined as publishing anything that prejudges the guilt or innocence of an accused; anything that either criticises or creates sympathy for an accused or a victim; any prior convictions, criminal history, or photographs or film of an accused; and any interviews with witnesses or potential witnesses. This definition is roughly consistent across most states in Australia but varies significantly in other countries. Sub judice rules in Australia usually apply from the time a person is charged with a crime through to the end of the appeal period after a trial has concluded.

Most mainstream publications have taken this definition to mean they need to be very careful about implying guilt in the accused or creating sympathy for victims. The requirement of not creating sympathy for the accused or criticising the victims often seems to carry less weight. This could partly be attributed to the fact that victims rarely have lawyers and contempt charges are rare in Australia, but it's also likely that violence myths about rape, still sadly too prevalent, are the basis for most headlines about sexual violence.

'GOOD' WOMEN AND 'BAD' WOMEN

Violence myths about rape are the preconceptions and subconscious biases we've learned through millions of tiny interactions with the world. Every advertisement that depicts women as passive sexual objects, every movie where the female villain is a femme fatale and the love interest is a passive princess, every song, poem, painting, photo, joke, headline, book, comic strip, news article, comedy sketch, or TV show that separates women into 'good' women and 'bad' women is based on the myth that women who have sexual agency are morally suspect. 'Good' women are pure, virginal, chaste, modest, nice, virtuous, maidenly, unsullied, sweet, wholesome, or any one of the dozens of other words we use to describe women who don't actively demonstrate that they want or enjoy sex. 'Good' women do not tempt men to do bad things, so they are very unlikely to be raped. If they are raped, however, the only possible perpetrator is an irredeemably evil monster, who is instantly recognisable as being different from all other men. A truly 'good' woman will never put herself in the path of such a man, but he may occasionally intrude upon her, even when she is being properly 'good'. It is only then that is she a 'real' rape victim and can receive the sympathy a 'real' victim deserves.

Any woman who is not a 'good' woman is a 'bad' woman, which means she has either demonstrated awareness of her own sexual desires or she has made choices based on the idea that she is a person in her own right rather than defining herself by how she affects the men around her.

These choices can be as simple as clothes that are playful, sexy or revealing because a woman can choose to be these things without inviting violence. The 'bikini barista' who fought off a man attempting to rape her at knife point (reported by the *Herald Sun* under the headline 'Bikini barista's terrifying attempted rape caught on CCTV') is just one example of how women's clothes are a priority in reporting acts of violence against them.

'Bad' women can't be raped, and if they are, the supposed rape would not have happened if they had been behaving like 'good' women, therefore they must bear at least some of the blame. The only exception to the 'good' vs 'bad' woman is the invisible woman, which is essentially anyone who is over forty, larger than average, has a disability, is not demonstrably cisgender and heterosexual, isn't white (except when they are fetishised and then they are most definitely 'bad') or is deemed to be too far from conventional beauty to count. In the view of the male-dominated media, these people are niche markets and incidents in their lives are not relevant to mainstream news unless they can be sensationalised.

The good/bad/invisible trinity forms the basis of all the other violence myths about rape. One of the most prevalent is the myth of 'real rape', which scholars and activists have been debunking for decades. This myth says rape is only real when a 'good' woman is physically attacked by a man she doesn't know. 'Real rape' victims must be able to show injuries and prove they fought back. They will always cry afterwards and will clearly remember every minute detail of the rape in the exact time sequence in which it occurred. They will not have had even a sniff of alcohol before the rape and they will have no history of trauma, mental illness or addiction. They will not have been out in public unescorted after sunset or alone in a house with a man not their family or husband at the time of the rape. They will never have displayed any sexual agency or confidence in photos or videos on social media. They will not have a sexual history that in any way deviates from the boy-meets-girl-and-falls-in-love trope. They will not have tattoos, piercings, unconventional hair or be wearing revealing clothing. There will always be objective bystanders who can substantiate the victim's account of the rape because even 'good' women are not reliable witnesses to their own experiences. These are the conditions of 'real rape' and anything that does not meet all these standards is probably not rape. Not really.

If any of this sounds over the top or even just slightly exaggerated, think back to the reactions in public discourse after the murders of Jill Meagher and Eurydice Dixon. In each instance, a man they had never met grabbed them as they were walking home, then raped and murdered them. And still, sententious voices were saying, 'Well she shouldn't have been out on the street by herself' and police publicly called upon women to 'maintain situational awareness' as if this (or the lack of it) was the thing that caused the rapes and murders rather than the choices of men who committed rape and murder. Do such people think these murders would not have happened if Jill and Eurydice had stayed home? Do they think the men who chose to rape and murder a woman they'd never met would not simply have found another woman to attack? I cannot believe people who ask why Jill or Eurydice were out by themselves would seriously advocate banning women from working or socialising on their own, or that they would suggest all women must be accompanied by a man every time they leave the house. What about women who cannot afford a taxi or an Uber home? Should they not participate in public life? Taxi and Uber drivers are also potential rapists, so that's no guarantee of getting home safely anyway. And the most likely location for rape to occur is in someone's home, so women who stay home all the time are even less safe than women who go out at night on their own. The fact is that there is nothing women can do to keep themselves safe from violence for the simple reason that the violence is never their choice: it is the choice of the person who enacts violence against them, and there is ultimately nothing we can do to protect ourselves from other people's choices.

The truth is that rapists can choose to attack people of all ages, genders, races, religions, classes, physical appearances and abilities. But across these groups, two factors remain constant: the first is that the perpetrator will almost certainly be a man, and the second is that it's very likely he will have known his victim before he raped them. Stranger rape is the least common rape in any western country. Research by the Australian Bureau of Statistics, which broadly matches similar research in the U.S., U.K., Canada and New Zealand, estimates that over 90 per cent of rapes are committed by men, and around 80 per cent of rapists were known to the victim; at least half of those were intimate partners. Around 70 per cent of rapes occurred in private homes. Less than 7 per cent occurred on public streets, parks or laneways.

While more than 80 per cent of rape victims are women, rape can (and does) also happen to men and children. Disabled women are at a disproportionately higher risk of being raped than able-bodied women. Women who are old, or not conventionally attractive, are raped. Sex workers are raped. Women who don't fight back are still raped and rape often occurs without leaving substantial physical injuries. Rape does not require physical violence; it can and frequently does happen through fear, coercion or lack of ability to consent and these things do not leave visible bruises. As discussed earlier in the book, freezing is a common response to fear, especially in women who have suffered abuse in the past, and these women are more likely to be the victims of predatory men in the future. In a 2013 paper commissioned by London's BPP University, Dr Nina Burrowes found that 'a lack of physical resistance is . . . normal and often out of the victim's conscious control'. The freeze response can frequently continue well after the rape so the victim appears cold and unfeeling. In other words, she doesn't cry and she can't remember all the details of the rape.

Alcohol is often a factor in rape but it is most frequently used either as a weapon to incapacitate the victim or focus blame on them later, or to diminish the perpetrator's responsibility for his choices. It's an excuse that would never work in any other crime – try getting up in court and arguing that you aren't to blame for driving drunk because you'd had too much to drink to be responsible for your choices – but it is accepted as an excuse for rape. In a famous 1984 study by sociologists Diana Scully and Joseph Marolla, for which they conducted in-depth interviews with 114 convicted rapists (covered more in Chapter 8), even the researchers were surprised by how often alcohol was used, either to weaken victims at the time or discredit them afterwards, or to provide justification for an 'aberration' by an otherwise 'nice guy'.

Despite this, and all the corroborating research since then, too many people still believe that a woman who is raped while she is drunk is at least partly responsible for the rape. For example, a 2014 study of social attitudes to sexual violence in Scotland found around 15 per cent of people attributed significant portion of blame to women who are raped when they're drunk. Nearly 40 per cent said the victim in these cases should bear some of the blame. Similar results were found in the Australian National Community Attitudes to Violence Against Women study and the U.K. Office for National Statistics. This is a gendered problem. Consider a scenario where a woman goes out drinking with a male acquaintance and, after they've both had far too much to drink, she falls asleep and he rapes her while she's unconscious. We might think of a similar scenario, but instead of a man and a woman going out for drinks, it's two men. In this scenario, if one of the men fell asleep and was raped by his friend while he was unconscious, it's highly unlikely that anyone in the community, media or the justice system would imply the victim brought it on himself by having too many pints in the company of another man. No one is likely to insinuate that being drunk or agreeing to go back to a man's house meant he was being sexually suggestive. These excuses are only offered to men who rape women.

There is no such thing as 'real rape'. There is just rape.

WOMEN LIE ABOUT RAPE

Another of the prevalent rape myths is that women often lie about being raped, either to punish a man who didn't follow through on a romantic relationship, or to protect their reputation after consensual sex. VicHealth's National Community Attitudes Towards Violence Against Women survey found only 59 per cent of people agree that 'women rarely make false allegations of rape', leaving around 4 in every 10 people who think women do lie about rape. Again, the beliefs don't match the facts. Because false accusations of rape are rare, it's difficult to establish exactly how many there are given that so few rapes are actually reported. The best guess puts it somewhere between 2 and 8 per cent of all reports. It's also worth noting that the very few cases where false allegations are made almost never have serious consequences for the man who was falsely accused (less than one percent of these reports resulted in charges being laid before the claims were found to be false). On the other hand, data from the Personal Safety Survey suggests over 85 percent of sexual assaults are not reported to police.

If you apply all those numbers to the just over 20·000 people who reported sexual assault to police in Australia in 2017, you'd find that on average, more than 150000 sexual assaults occurred and 11 men were charged (but not convicted) over false accusations. In other words, you could fill the MCG one and a half times over with victims of sexual assault from a single year and fit the men falsely accused in a little minibus outside. This does not justify the false reporting or minimise the suffering of those men who were falsely accused, but it does put it into perspective to think that for every man who has gone through a false allegation, around 12 000 women have silently suffered the trauma of sexual violence. The few men who were falsely accused undoubtedly suffered, but they were also publicly vindicated and usually celebrated in the media. This occurred with Adam Rowe, when the judge in his trial for raping a woman who had been drinking declared the woman's evidence was not reliable enough for the trial to continue. *The Sun* reported it under the headline, '"17 MONTHS OF HELL" Man, 29, accused of raping a "10-out-of-10 drunk" woman on night out is cleared'. The judge was quite clear in saying that he did not think the woman was lying, so declaring the accused was 'cleared' is a bit strong. The woman described herself as '10-out-of-10 drunk' (in which case, how could she give consent?), but the headline and the article itself make no mention of how the trial and its subsequent dismissal affected her. It is the man accused of rape who becomes the object of sympathy in this headline, not the woman who says she was raped.

RAPE HAPPENS BECAUSE MEN CAN'T CONTROL THEIR NEED FOR SEX

Again, this myth plays into stereotypes about gendered sexuality – men need sex and women just use it. Sadly, far too many people still believe this to be true. The National Community Attitudes to Violence against Women study found that 40 per cent of people agree that 'rape results from men not able to control their need for sex'. Now that's an interesting one. Do we believe that all men are potential rapists because they are unable to control their need for sex? Or do we believe the wide body of research that shows rape is about power and control, not sex, and that the men who commit rape choose to do so and should be held accountable for their choices?

A study by Boston University researchers on 133 rapists concluded that the motivation for rape has far more to do with power than sexual desire. The offences could be categorised as power rape (sexuality used primarily to express power) or anger rape (use of sexuality to express anger). There were no rapes in which sex was the dominant issue; sexuality was always in the service of other, non-sexual needs.

Research since the 1970s has concluded the motivations for rape are more complex and often dependent on situational factors. A 1984 paper by Virginia University researchers found significant links to revenge/ punishment of all women by hurting an individual woman. Another study by Marquette University in 2010 found that men are more likely to commit rape if they believe rape myths to be true or if they associate sex with power.

RAPISTS ARE ALL INSTANTLY RECOGNISABLE MONSTERS

It is a terrible thing to believe that men we know and love could commit rape. Far more comfortable is the idea that 'real' rapists are recognisable monsters, stereotypical balaclava-clad aberrations lurking in the shadows. They're not. They are our friends, relatives, partners and members of our sports clubs. They are our gym buddies and our drinking buddies. Rapists look like Brock Turner and Mitchell Peggie. They have friends and family and communities who respect them, love them and would never believe they could commit a crime as horrendous as rape. Data from the Personal Safety Survey indicates that more than 2.1 million people in Australia have experienced sexual violence at age of fifteen or older, and over 1.4 million experienced sexual abuse as children. It takes more than just a few aberrations to commit millions of crimes. If you live in Australia and you know more than eight people, you probably know someone who has been subjected to sexual violence. If you know more than eight Australian men, you probably know someone who has committed sexual violence. It's a deeply uncomfortable thought, but turning away from it does not make it any less true.

Rape committed by an attractive, charismatic man with loving friends and family is still rape.

RAPE IN THE NEWS

In 2016 Mitchell Peggie was convicted of rape and sentenced to seven years in prison. A week before the rape for which he was convicted, he had been acquitted of raping another young woman under similar circumstances. During the successful trial, his 21-year-old victim was asked whether her cries were her 'moaning and gasping' with pleasure. She was told that wearing 'sexy lingerie' implied she intended to have sex. The defence lawyer insisted she was lying about the rape to take revenge against Peggie for treating her 'like rubbish' after consensual sex. When she testified that she had masturbated him because she was scared he would hurt her and hoped it would placate him, it was used against her as evidence that she was a willing participant. All of this was reported lasciviously in various publications around Australia.

The Courier Mail: Mr Wilson suggested text messages between the pair in the hours before the alleged rape showed 'some implied acceptance that you intended to have some sexual activity' with Peggie that night, a claim she denied.

News.com.au: The court heard they organised to meet after exchanging more than 200 text messages in which Peggie told her he liked 'rough fucking' and wanted to meet an 'adventurous' girl.

9 News: Mr Wilson also accused her of moaning with pleasure
during the alleged assault – a claim she denies – and questioned why
she didn't call out for help. He also asked her why she had chosen to
wear a red and black lace G-string and bra.

Brisbane Times: There were tears in the public gallery as the jury
announced their verdict, which included not guilty findings for two
counts of sexual assault and another rape charge. [These tears were
from Peggie's family. There was no mention of the reaction from the
victim or her family, or the effect this rape had on them.]

The woman's underwear was displayed at the trial and lurid descriptions of the size and colour of her underpants were included in the news
reports of the trial. There's certainly a public interest in reporting on how
rape victims are treated in court, but it is possible to do this without
sensationalising the evidence. To be fair, precising even one day of testimony, let alone an entire trial, which can go on for weeks, is a difficult
job. Summarising is an essential part of court reporting but so is including some context. If court reporters are reporting on a day where the
defence is questioning a witness, they can (and do) paraphrase, they can
(and do) choose which quotes to include and which ones to leave out,
they can (and almost never do) explain that this particular report is only
the defence case because the prosecution did not have a chance to cross
examine or present witnesses that day. The woman Mitchell Peggie raped
said later that she was utterly traumatised by the way the defence lawyer
treated her in court. She wrote about it for SBS two years after the trial:

I felt so alone and isolated up on that witness stand, like everyone
in that room was judging the person I was based on that one night,
that one thing that happened to me. A survivor of something like

sexual assault should not be made to feel this way. I personally felt like I was dirty, not worth being there and that I should just give up and call off the trial.

There is a line between reporting on what happens in court and colluding with a defence lawyer's tactics of shaming and scaring rape victims in an effort to discredit them. It's a line far too many journalists cross. The confluence of rape myths that underpin defence tactics in trials (discussed further in Chapter 9) and the way rape trials are often reported result in a proliferation of rape myths under the guise of what looks, on the surface, like straight court reporting. In Mitchell Peggie's trial, for example, the details of the defence case were given far more space and weight in news reports than those of the prosecution's. It makes for sensationalist reading and garners clicks and support from the male-dominated readership of hard news.

FIXING THE HEADLINES

These are examples of the way Fixed It posts work. I take a screenshot of the headline and use a simple photo editor to red-pen the edits into the image. When I upload them to the website I usually include a short description of why the original headline was inaccurate and the purpose served by making the fix.

As discussed in Chapter 2, journalists almost never write headlines for their own articles. They're written by editors whose primary concerns are to encourage people to click through and read the full articles or to boost SEO rankings. Given how many headlines we see in our social media feeds each day (far more than we ever click on) I concentrate on the headlines because of how often we see them without finding out any of the context or further details. The violence myths that permeate so many headlines have an effect on us even when we don't notice them. Perhaps especially when we don't notice them.

These headlines were not selected for the book because they were the worst I could find (all these types of headlines are the worst I can find because every single one of them is about a person experiencing probably one of the worst moments of their lives). These are randomly selected from the hundreds I have collected over the last few years.

The Cairns Post: ~~POLICE CHARGE YOUNG MALE WITH ILLICIT ATTACK ON YOUNG MOTHER~~
Fix: *MAN CHARGED WITH ATTEMPTED RAPE OF A WOMAN*
Well there's a nice euphemism for you. 'Illicit attack'. Did he flick a rubber band at her across the classroom? The terminology of legislation can sometimes make it difficult for journalists to accurately report on rape if the charges do not include the word rape. There is, however, no charge, in any criminal code in Australia, of 'illicit attack'. He was charged with attempted rape. Softening the language to this extent has no public interest or social benefit. All it does is reduce a violent crime to schoolyard level and, once again, diminish the perpetrator's responsibility for a violent crime.

News.com.au: ~~BIKINI BARISTA'S TERRIFYING ATTEMPTED RAPE CAUGHT ON CCTV~~
Fix: *ARMED MAN'S ATTEMPT TO RAPE WOMAN CAUGHT ON CCTV*
The first word in this headline references what the victim was wearing. Calling her a 'bikini barista' is a sensationalist way to suggest her choice of clothing was responsible for the man's violent actions. Further, the man who attempted to rape her at knifepoint is erased from the story and all we're left with is the woman who caused the problem (except, of course, she didn't).

Yahoo News: ~~ALLEGED TINDER RAPIST TO FACE VIC COURT~~

Fix: *ALLEGED RAPIST TO STAND TRIAL*

If a man and a woman meet on Tinder and the man ends up raping the woman, it is guaranteed the word Tinder will appear in the headline before the man, the woman or the rape. If he met her at a party, a book shop or in front of the cabbages at Aldi, their meeting wouldn't rate a mention. But Tinder creates a frenzy because women who actively and confidently act on their sexual desires are the epitome of 'bad' women. 'Good women' wait passively for men to want them. They are the objects of desire, not autonomous people with their own feelings. Women who seek out sex on Tinder are therefore perceived as inviting violence. It's an insidious and pernicious form of victim-blaming.

BBC: ~~FLECKNEY MURDER INQUIRY: MAN CHARGED OVER BUNGALOW DEATH~~

Fix: *MAN CHARGED OVER RAPE AND MURDER OF A 72-YEAR-OLD WOMAN WHO WAS A PERSON NOT A HOUSE*

Here is another common trope. If the perpetrator is not erased, the victim is. This man was not charged with murdering a bungalow, he was charged with raping and murdering a woman, but with a headline like this we don't have to think about the terrible crimes committed by violent men because the victim doesn't exist.

Townsville Bulletin: ~~DRINK WAS THE DOWNFALL OF SEX ABUSE FORMER CARER~~

Fix: *MAN WHO CHOSE TO RAPE DISABLED WOMAN FOUND GUILTY OF RAPE*

Drink was not the 'downfall' of the 'sex-abuse former carer'; he is not the victim and what he did was rape, not 'sex' abuse. He chose to rape a disabled woman; he may have been drinking when he made that choice, but the choice was still his. Women with disabilities are at significantly higher risk of sexual violence, usually because they are vulnerable and less likely to be able to ask for help or be taken seriously when they do. The only blame for this rests on the men who choose to take advantage of that vulnerability to commit crimes against them.

Sydney Morning Herald: ~~FORMER RUGBY UNION STAR CRAIG WELLS JAILED FOR RAPING DRUNK TEENAGER~~
Fix: *CRAIG WELLS GUILTY OF USING ALCOHOL AS A WEAPON IN BRUTAL RAPE OF 14-YEAR-OLD GIRL*
'Drunk teenager'? She was fourteen years old! 'Drunk teenager' implies that she was wanton and complicit in the crime Wells chose to commit. Six months after the rape in which alcohol was deliberately used as a weapon against her, this fourteen-year-old girl, this child, tried to kill herself. He was in his forties. Implicitly blaming a child for an adult man's choice to rape her is utterly revolting.

9 News on Facebook: ~~A BRISBANE MAN WHO SAID HIS ALLEGED RAPE VICTIM, A 20 YEAR OLD VIRGIN, WALKING TO THE BUS, HAD BEEN 'PROMISCUOUS'. HE HAS JUST BEEN GRANTED BAIL.~~
Fix: *ONE OF THE MEN ACCUSED OF RAPING A YOUNG WOMAN HAS BEEN GRANTED BAIL. HIS CLAIMS ABOUT HER SEXUAL HISTORY ARE NOT IN ANY WAY RELEVANT TO THE CHARGES AGAINST HIM*
Very few rapists gleefully describe themselves as rapists. They believe the myths that 'bad' women asked for or deserved rape. This doesn't mean journalists need to repeat or endorse their delusions. Whether she was a virgin or had had many lovers is irrelevant to the crime. Rape is rape. Note also the word 'promiscuous', a word that is almost never

applied to men. It's a euphemism for 'slut' and is completely irrelevant to the report.

ABC: ~~CANBERRA BROTHERS MOHAMMAD AND KHALID AL-ABBASI JAILED FOR RAPE OF SEX WORKERS~~
Fix: *CANBERRA BROTHERS MOHAMMAD AND KHALID AL-ABBASI JAILED FOR RAPE OF WOMEN*
The only thing surprising about this headline is that they called these women 'sex workers', rather than 'prostitutes', which most sex workers consider to be a slur. Despite this, the word 'prostitute' was still used extensively in the media until very recently. For example, when Tracy Connolly was murdered, as I wrote about in the introduction to this book, almost every single mainstream news article about the murder described her as 'St Kilda Prostitute'. Regardless of the terminology, this is very similar to the Tinder headlines issue: if a woman is raped or assaulted and she works in the sex industry, her work will always make the headlines, thereby erasing her personhood and implicitly blaming her for putting herself in a dangerous situation. As Sally Tonkin, then CEO of St Kilda Gatehouse, a drop-in centre for street sex workers, said in her TEDx talk, sex workers are always told their work is dangerous, as if the women are the ones making it high risk. But sex workers don't make their work dangerous. It's dangerous because they're working with men – not hardened criminals, but men in our community who get up every morning, drive to work and drive home again. They shop in our supermarkets and drink in our pubs. They are the men we see every day and they are the reason sex work is dangerous.

It's also worth noting that this is one of the few cases where the rapists are clearly identified and named at the front of the headline. If their names had been John and Peter Smith, it's unlikely they'd have featured so prominently. Rapists are often given nicknames – the Churchyard

Rapist (Mitchell Peggie), Tinder Rapist (any man who raped a woman he met on Tinder), but men of colour, particularly Muslim men, are named and put firmly at the front of the headline. It's not just about reinforcing the myth of Muslim men as being dangerous to 'our women', it's also ensuring we maintain the distance between 'normal' (i.e. white, straight) men and 'monsters' who rape women.

The Chronicle: ~~TOOWOOMBA CABBIE HIT WITH SEXUAL ASSAULT CHARGES~~
Fix: *TAXI DRIVER CHARGED WITH SEXUAL ASSAULT OF TWO WOMEN AND HE IS NOT THE VICTIM HERE OMG*
He was 'hit' with sexual assault charges? He sexually assaulted two women. Are we supposed to feel sorry for him that he's been 'hit' with charges? Again, the victims here have been erased from the headline, and the perpetrator is set up as the object of sympathy in a story about a man sexually assaulting two women. Yes, this does get incredibly frustrating sometimes.

THE HEADLINES THAT DON'T EXIST

There's representation, misrepresentation and then there's no representation at all. According to awareness and advocacy group Our Watch, Aboriginal and Torres Strait Islander women are around thirty-five times more likely to be hospitalised due to family violence (which frequently includes rape) than other Australian women. They are also significantly over represented in family violence homicides and reported instances of child abuse. The reasons for this are complex and best explained by this statement from the Strong Families, Safe Kids policy, which was a collaboration between National Voice for our Children, National Family Violence Prevention Legal Services Forum and National Aboriginal and Torres Strait Islander Legal Services:

The trauma of colonisation and oppression is directly linked to the complexity and prevalence of family violence that exists today. The impact of colonisation on Aboriginal and Torres Strait Islander peoples' cultural practices, laws, customs and ways of life has been devastating, generating multiple layers of trauma spanning generations. Families and communities have been fractured and torn apart by dispossession from traditional lands, breakdown of cultural practices and kinship systems, the forced removal of children from their families, and ongoing racism (including structural racism and systemic discrimination), leading to social and economic exclusion. Added to this are experiences of entrenched poverty and political marginalisation, high rates of substance abuse and the loss of traditional male and female roles, which all influence the prevalence of family violence in Aboriginal and Torres Strait Islander communities.

There is a reason almost none of the headlines in Fixed It are about violence committed against Aboriginal and Torres Strait Islander women and it's not because such headlines never need fixing. It's because these stories almost never make the news. Despite the grievous levels of abuse suffered by Aboriginal and Torres Strait Islander women, mainstream news almost never reports it. While no one would wish further abuse upon Aboriginal and Torres Strait Islander women in the form of victim-blaming reports, the fact that their lives and the violence they live with are erased completely from white Australian journalism is further proof of the problems outlined in the above statement from the Strong Families, Safe Kids paper.

Trans women are another group of women who suffer disproportionate levels of violence but are rendered invisible in mainstream news. On the

very rare occasions this violence is reported, it is almost always dehumanising and retraumatising. *The Courier-Mail*'s coverage of Marcus Volke's
murder of Mayang Prasetyo under the headline 'Monster Chef and the
She Male' was revolting. It rightly became the subject of multiple complaints to the Australian Press Council. Other headlines that came out of
News Corp included 'Ladyboy and the butcher' and 'Killed and cooked
trans woman was high-class sex worker'. Mayang was a woman and a
person; she had the same full range of emotions, hopes, failings and suc-
cesses as any other person. She had a past and she should have had a
future and, to say the very least, nothing she did warranted this devaluing
and dehumanisation in the aftermath of her murder.

The complaints to the press council were upheld and the online ver-
sions of those headlines were all edited. *The Courier-Mail* never issued an
apology. Instead, they added a few lines at the bottom of a long article full
of salacious details about Mayang Prasetyo, recognising that she was an
'innocent victim' of a terrible crime committed by a man she should have
been able to trust. They mentioned that she should have been remembered for her 'cheerful and friendly disposition' and acknowledged that
she had friends and family who loved her. They then went on to say:
'Many believe that yesterday we presented Mayang's story in a way that
was disrespectful to her memory. *The Courier-Mail* had no intention of
diminishing the value of Mayang's life, or to add to the grief being felt by
her family.'

If you ever wondered what #SorryNotSorry looks like, now you
know.

Men's violence against women with disabilities, who are a highly
at-risk group, does sometimes make the news, but the disability is
almost always framed as an excuse for the violence, thus the person

with the disability is presented as a burden that caused a violent break-down. Rarely is violence against people with disabilities portrayed as predatory behaviour that deliberately takes advantage of people's vulnerabilities. Even more common is reporting on the disability rather than the person. In Georgia, United States, the *Macon Telegraph*'s report on David Lee Davis's rape of a twenty-year-old woman with disabili-ties included a quote from the rapist's mother. It described her saying 'through sobs' that he had a young child and helped around the house, but that her remarks fell flat as she tried to make sense of what her son did: '. . . It's just the wrong girl at the wrong time. I don't know what else to say. He don't really know no better.'

The report did not mention anything about the woman other than the effect her disability had on the language she was able to use to describe the crime. It did, however, at least include this quote from the prosecu-tor: '"Something is wrong with him," Milton, the prosecutor, said, "and that is that he is . . . a brutal, savage, inhumane rapist who is not fit to live in society."'

Indeed.

For every 100 rapes that occur in Australia, eighty-eight will be commit-ted by someone known to the victim, forty-five will be committed by the victim's intimate partner, five will be reported to police, two will go to court, one rapist will be found guilty and 0.5 rapists will go to prison. For every single false report of rape, 130 rapes are actually committed. No rape or sexual assault legislation in Australia or other western dem-ocratic society requires men to go to great lengths to ensure their sexual partners are consenting or determined that it is only then not rape. Rape convictions require that the prosecution prove that sexual intercourse took place, that the victim did not consent and that the perpetrator knew she did not consent. Most rape trials turn on those last two elements because they are almost always about victim's credibility. Does she look like the sort of woman who would say yes to sex under those circumstances? Is she a 'good' woman? Does she sound like she was really raped? Is she a 'bad' woman?

The few times a rape does result in a criminal trial, the victim is treated like a dubious item of evidence rather than a person who has been brutalised. Police, lawyers, judges and juries often do not believe women and children can be reliable witnesses to their own trauma, and men who commit these crimes seem to view women as objects, partners as property they have the right to control, and violence as an expression of their rightful power. All of these things are informed by, and in turn inform, the rape myths outlined earlier in this chapter. While there are notable exceptions, too much of the mainstream media reporting of men's violence against women supports or implicitly endorses these views and gives them legitimacy in the eyes of the perpetrators of violence.

Chapter 5
It's just a domestic

The gutter press and tabloid hacks have long been part of news media and sensationalised violence has always been one of their staples. Jack the Ripper, the Boston Strangler, Ned Kelly, Bonnie and Clyde, Al Capone, Madeleine McCann, the list of human tragedies manipulated to sell newspapers is endless. There's something very human in wanting to read about the horrors we hope happen only to other people. It reminds us we're still alive and safe while also reinforcing the fears we can enjoy, because we never really believe they will become reality for us. The real things we should be afraid of – like climate change, corrupt or even just dysfunctional governments, failing economies, and the violent men we live with – are too real and it's easy to feel powerless to protect ourselves from them. They often don't make for great news stories, because few people really want to think too much about dangers we can't change.

Domestic violence is too common in Australia, so common that the statistics about it almost roll off the tongue without meaning. One woman a week is killed by a man who claimed to love her. One in three Australian women have experienced violence from a man they know. Women are almost three times more likely than men to have experienced

violence at the hands of a partner since the age of fifteen. Intimate partner violence contributes more to the burden of disease of adult women
than any other risk factor.

As with the rape myths discussed in the last chapter, myths about
domestic violence are common and contribute to the way it is understood and reported in news media.

VIOLENCE MYTHS ABOUT DOMESTIC VIOLENCE

- When a person is violent to someone in their family it is an
  isolated event with no wider social context.
- Domestic violence only comprises physical abuse.
- Women are able to leave violent men if they want to. If they don't
  leave, they are responsible for the violence committed against
  them.
- Women are just as violent to men as men are to women.
- Men who beat their wives are often provoked into it by nagging,
  unfaithfulness or cruelty.
- Women frequently lie about domestic violence, particularly if
  they are seeking custody of children.

ISOLATED INCIDENTS

Most of us who consume news have heard the term domestic violence,
but it's relatively new to the mainstream media and its meaning is vague.
It's a phrase that still carries connotations of class and race, seen as a problem for the poor, the drug-addicted and alcoholics. It is also too often
understood as purely physical violence, the stereotypical example of a
drunken man beating his wife. In truth, domestic violence is far more
complex and very difficult to write into legislation. Emotional abuse is
poorly understood. It is not the same as hurt feelings, it's an ongoing process of instilling fear and dismantling the victim's trust and confidence in

themselves and their ability to cope with life without their abusive partner. Financial and sexual violence are also common tools used by abusers
to maintain power and control over their victims. These forms of violence can be difficult for victims to recognise as abuse if they are groomed
to believe it is normal behaviour or something that is their fault. Because
it is so difficult to define and legislate, it almost never results in criminal charges and is therefore rarely reported as news. Physical attacks are
much easier to define and take to trial, but the nature of the criminal
process means it is usually a specific incident that goes to court and this
perpetuates the notion that domestic violence is a single physical event.

Until very recently, domestic violence was rarely reported as a social
issue. This was mostly due to its nature – it lacked the sensationalism that
news required – but also the media was uninterested in violence that took
place in the home. When it was reported at all, it was not depicted as a
social issue but rather as a series of isolated incidents. Mainstream media
did not recognise or report on the connecting factors of gender, attitudes
to women, and the broader social context.

A 2012 study by University of Melbourne researchers Jenny Morgan
and Violeta Politoff demonstrated how prevalent this kind of reporting
is, even in Australian media which, by international standards, reports
men's violence against women quite well. The study looked at nearly
2500 articles published over twenty years and analysed the way men's
violence against women was reported. They found remarkably low
rates of sensationalism and victim blaming when compared to similar
studies from the U.K. and U.S. Despite this, the overwhelming majority (85 per cent) of texts were event-based rather than what they called
'thematic'. In other words, each article presented an individual case of
violence as a stand-alone incident, where the cause and effect were limited only to that particular perpetrator and victim, and only to that
particular incident. The thematic articles, which were rare, included

context about family violence, such as data on how common it is in Australia or how likely it is for such violence to be gender-based and related to men's need for power and control over an entire relationship. The event-based articles put responsibility for causing and preventing the violence solely onto the specific people involved in that one incident. Thematic articles make family violence a social issue that requires the entire community to give attention and effort to the changes needed to stop this violence occurring.

INVISIBLE PERPETRATORS

Listed below is a small selection of the hundreds of headlines I've collected over the last few years. In these examples, the male perpetrators of violence are erased and replaced with locations, houses, cars, or sometimes utterly unrelated facts. I could fill chapters with just these headlines but there's only so much of it you can read before your eyes glaze over and your brain seizes up. These headlines come from mainstream publications all over the world. While they might be more prevalent in the tabloid press, they are by no means solely to be found there. Some of them are lifted from the most reputable and otherwise professional sources of journalism in their countries. These are not the ten worst, they're not even the ten most recent, they are just ten chosen to represent a cross-section of the several hundred in my research.

MyGC: ~~WOMAN FIGHTS FOR LIFE IN HOSPITAL AFTER HORROR DOMESTIC VIOLENCE ATTACK~~
Fix: *MAN CHARGED WITH ATTEMPTED MURDER AFTER ALLEGEDLY BREACHING DOMESTIC VIOLENCE ORDER AND NEARLY BEATING EX-WIFE TO DEATH*
Yes, it was a horrific attack, but who attacked her? And what was the context? There's no perpetrator mentioned here and no history or context.

The headline suggests an isolated attack, and the man who tried to kill his ex-wife is erased from the story.

Daily Mercury: ~~INFANT CAUGHT UP IN DRUNKEN ASSAULT~~
Fix: *MAN REPEATEDLY PUNCHES WIFE IN THE HEAD AND INJURES 4 MONTH OLD BABY*
The infant wasn't 'caught up' in the assault, a violent man deliberately assaulted his wife while she was holding their baby, thus putting the infant at risk of harm. And while he might have been drinking when he chose to assault his wife and child, the assault was still his choice. Similar to rape reporting, here alcohol is mentioned in the context of excusing the actions of the perpetrator.

The Sunday Telegraph: ~~'GOOD' BLOKE SHOT WIFE, DAUGHTER AND HER FOUR KIDS, THEN HIMSELF~~
Fix: *PETER MILES SHOT WIFE, DAUGHTER AND HER FOUR KIDS, THEN HIMSELF*
This was the worst mass shooting since Port Arthur. No one would ever describe Martin Bryant as a 'good bloke' in a headline. 'Good blokes' don't kill women and children, and the fact that someone thought he was a good bloke does not belong in this headline. It's inaccurate, misleading and irrelevant to the story.

Savannah Morning News: ~~TROUBLED PORT WENTWORTH MARRIAGE ENDS IN MURDER~~
Fix: *MAN WITH HISTORY OF DOMESTIC VIOLENCE MURDERS WIFE*
'Troubled marriage' and 'volatile relationship' are euphemisms for intimate terrorism frequently used in court and in the media. It softens the appearance of violence and shifts blame from the perpetrator to a shared

responsibility with the victim. This man had a history of being violent to his wife before he killed her. She was not in any way responsible for that violence and the marriage didn't 'end': he murdered her.

The Newcastle Herald: ~~MURDER VICTIM AMANDA CARTER SUSPECTED AFFAIR, COURT TOLD~~
Fix: *MAN ACCUSED OF STALKING AND MURDERING AMANDA CARTER*
Another invisible murderer. This time, the facts are also twisted to place blame for her own murder on a jealous woman, rather than on the man who chose to stalk her and kill her after she left him. (I don't think it helps to get into he said/she said about the infidelity, whatever her reason for leaving him the point is that it doesn't mean it's okay for him to kill her and OMG we have to tell people that FFS.)

ABC News: ~~MURDER CHARGE LAID AFTER FIVE MONTH OLD BOY FOUND DEAD ON BRISBANE'S BAYSIDE~~
Fix: *MAN CHARGED WITH MURDER OF FIVE-MONTH-OLD BOY IN BRISBANE*
Who was charged with murder? Another invisible, anonymous being? At the time of the report, police had not released any details about the man or his relationship to the baby, but they had said that a 32-year-old man was charged with murder. Why is that highly pertinent detail not in the headline? The headline is written in the passive voice, as headlines about men's violence against women so often are. We're warned against using the passive voice in journalism from almost the first day of classes, but it seems impossible to eradicate from these headlines. The very simple fix here demonstrates how easy it is to change the headline back to the active voice and how clearly that puts men's violence back into the headline.

Daily Telegraph: ~~WOMAN DIES IN HOSPITAL AFTER STABBING ATTACK IN NSW~~

Fix: *MAN CHARGED WITH MURDER OF HIS OWN GRANDMOTHER*

She didn't just die, she was killed, and her own grandson was charged with her murder. Yet again, a man charged with committing violence was erased from the headline of the article about the violence he allegedly committed.

News Mail: ~~SHOCK END TO TWISTED INCEST CASE~~

Fix: *MAN MURDERS HIS DAUGHTER, THEIR BABY AND HER ADOPTIVE FATHER*

This was a complex case and one that was difficult to sum up in a single sentence, but it's worth taking an extra minute or two to think about how to do it properly. A triple murder is not a 'shock end': it is a choice to end three lives, a choice made by one person who has been omitted from the headline.

The Australian: ~~FUNERAL OF MANRIQUE-LUTZ FAMILY HEARS OF ENORMOUS STRESS~~

Fix: *MANRIQUE-LUTZ FAMILY UNITE FOR FUNERAL OF WOMAN, CHILDREN AND THE MAN WHO KILLED THEM*

Many, many families in Australia are under stress. It fact it would probably be quite difficult to find a family with two young children who didn't experience stress from time to time. And there are certainly far too many families finding it difficult to access adequate disability support services. You know what they don't do? They don't kill their wives and children. They find ways to cope that are not meticulously planned murders, and they love their children, not in spite of their disabilities, but because they just love their children. People who murder their own children are not just suffering stress, there is no excuse for it, and they shouldn't be erased or excused. They are murderers.

Brisbane Times: ~~QUEENSLAND MUM FATALLY BEATEN OVER BACON PACKET~~
Fix: *QUEENSLAND MAN CONVICTED OF MURDERING HIS PARTNER*
How to trivialise a murder in one easy step: blame it on the bacon and take the murderer out of the headline. Simple.

Invisible perpetrators are a constant feature in Fixed It, and this has a real impact on how we think about and understand violence. Among the first things journalists are taught are clarity in reporting and avoiding the passive voice. This is why the persistent use of passive voice and unclear reporting on men's violence against women stands out so starkly. If all the violent crimes committed by men were reported in the active voice, with the perpetrators and their crime the subject of every headline, it would overwhelm daily news reporting. Because it *is* overwhelming. This kind of reporting would make inescapable the uncomfortable truth that most violence is committed by men; but it is not the job of journalists to erase the truth to avoid making readers uncomfortable. A journalist's job is to describe what is happening in our society, and the truth is that around 90 per cent of violent crimes are committed by men.

Invisible perpetrators of men's violence against women are more common in headlines than in the body of the report. Headlines are supposed to be a short summary of the article. When the article is about men's violence against women and the violent men are rendered invisible, the headline is not telling the story, it's erasing the story. Fixed It focuses on headlines because most people don't consume news by reading a print newspaper from cover to cover. Whether we get our news from social media links or by running our eyes over the website of a news publication, the first and most common thing we see are headlines.

There's a lot of variation among individuals, but many people only read the headlines on somewhere around 60 per cent of the articles they see. When we skim over headlines like this, we might not be thinking very much about what they say, but we see them. When they fit our subconscious bias or when they're underpinning violence myths and repeating them over and over again, they reinforce those myths without us even noticing it.

The things we don't notice are far more dangerous than the things we do notice.

He was such a Good Guy

The Good Bloke, the Great Guy, the Loving Father, the Amazing Hubby, the Pillar of Society. Also known as: the man who killed his partner and/or children. The Good Guy trope is so ubiquitous in news reports about men who committed suicide after murdering their partners and children that it was almost impossible to find a media report on this crime that didn't include a Good Guy reference.

In Wangaratta during April 2017, Ora Holt and her children were chased from their home at gunpoint by Greg Floyd, her husband and the father of the children. Ora fled to a neighbour's house and put herself between her armed husband and their children. He shot her, then himself.

The ABC quoted a Wangaratta local as saying, 'He seemed to me to be a decent young fellow, who worked hard in order to protect and feed his family.' The *Herald Sun* quoted Floyd's sister: 'Everyone will tell you he was an excellent person, there wasn't a bad bone in his body.' News.com.au reported a former neighbour saying there had never been signs of trouble at the property. '"They're pretty good people," he said.' Kidspot wrote, 'The family have been described as loving and normal. Neighbours say they had never even heard Floyd yell at his kids.' *The Age* quoted a local resident as saying, 'They were very nice people.' In other words, every major news outlet in the state included some form of Good Guy quote in an article about a man who chased his wife and children out of their home with a gun before killing his wife in front of their children. The only reason Floyd got the Good Guy treatment was because he was her husband. If he had been a stranger, or worse, a Muslim stranger, he'd have been demonised in the press as a monster and a terrorist. The fact that some of his neighbours liked him is not relevant to the crime he committed, and yet it was reported in almost every single article about the murder he committed.

In October 2016, Fernando Manrique planned an elaborate construction of pipes to deliver poisonous gas into the home where his wife, Maria, and their children, Martin and Elisa, were sleeping. The murders occurred not long after Maria had told him she wanted a divorce. The headline of the report in a leading newspaper was: '"A horrific thing": the death of the Manrique-Lutz family'. It truly was a horrific thing, but it was not a simple 'death' of the family. It was not a tragic accident or unforeseeable disaster, but a meticulously planned murder. Again, if it had been committed by anyone but the husband and father, it would have been called a massacre, not a death, and the murderer would have been vilified in a series of outraged articles about the vicious and unforgivable nature of the murder of innocent women and children.

Also included in the article was an interview with a friend of Manrique who 'remembers Manrique as a private but warm man who cared deeply for his children'. This 'warm man' spent weeks planning their murder. It should go without saying that this is not how men who care for their children behave.

Kidspot, under the headline 'Davidson Family Tragedy: Was Mum struggling to cope?' (Davidson is the location of the murder, not the name of the murdered family), quoted neighbours saying, 'Maria had been feeling the burden of raising two children with autism.' While it's certainly true that services for autistic children could be improved, describing murdered autistic children as a 'burden' rather than assuming they were, as was the case with these children, beloved sons and daughters, is particularly abhorrent. As evidence gathered over time proved, Maria was in fact a devoted mother, entirely prepared to care for her two children by herself.

In March 2016, Arona Peniamina stabbed his wife, Sandra Peniamina, to death in front of their ten-year-old son. They also had another three younger children. Paramedics who attended described the attack as one of the worst they had ever seen. SBS reported that his aunt described Peniamina as 'a really good man'. The *Brisbane Times* repeated the quote and added that he 'just wanted to work hard for his family'.

In September 2014, grain farmer Geoff Hunt killed his wife, Kim, and their three children at their home in Lockhart, in the New South Wales Riverina region, before shooting himself. Under the headline 'Strains that grew inside Geoff Hunt ended in five deaths on a farm' and a picture of a happy-looking couple, the *Sydney Morning Herald* reported that one of his friends said, 'You couldn't get a better bloke. The most gentle, considerate bloke . . . a pillar of society.' The *Weekend Australian* reported, 'He has done a horrific thing, yet Lockhart remembers Geoff Hunt as a good man,' followed by a quote from one of Hunt's friends saying, 'Geoff is one of the kindest, most caring fathers you would ever find.'

Damien Little, who shot his two sons then drove off a wharf with their bodies in his car, was described by Australia's national broadcaster as 'respected and well liked'; coverage quoted a friend as saying, 'You couldn't have asked for a better bloke.'

The arrest of Chris Watts in Colorado, United States, who confessed to killing his pregnant wife, Shanann, and two small daughters, was reported by the BBC under the headline: '"Amazing hubby" held after missing family "found dead in fuel tanks"'. The article included copies of several social media posts by Shanann praising Watts as a loving husband and father. At the time, Watts had been arrested but had not yet confessed to the murders. In sharing these posts by a murdered woman, the BBC showed a staggering level of ignorance. Do they think women in violent relationships commonly post pictures of their bruises and details of the abuse they suffer?

In Ireland in early 2016, Alan Hawe stabbed his wife, Clodagh, to death. Then he walked upstairs with a knife and a hatchet and murdered their three sons. The youngest, Ryan, was six years old and he had defensive wounds, indicating he was probably awake and trying to defend himself when his father killed him. Hawe then wrote a note saying he'd killed his family because he didn't think they could live without him, and hanged himself. News reports across Ireland lauded him as 'a brilliant dad', 'a valuable member of the community', 'the most normal person you could meet', 'quiet and a real gentleman' and ran photos of Hawe and his sons, but none of Clodagh. Journalists ascribed the murders to mental illness and, had it not been for an impassioned blog by Irish feminist Linnea Dunne, the story might have ended there. Dunne's post, called 'Rest In Peace, Invisible Woman', eviscerated the media reporting of Hawe's crimes. She pointed out how often the mentally ill are targets of abuse but rarely the perpetrators of it, and that the idea a family had no right to live if their father chose to die was patriarchal bullshit, not mental illness. The post went viral and the hashtag #HerNameIsClodagh began trending on Twitter as women in Ireland, followed by women all over the world, protested Clodagh's erasure from the reports on her murder while the man who killed her was given empathy and excuses.

A man murders four people in Cavan, and we are fed questions and statements of disbelief alongside praise of the murderer as a community man. On the front pages, we see the man and the three children he murdered. Two days in, Clodagh has all but become invisible. And you ask why feminists are so loud and angry?

These are just some of the countless examples of the Good Guy narrative in reports of murder–suicides. They occur across all spectrums of media around the world and listing all of them would fill this entire book plus a sequel.

Until recently, this was the standard template for reporting on men who commit murder–suicides. It rarely, however, applied to the few women who did it. Some of the impetus for the Good Guy story comes from the issue discussed earlier – reporting each killing as a separate incident rather than part of a recurring pattern of male violence – but there are other factors at play. Murder–suicides, particularly when they involve children, make for emotive news. They are one of the very few instances where men's violence against women will make the front page. Journalists operate on tight deadlines and usually with little information. Police are understandably reluctant to release details in the first few days after a multiple murder, when they have not had time to process evidence, interview witnesses or confirm theories. Neighbours and friends are often gathering on the street in shock, trying to make sense of what happened. They make easy targets for journalists looking for quotes. And unless the journalists have had training or experience in dealing with family violence, it probably doesn't occur to them that men who are violent with their partners and children rarely display such behaviour in public. In fact, such men often go out of their way to portray themselves as loving fathers and husbands, because it makes it that much more difficult for their partners to ask for help and less likely to be believed if they do. It's also possible these men also do possess some good qualities, which are discernible and evident to the people around them. The idea that violence against women is only committed by observably evil men is one of the reasons women find it so difficult to report family violence and find acceptance when they do.

Journalists reporting these stories search for quotes to explain why this particular murder happened, what went wrong for this particular man and what this particular woman did to provoke him. They might find quotes to suggest mental illness or depression but almost never ask why, if that were the cause (which is isn't, people with mental illness are far more likely to be victims than perpetrators of violence), the man in question chose to kill his family. Why wasn't he attacking people on the street or in his workplace or at his church or sports club? The reason is that he didn't 'snap'. He made a choice.

Including descriptions of a perpetrator's good qualities is not sound journalistic practice, according to the University of Melbourne's Dr Denis Muller.

> The ethical duty of a journalist is to consider the impact of what they write on all parties. To allow a perpetrator of a crime like this to be portrayed as someone who had good qualities is getting into the territory of irresponsibility. They may have had good qualities – most people do. But the context is of a gross crime. And so it doesn't seem to me to be the responsible thing to do, to in some way build up the perpetrator in a positive light.

Rather than reaching for the easy Good Guy quote from distressed but ill-informed friends and neighbours, some responsible journalists have recently started including more information on the context of murder–suicides in family violence by linking them to previous cases and evidence-based data on the typical history of family violence in such crimes. They've also started including quotes from family violence experts who can put the crime into perspective by explaining the gendered history and that while men killing their partners and children is tragically common (around twenty per year in Australia), it is almost unheard of for women – it is true that women sometimes kill themselves and their children, but the circumstances are usually different and they almost never kill their partners as well; this is a uniquely male crime. Adding this kind of commentary to reports of murder-suicides avoids the event-based reporting that focuses solely on the individuals, while also helping both public and friends and family understand these crimes as expressions of violent power and control underpinned by misogyny.

Monash University researcher Gary Dickson's study of the news media's reporting on 'one punch' hits found that over the summer of 2013–14 the *Sydney Morning Herald* and the *Daily Telegraph* published fifty-four articles between them about the killing of Thomas Kelly in 2012 and Daniel Christie in 2013. Both publications called for drastic reform in how the justice system dealt with one punch hits fuelled by drugs and alcohol. Within weeks of this barrage, then Premier Barry O'Farrell announced new laws would be introduced to combat alcohol-fuelled violence. When Dickson compared the reporting of one-punch hits and men's violence against women, he found 'that in cases of men's violence against women, the men are given a greater opportunity to speak for and represent themselves than in cases of violence against other men', the implication being that when men are violent to women there is a reasonable excuse that does not exist when they are violent to other men. He also showed that men's violence against women is more likely to be sensationalised than men's violence against other men.

BLAMEABLE VICTIMS
As with the earlier examples of Fixed It headlines, these are not exceptional. They are just a random selection of more recent headlines that blame women for the violence men have chosen to enact against them.

The Age: ~~SHANE ROBERTSON BASHED MOTHER OF HIS CHILDREN BECAUSE SHE WANTED TO LEAVE HIM~~
Fix: *SHANE ROBERTSON BEAT MOTHER OF HIS CHILDREN TO DEATH BECAUSE HE CHOSE TO COMMIT MURDER*
Robertson did not just 'bash' his wife, he murdered her, and he admitted to it so there is no doubt here. Men who murder their female partners often do so when their partner leaves or says she wants to leave, but the phrasing of this headline suggests wanting to leave causes murder. It doesn't. Choosing to commit murder causes murder. Men kill women who want to leave them to maintain control. They would rather take her life than allow her to live it on her own terms. This is a choice made by the murderer, not the woman he killed. Implying her choices were in any way to blame for his choice to murder her is both abhorrent and inaccurate.

Daily Telegraph: ~~MAN WHO BUGGED CHEATING PARTNER'S CAR SENTENCED FOR DOMESTIC VIOLENCE~~
Fix: *MAN CONVICTED OF STALKING, INTIMIDATION AND THREATS TO KILL PARTNER*
Faithless women, what can you do, right? Well, perhaps you could refrain from stalking, intimidating and threatening to kill them. If you choose not to refrain from committing these crimes, you should at least expect them to be accurately described when they're reported in the media. You would think.

The Guardian: ~~MAN WHO KILLED WIFE OVER FACEBOOK POSTING JAILED FOR LIFE~~
Fix: *MAN WHO CHOSE TO MURDER HIS WIFE JAILED FOR LIFE*
He didn't kill her because of what she posted on Facebook; he killed her because he chose to commit murder. His choices are the cause of the murder, not hers.

Warwick Daily News: ~~MAN SLAPS PARTNER WITH DISABILITY TO STOP HER SWEARING~~
Fix: *MAN GUILTY OF DOMESTIC VIOLENCE OFFENCES AGAINST PARTNER*
This man's partner has a disability – this is not a defence or an excuse for violence. Neither is it a defence that she was swearing. But in the original headline we know all about his excuses and nothing about her as a person. She is far more than her disability, but that's very difficult to see in this headline. It's arguable whether the victim's disability should be in the headline at all. It's relevant because women with disabilities have a higher risk of being abused, but its usage here seems to be to excuse the violence and put the blame on her disability rather than his choices. I would hope that if the woman's disability was mentioned at all, it would be giving the context of how much higher the risk of violence is for women with disabilities. Sadly, but not unusually, that context was not given in this article.

News.com.au: ~~MAN KILLED WIFE OVER LESBIAN AFFAIR AND 'SMALL PENIS' TAUNTS, COURT HEARS~~
Fix: *MAN DECIDED TO MURDER HIS WIFE, COURT HEARS*
Again, affairs and cruel words are hurtful and damaging, but they don't cause murder. The victim's sexuality is in no way relevant to the crime and in this case appears to be included only to sensationalise and sexualise the murder.

Reuters: ~~SPURNED ADVANCES PROVOKED TEXAS SHOOTING~~
Fix: *DIMITRIOS PAGOURTZIS CHOSE TO COMMIT MASS SHOOTING AT TEXAS SCHOOL*
'Spurned' lovers: they come up all the time in reporting of men's violence against women. Spurned they were, by the evil women who provoked them into killing people. Bullshit. The girl who did not want to date

him had every right to choose who she did or did not want to date. Her choices had nothing to do with his decision to load a gun, take it to a school and kill people.

Sunshine Coast Daily: ~~'LOVE MADE ME DO IT': MAN SHOVES HOSE DOWN WOMAN'S THROAT~~
Fix: *MAN CONVICTED OF ASSAULT AFTER SHOVING HOSE DOWN EX-PARTNER'S THROAT*
Love did not make him do it. Love might make you interested in someone's life or care about their feelings, but it does not make you assault them. Wanting power and control over your partner makes you assault them. Quoting men's excuses and justifications for the violence they've committed is another common trope in Fixed It and it's not something we'd see in reporting of any other kind of violence.

Journalists I've argued with about this claimed it was legitimate reporting of what was said in court. That may be true if it's in the body of the article and includes context for the quote (e.g., that there is no excuse for violence and love is never violent), but in a headline like this, all it does is reinforce and give legitimacy to violence myths. Also, making the relationship between them clear and showing the consequences for the violence (a criminal conviction) is a far more accurate and responsible way to report violence than to link it to expressions of love. There is never any connection between love and violence.

Daily Mercury: ~~MINER'S BRUTAL REACTION TO FINDING FRIEND WITH EX-GIRLFRIEND~~
Fix: *MAN BREAKS INTO EX-PARTNER'S HOME, SEVERELY ASSAULTS HER AND HER COMPANION*
He didn't just 'find' them, he broke into her home then he assaulted her and her companion. The implication that she was cheating (she wasn't,

but even if she was, it's no excuse for violence) and the twisting of facts that suggest he just happened to see them, rather than the truth – that he stalked her and broke into her house to assault her – suggests the blame lies with the victim, rather than keeping it squarely where it belongs: with the person who chose to use violence.

The Mirror: ~~SPURNED LOVER PUNCHES HIS GIRLFRIEND IN THE FACE WHEN SHE TURNS DOWN MARRIAGE PROPOSAL~~
Fix: *VIOLENT MAN PUNCHES HIS GIRLFRIEND IN THE FACE BECAUSE HE CHOSE TO COMMIT ASSAULT*
Another 'spurned lover' and another evil woman whose cruel rejection left him with no choice but to punch her in the face. No. Just, no. Rejection hurts. It's an awful feeling, one all of us can relate to, but it is not an excuse for punching someone. Once again, the choice to be violent is the only thing to blame for violence.

Cheating girlfriends, unfaithful wives, cruel women who reject loving advances, women who have the temerity to want to leave abusive men – this is how victims of domestic violence are blamed for the actions of others. These are just a few typical examples of the countless victim-blaming headlines I've collected over the years. The implication is always that these men did not mean to be violent but were pushed to it by women who hurt them so much they 'just snapped'. As we saw above, the blameable victims are all presented as individual cases rather than as a pattern of men's violence against women in intimate relationships. This sort of violence is how men exert power and control over their partners. Violence (outside self-defence) is always a choice and is never the fault of the victim, but none of these reports reflects this or interrogates that choice. None of them asks what else he could have done. Could he have walked away? Could he have just told his partner how sad and angry he was? Or found a friend to talk to? Could the man have sought out counselling to help him deal with his pain? Maybe even gone for a walk or a run or a swim or a drink? Maybe even curled up on the couch with ice cream and Netflix? All these options, and so many more, are the ones most people take when they feel rejected, jealous or lonely, and they were all available to the man who instead chose to be violent. That choice is something we need to understand in the context of all the complexities of domestic violence. Violent men are not 'provoked' into violence, they are taught from childhood that it is their right and their natural response to fear of losing control over their partner. Men who are not violent, who also suffer through loss, rejection, infidelity and pain, make different choices. There is no reason to accept that violence is an acceptable or understandable response from 'spurned lovers'.

Rape and domestic violence are the forms of men's violence against women most prominent in the media. As discussed in earlier chapters, this is partly to do with the media focus on crime and court reporting in what is known as 'hard news', while the wider social and systemic context are often relegated to the women's pages and deemed to be 'women's issues' rather than news. Male-dominated newsrooms, women's news, violence myths, the justice system, representation in government and other power structures, economic disadvantage, the depiction of women in popular culture, even the dismissal of women's sport, are small pieces of a much larger picture. And it's that big picture we need to look at.

Chapter 6

Sexual abuse of children is not sex

This chapter looks at how the media reports sexual violence against children. I will not be giving any graphic details of rape or abuse, but I will talk about incest, sex abuse by religious figures and the rare occurrences of 'stranger danger'.

People who have experienced abuse as children should take care in reading this chapter.

Myths about child abuse

- Strangers are the most likely person to sexually abuse children, therefore children can be kept safe by keeping them away from strangers.
- Caring adults will immediately know if their children are being abused.
- Children will always and immediately tell their parents if someone is abusing them.
- Children often make up stories about sexual abuse and can be easily coached to lie about fathers abusing them if their mothers are in custody battles.

- Children who have been abused will be terrified of their abuser and will scream and fight if he tries to come near them after the first instance of abuse.
- Rape and sexual abuse of children are the same as sex.

Another day, another headline about adults having 'sex' with children.

ABC News: ~~PNG MAN USED FACEBOOK IN AN ATTEMPT TO PROCURE SEX FROM 10YO BOY~~

Fix: *PNG MAN USED FACEBOOK IN AN ATTEMPT TO RAPE 10YO BOY*

Children can do a lot of things. They can forget to do their homework. They can be rude, silly, playful, funny, adorable or irritating. What they *cannot* do is have sex with adults. Sex requires consent and children cannot give consent, so it's not sex. Sex is not a crime. You can't be charged with having sex. You can only be charged when one of the people involved does not or cannot give consent. Sex and rape are not the same thing and these words cannot be used interchangeably.

When the media persistently labels sexual abuse of children as 'child sex', it weakens the public understanding of the extent and effect of such abuse. The effects of this go far beyond the media. Juries comprise people who read newspapers and watch television. They bring to the jury room all the unconscious biases and preconceived ideas they've learned about a topic that is rarely discussed outside media reporting of specific incidents. A study conducted for the Australian Royal Commission into Institutional Responses to Child Sexual Abuse found that juries who have a better understanding of the reality and effects of child sexual abuse are less likely to make mistakes in their assessment of evidence given in court. They are more able to recognise that children have trouble finding the right words to describe what happened to them and do not expect a perspective or vocabulary that only an adult could provide. The Royal Commission research also found that well-informed juries know abused children frequently cannot remember all the details of the abuse and understand that moments missing from the victim's memory is likely to be a result of trauma, not an indication the victim is lying.

In the U.K., the Criminal Injuries Compensation Authority (CICA), a government agency dedicated to compensating victims of crime, refused to give compensation to almost 700 victims of child abuse because it determined that the victims consented 'in fact' if not 'in law'. One of those 700 victims was a fifteen-year-old girl who had been abused by her 35-year-old teacher. He groomed her and then abused her and was convicted for both those crimes. The CICA refused to pay any compensation to the girl because they ruled that she had consented to the abuse.

Dino Nocivelli, an associate solicitor in the child abuse department at Bolt Burdon Kemp, wrote in *The Guardian* in 2017 about his experience in dealing with the Catholic church's attitude to child victims. He said the church frequently appeared to believe that children were consenting to sex (something they cannot legally or morally do) or even responsible for inciting the abuse. 'In my experience of working with survivors, the Catholic church's views on consent frequently hold survivors back from disclosing their abuse at the hands of priests for decades, if they report at all, as they feel they are to blame for the abuse taking place or for "leading the abuser on".'

Sexually abusing a child is a violent act perpetrated on an innocent victim who was unable to defend themselves. That victim will suffer for years, sometimes decades, because of an adult's choice to abuse a child.

That word, 'choice', is the key. Sex is a choice made by every person involved. Rape and abuse are a choice made only by the perpetrator(s).

The victim has no choice. No child has ever chosen to be abused. No child has ever done anything that caused or incited abuse. No child has ever wanted to be abused. No child has ever willingly participated in their abuse, even if they are groomed to believe they did. No child has ever been in any way responsible for abuses committed against them by adults.

The tragedy of abuse, though, is that so many victims do feel responsible for what was done to them. The shame that should belong only to the abuser is taken on by the abused child and incorporated into their view of themselves and their worth as a person.

Words matter.

When we name abuse as 'sex', we imply victims had a choice. We tell them the violence someone else chose to do to them when they were a child is the same as sex they can choose to have as an adult. It isn't.

Raping children is a horrific concept, but we can't protect vulnerable children or deter predators by diminishing the reality of sexual abuse. We further damage survivors with the implication that the crimes committed against them are something less than a horrific and violent offence.

Research by the U.S. Crimes Against Children Research Centre estimates that in the U.S. at least one in five girls and one in twenty boys have been sexually abused. That means there are over nine million children, more than the entire population of New York City, living in America right now who have been sexually abused. When you add up all the adults who were abused as children and all the children suffering abuse now, it's more than the entire population of California. There are entire countries with smaller populations than the number of Americans who have suffered childhood sexual abuse.

In Australia, you could fill the Melbourne Cricket Ground eight times over with the number of children living who have been or will be sexually abused. You could empty out Brisbane, our third largest city, and refill it with adults who have suffered sexual violence in their lifetimes. All these people see the headlines about other victims. Even more horribly, they sometimes see headlines about their own abusers.

BAY 93.9: ~~PEDO SCOUT LEADER GUILTY ON CHILD SEX COUNTS~~

Fix: *PEDO SCOUT LEADER GUILTY ON 24 COUNTS OF SEXUALLY ABUSING CHILDREN*

This was how the conviction of scout leader Neville Raymond Budge, fifty-six, was reported by one of the local radio stations. Obviously, a radio station would concentrate most of their reporting on audio not written articles, but they still posted this on their website as news.

Compare it to the headlines from scout hall's local paper and the state-based paper:

Geelong Advertiser: FORMER BELMONT SCOUT LEADER NEVILLE BUDGE GUILTY OF 24 INDECENT ASSAULT CHARGES

The Age: FORMER SCOUT LEADER GETS SEVEN YEARS IN JAIL FOR 'ABHORRENT ABUSE' OF EIGHT BOYS

Both headlines are pretty good examples of reporting on crimes against children with accuracy and respect. The *Geelong Advertiser* named the convicted paedophile and gave some context of where his abuse took place (scout leader) and the scale of the abuse (24 counts). The *Age* headline didn't name him, but included a quote from the judge about the abuse and gave some context by telling people where he was from and how many boys he abused. Ideally the two headlines would be combined to something like this: 'Former scout leader Neville Budge found guilty on "abhorrent" abuse of eight boys'. It puts the perpetrator at the beginning of the sentence and names him, so he's completely visible and identifiable. Then it makes clear that he was found guilty of the crimes and that they were vile and inexcusable.

Despite all the examples of awful reporting in this book, the media can report on crimes like child abuse and do it well. The two articles quoted above show how it can be done properly.

The full article in the *Geelong Advertiser* gave details of the abuse Budge committed against the boys but avoided sensationalising it by including several excerpts from the victim impact statements, some of which were also included in the article from *The Age*. Victim impact statements are written by victims and submitted to the court for the judge to consider in sentencing. They give the victims an opportunity to tell the court how the crime committed against them has affected them and are supposed to help judges impose sentences that match the scale of the crime.

These statements are a testament to the lifelong injuries suffered by some of those who were sexually abused as children. Drug addiction, alcohol dependence, gambling problems, depression, crippling anxiety, relationship breakdowns, suicidal thoughts, shame, self-hatred, mistrust of others and long-term emotional damage are common in survivors of child sexual abuse.

While victim impact statements are meant to inform the judge, they can also be a powerful part of media reporting of criminal cases. They help readers understand the reality of crimes that might otherwise seem imper-sonal. Sometimes judges will hold victim impact statements back from the media to protect the identity of the victims, or the victims themselves will ask the court to keep them private. Obviously, media outlets must obey the courts and respect the wishes of the victims, but where they are available they should always be part of the reporting on the story.

It's the difference between a dispassionate report of the facts and tell-ing the victim's story so the audience understands the nature of the crime. The first one might be shocking but it's not personal and it doesn't tell the readers what happens to real people after abuse. Hearing someone's story in their own words has enormous power. Quoting from the victim impact statements allows journalists to give the victims a voice without questioning them about their experiences, which can be traumatic.

In the scout leader case above, Neville Budge was found guilty of twenty offences against children aged between ten and fifteen. By the time he went to court most of the victims were in their twenties and thirties. One victim in the Budge case told the court he had tried to kill himself while he was still a child and described a lifetime of addiction because of the abuse. He said he had lost more than $100 000 to gambling.

> I've spent many years with hatred deep inside me. The nightmares began almost immediately following the sexual abuse and I've suf-fered from them weekly on and off over the last 17 years. I turned to alcohol, as being drunk relieved the anxiety; I turned to marijuana, as being high relieved the depression.

Giving this victim a voice gives him back some of the power his abuse took from him. His words also help the public's understanding of such a crime and the true nature of child abuse. Apart from being the right thing to do, sharing such statements allows journalists to ful-fil the requirements of our profession outlined in Chapter 3 and describe society and the lives of the people who live in it.

STRANGERS ARE NOT THE DANGER

No one really knows the truth about how many children are sexually abused. Almost every country in the western world has conducted sur-veys about child abuse in an effort to understand how often it happens, but at best these surveys are an indication, not absolute proof of preva-lence. False answers about abuse that didn't occur are rare but possible. False answers about abuse that did occur are frighteningly common. Young children barely understand what is happening to them at the

time; surviving the abuse often means shutting away the memory of
it and even as adults it can be too unbearable to remember. But the
information we do have, replicated repeatedly in the U.S., Canada,
the U.K., Australia and New Zealand, all shows that the people who
abuse children are almost always someone the victim and their families knew well. This makes it incredibly difficult for the child to tell
anyone about the abuse and, if they do, it can be difficult for people to
believe them.

On the rare occasions a child is kidnapped and abused by a stranger in a movie-style snatch from a street or playground, the response
is very different. Police are called; there is no question about the child
lying or exaggerating; the perpetrator is immediately and unquestion-
ingly identified as a monster; his actions are recognisable as abhorrent
and indefensible.

Global News: JARROD JOHN CHARLES, SASKATCHEWAN
KIDNAPPING SUSPECT, FACES SEX ASSAULT, CONFINEMENT
CHARGES

This is how crimes against children should be reported. There's no
excuses or dilution here. He's accused of kidnapping and sexual assault.
He's named and the crimes he was accused of are clearly laid out with no
qualifications.

Strangers are an easy danger to understand. There's no emotional
conflict. He's not someone loved and trusted. He's not part of a community. No one will defend him or believe him. We all want to believe
the people we love are good and most of us instinctively want to protect
children from evil. So it's almost impossible to reconcile these two beliefs
when someone we love does something we recognise as evil. It's incomprehensible. We cannot conceive of such horror and so, too often, we will
not believe it.

The unknown monster is easy to believe in, unlike the monster we trust and love and invite into our homes.

Most people who rape children are beloved uncles, revered priests, trusted friends or, most commonly, fathers, stepfathers and brothers of the victim. These men are so much more difficult to portray as monsters and, all too often, their crimes are excused or diluted.

Perth Now: ~~DAD ABUSED DAUGHTER AFTER FAMILY BREAKUP~~
Fix: *DAD RAPED DAUGHTER AFTER HE MADE THE CHOICE TO RAPE HIS OWN CHILD*
The first paragraph of the article reports that the man admitted to sexually abusing his daughter and describes it as 'a relationship that started when he looked for comfort after his partner left him'. He was jailed for thirteen and a half years.

According to the original headline the rapist is a 'dad', not a child abuser. He didn't rape a child, he sought 'comfort' from a teenager after his partner left him (implying it was her fault he was in such need of 'comfort' that he would rape his own child) and it wasn't rape, it was a 'sexual relationship'. I cannot think of a more revolting and factually incorrect way to report the horror of a father raping his own daughter.

The article goes on to describe the abuse as a 'sexual relationship' and notes that he had even 'filmed their sexual contact'.

'The pair' did not 'start a sexual relationship': this child was not complicit in her own abuse. He chose to rape her. It was not 'sexual contact'. It was rape.

Millions of marriages around the world break up, but it's difficult to imagine any reasonable person thinking that is a reason to rape your child. This, however, seems to be the implication in this article. He's lonely and sad, he needs comfort, so he turned to his fourteen-year-old daughter. Well yes, he probably did need comfort. But the tone of this article makes raping your own daughter an understandable mistake, not the horrific and life-shattering trauma of rape and incest.

The Herald: ~~JAIL FOR DUBLIN MAN WHO HAD SEX WITH DAUGHTER AT PARTY~~
Fix: *JAIL FOR DUBLIN MAN WHO RAPED INCAPACITATED DAUGHTER AT PARTY*

Andrew Durran of Dublin left his wife and children when his daughter was ten. After five years of almost no contact with her, she got his phone number from one of her cousins and tried to create a relationship with her father. A few months after they got in contact again, he took his fifteen-year-old daughter to a party and watched as she drank so much vodka she could no longer stand. She went upstairs to lie down. He followed her, removed her clothes and raped her.

In her victim impact statement, she said about when she first got in contact with him again: 'I really felt the father–daughter bond and I believed he felt it too.' Who couldn't understand a teenager trying desperately to reconnect with a father she thought had abandoned her? When he was buying her alcohol and cigarettes and encouraging her to drink with him, of course she didn't want to say no. She was a child, vulnerable and trying to reach out to the father she'd lost. Durran, a man in his forties, an adult and a father, responded to his daughter's need for love by raping her. As she said, again from the victim impact statement reported by some media outlets, 'The day my father will walk free, I will be serving the life sentence he imposed on me.' She said she still struggles to sleep and feels uncomfortable around men, and that deep depression can hit at any time.

It's a terrible and tragic story of an abhorrent and criminal act with lifelong consequences for the woman, but to *The Herald*, it was nothing more than fodder for sensationalist headlines.

Again, it is reported as 'sex' not rape, and the irrelevant details about her choices dilutes the real story of shocking betrayal and pain. Durran's act was even more repellent than a stranger attacking a teenage girl. He raped his own daughter. But he's not portrayed that way in the headlines. He's a 'dad'. It's a 'party'. She's drinking vodka! It all sounds just a bit of fun gone wrong.

All sexual violence leaves injuries, not just on the body but also in the mind. While the victim of a publicised attack by a stranger may well feel shame that everyone knows, they are believed, and the crime committed against them is acknowledged. It's not a hidden shameful secret the victim has to keep to protect their abuser.

Victims of incest are often hidden. The secret becomes their shame and their fault. Acts they could not comprehend were forced upon them by someone who loved them and may have behaved like a normal dad the rest of the time.

Research on the effects of child sexual abuse has been going on since the 1980s, but it can be difficult to isolate the damage done by sexual abuse from other types of abuse experienced by the victim. Predators often search for vulnerable children in families where parents are not able to provide a high level of care. An Australian study of twins from all over the world found nearly 6000 twins where only one twin had been sexually abused, and measured the outcomes for the lives of each twin. The results conclusively showed a range of mental illness, addiction, bad relationships and suicide were significantly higher for a twin who had suffered sexual abuse.

The betrayal these children must feel is almost unfathomable. We expect our parents will love us and protect us from harm. When they become the source of harm it can feel like a life-threatening act. And when the source of harm is another family member, even non-abusive parents become a threat if they refuse to see or believe what's happening.

Researchers at Harvard University have done many studies of the long-term effects of sexual violence in childhood. They found that it's common for young victims of incest to detach from emotions too horrible to bear. They separate themselves from their bodies, memories and feelings because it is the only way to endure what is done to them. But what was once necessary for their very survival becomes a block to normal life as they get older.

Eating disorders are common in survivors, and develop either as a means of creating some control in a world that feels utterly beyond their control, or to punish their bodies for attracting abuse they believe was their fault. Self-harm and drug and/or alcohol abuse are other common occurrences.

Depression and anxiety are almost universal in survivors of abuse. Deeper mental illnesses like bipolar, schizophrenia and psychosis are not uncommon. Young minds subjected to constant trauma cannot grow and learn the way a happy child's can. They are imprisoned in the abuse and powerless to stop it or do anything about the effects it has. Intimate relationships in adulthood can become impossible. Children who have been so utterly betrayed by the people who were supposed to teach them that love is safe and protective can find it difficult to respond to love. They learned it is something damaging and painful so they often treat it with suspicion and dread. It's also common for abused children to end up in abusive relationships as adults because the familiarity of abuse is less frightening than the strangeness of sustaining love. Or if they do find love with someone who doesn't hurt them, they can't cope with it and leave rather than wait for what they believe is an inevitable betrayal.

When victims of abuse use such methods to cope with the horrors inflicted on them they become unreliable witnesses to their own abuse. A thirty-year-old with a history of drug addiction, divorce, self-harm and mental illness who suddenly reveals they were abused by a family member will not find easy acceptance – especially if the abuser was loved and trusted by the rest of the family.

When the circumstances of their abuse isolates them from friends and family, and they have nobody to believe them, recovery can feel impossible.

SEXUAL CHILD ABUSE IN THE CLERGY

Reports of priests sexually abusing children started appearing in the media as early as the 1980s but it wasn't until the mid-1990s and early 2000s that the systemic cover up by church hierarchy was investigated and reported. Since then, media reports of paedophile priests charged with rape, sexual abuse and grooming have made regular headlines.

Sexual abuse of children by revered and respected priests is a unique injury. Children of religious households are taught a special reverence for priests. They are taught that the priest has a moral authority far beyond any other person, that he is a representative of God. This moral authority given to priests in religious communities contributes to victims' inability to tell someone what was happening or had happened. Priests commonly sought out children who were already suffering, because of absent fathers, unwell mothers or alcoholism in the family. Such children were unprotected and isolated: they were the perfect prey.

The Catholic church was not the only institution abusing children. Abuse by men (and some women) cloaked in the power of God has happened in all denominations of Christianity as well as Judaism and Islam. The nature of the religion is irrelevant; it's the abuse of power and the corruption of the hierarchy that excuses, hides and dismisses the abuse that does such harm to the victims. Diluting the suffering of these victims to a 'sex' headline adds to the harm experienced by victims. It transforms their abuse into a salacious and meaningless encounter.

Cincinnati.com: ~~PRIEST CHALLENGES CONVICTION IN CHILD-SEX CASE~~

Fix: *PRIEST CHALLENGES CONVICTION IN CHILD SEXUAL ABUSE CASE*

The text of the article referred to the priest being convicted for 'transporting a minor in interstate commerce for the purpose of engaging him in sex'. This little boy was ten years old. He can't have sex; he would barely understand was sex is. He had no capacity to consent and no ability to withhold consent.

The Seattle Times: ~~FEW CLERGY ON CATHOLIC CHILD SEX LIST EVER PROSECUTED~~

Fix: *FEW CLERGY ON CATHOLIC CHILD PAEDOPHILE LIST EVER PROSECUTED*

Again, the phrase 'child-sex' has been used. It's not sex, it's rape.
You have to wonder what happens in the minds of editors who write headlines like this.

Daily News: ~~PENNSYLVANIA PRIEST ARRESTED FOR ALLEGEDLY TRAVELING TO HONDURAS TO HAVE SEX WITH KIDS~~

Fix: *PENNSYLVANIA PRIEST ARRESTED FOR ALLEGEDLY TRAVELING TO HONDURAS TO RAPE CHILDREN*

It's unlikely that every one of the hundreds of editors who have written headlines like this genuinely does not understand the difference between rape and sex. It might be ignorance or possibly that this is just how it's always been done so this is how we'll continue to do it. It might even be a cynical attempt to manipulate Google rankings by using the word 'sex'. One news editor I spoke to said, 'It's not that we're saying it's okay to rape children, that's abhorrent, but everyone knows what we mean when we say child sex.' Maybe so, but everyone would know what they meant if they said 'child rape' too, and that would be the only accurate term to use.

Yes, it's shocking to name it as rape – perhaps too unbearable if you're reading the news over your morning toast. But the unintended consequence of making the truth sound more palatable is that the gravity of the offence is lost.

'CHILD SEX' IN THE MEDIA

These are headlines that come up day after day. All over the world. They are seen by millions of victims. Regardless of who committed the abuse, the one thing abusers have in common is their ability to convince their victims that what is done to them is normal, possibly even loving, but always the child's fault. It's an incredibly rare child-abuser who takes full responsibility for their actions as they are committing their crimes.

News Mail: ~~STEP-DAD GUILTY OF SEX WITH FOUR GIRLS FREED ON PAROLE~~

Fix: *STEP-FATHER FREED ON PAROLE AFTER CONFESSING TO RAPE AND SEXUAL ABUSE OF FOUR CHILDREN*

Skipping over the grammatical problems (it was not the four girls who were freed on parole), this man was not a child-friendly 'dad', he raped and sexually abused his own step-daughter and three other girls, who were between the ages of six and thirteen. It's unspeakably heartbreaking that children are abused this way so often, but when the abusers are caught and charged, surely the very least we can expect is truthful reporting. Victims deserve dignity rather than messages that tell them they are responsible for the abuse they suffered. Surely, at the very least, journalists can tell the truth about one of the most horrific crimes humans can commit – the abuse of innocent children.

Chapter 7

Male victims of violence

If you want to read about male victims of violence, go to the comments section under any mainstream news article about men's violence against women. It's about the only place male victims are ever discussed. Unsurprisingly, the 'facts' presented there are almost always wrong. Not only does this derail the conversation about female victims, which is its intention, but it also does a vast disservice to genuine male victims. Violence myths are always dangerous to victims, regardless of their gender. The rare male victims of female violence might well believe, after reading too many of these comments sections, that they are one of many, and feel justifiable anger that their pain and experiences are being ignored. Men who are the victims of male violence (as most of them are) could also feel, again justifiably, that their pain and experiences are being ignored because they are never talked about. Equally, perpetrators of violence against men could see their crimes being ignored and, believing this means their crimes are not real, feel entitled to continue their abuse. None of these outcomes help men.

MYTHS ABOUT MALE VICTIMS
- Men are always strong and able to defend themselves from abuse.

- Men don't need to talk about abuse they suffered in childhood. They can deal with the effects on their own.
- When women are abused it is almost always men who do it, therefore the opposite is true and when men are abused it is almost always women who do it.
- Men are only violent when they are angry.
- Men's rights activists care about men. They look after each other and advocate for the services men desperately need.
- Men who commit violence are either unbearably provoked by manipulative women, or they are evil monsters, clearly and recognisably different from other men.

Male victims

It would be wrong to argue that women are never violent and men are never victims. Both these statements are demonstrably untrue and demeaning to both men and women (women are no more inherently gentle than men are inherently violent). Men are far more likely to be the perpetrator of violence than women, especially sexual violence and the more severe forms of physical violence. This does not mean the men who have suffered violence from women should be ignored or have their pain minimised. Men who have been through domestic or sexual violence have a difficult time finding a supportive community, which can lead to more feelings of isolation and feeling, as one survivor described to me, 'like a freak, a weak, weak freak'. If these men were reassured that they are one of a small group but that this does not mean there is something wrong with them, which is true of all violence victims, they might find it easier to understand their experiences in a wider context.

Those with an understanding of domestic violence know that Aboriginal and Torres Strait Islander women, women with disabilities, and people from the LGBTQIA+ community are in disproportionately high-risk groups, with very specific needs that cannot be met with a one-size-fits-all approach. It's a shame it's so difficult to adopt a similar approach with male victims of female violence. There may be far fewer of them than female victims, but they do exist and their needs cannot be met by the same services designed for women victimised by violent men.

Part of the reason male victims of this type can be overlooked is that so many advocates for male victims seem to feel that they have to prove that women are *exactly* as violent as men to get recognition that *any* women are violent to men. The proof does not exist – in fact the evidence proves quite the opposite – so the debate becomes angry, polarised and ideological: three qualities that make empathy and resolution impossible. Feminists and advocates of women experiencing violence from men are understandably frustrated by this response. Men's rights activists are reacting against the recent increase in public discussion of female victims. They feel threatened and ignored when there is no equivalent increase in public recognition of male victims. Almost everyone involved has some experience with trauma, so the debate is emotive and personal, and usually ends in bitter frustration on both sides.

Research on male victims of female violence is complex and divisive. It is common for men who abuse their female partners to claim (and believe) that they themselves are the primary victim. It's also not unusual for women who are being abused by men to react with violence, which abusers can claim as proof they are being victimised when in fact the women were acting in self-defence. Trying to recognise the difference between these men and the men who are genuinely being abused by their female partners, and get it right every single time, is an almost impossible task. It's also highly likely that women who abuse their male partners would present themselves as the victims, and when police are involved, there's conflicting evidence on who is more believable in this situation. Men abusing women is the scenario they're used to seeing and the one most

people understand as 'typical' domestic violence, but the prevalence of the myth that women lie means there's an inconsistent response. Research on male victims is inconsistent for the same reasons. Surveys of self-reported violence can indicate that up to 40 per cent of domestic violence victims are men, but in-depth analysis of domestic violence homicides (where reported violence requires corroboration) such as the New South Wales Coroner's Court Report on domestic homicides, found not one single case of a man being murdered by an abusive female partner in the last fourteen years. Over that time, 162 women were killed by male partners and 98 per cent of them had been abused by the man who ended up killing them.

The data most commonly misused in Australia to inflate the prevalence of male victims of domestic violence is the Australian Bureau of Statistics Personal Safety Survey. The survey does a very good job of doing what it was designed to do: present an estimate of how Australians perceive the presence of violence in their lives. Too often, however, it is interpreted as a factual account of objectively observed violence, which it is not and was never intended to be.

There are thirty-nine tables in the Personal Safety Survey, many of them containing hundreds of separate data points. No one can or should take a single piece of data from one table and use it as a standalone piece of information without considering the context of all the other information provided by the survey. Doing so is, at best, misunderstanding the data. At worst, it's using it to mislead people's understanding of violence in Australia. Men's rights activists, for example, frequently cite the Personal Safety Survey's record that men are one in three of the people who report experiencing violence from a current partner in the last twelve months. The problem with looking at this single piece of data in isolation is that it does not distinguish the sex of the perpetrator. It also ignores how people in existing abusive relationships recognise the abuse as abuse, and it does not account for the difference between a single incident of violence and an ongoing pattern of controlling behaviours that often includes violence. The Personal Safety Survey does provide these details, but you have to look at more than one piece of data to understand it. The one-in-three statistic that the men's right's activists cite so frequently is taken from the number of people who report experiencing violence from a current partner in the last twelve months. This is true, as it stands in that particular dataset, but it doesn't explain the full story. Many people in an abusive relationship are groomed to believe either isn't really abuse or it is caused by their own behaviour and is therefore their own fault. If this is their perception of violence, this is how they will report it if they're interviewed for the Personal Safety Survey. It's easier to obtain a more accurate understanding of abusive relationships after the relationship has ended and the abuser is no longer controlling (or gaslighting) their victim's perception of the abuse. So, when we look at the number of women who report having experienced violence from a male intimate partner since the age of fifteen, they are 75 per cent of people who have experienced intimate partner violence. Men who have been the victim of violence by a female partner are 23 per cent. When we drill down further, of the people who have experienced intimate partner violence, women are three times more likely to have been subjected to repeat attacks and four times more likely to report that violence occurred all or most of the time. They're four times more likely to have had to take time away from paid employment because of intimate partner violence and eight times more likely to suffer anxiety and fear due to intimate partner violence. They are also five times more likely to experience violence from a male family member than men are to experience violence from a female family member. Both men and women are three times more likely to be subjected to violence by a man than by a woman. Overwhelmingly, the person most likely to be violent to a man is another man he doesn't know, followed by a male acquaintance or neighbour. The person most likely to be violent to a woman is her male intimate partner, followed by a male acquaintance or neighbour.

The point of all of this is not to deny that men suffer intimate partner violence. Clearly, they do. But it is deeply misleading to say they are one in three victims of domestic violence. Cherry-picking data like this does nothing to advance the men's rights movement; it only proves they are unwilling to recognise the way men and women experience violence in Australia.

It's important to reiterate that these are self-reported accounts of violence and the victim's feelings about it. Men might be more likely to underreport feeling anxious or afraid of their partner because they are socialised to consider it 'weak' to admit to such feelings. According to the Personal Safety Survey, they are certainly less likely to ask for help or support about the violence they experience. The full dataset in the survey, however, strongly supports wider research that shows male victims of female violence absolutely exist, but they are rare and far less likely to suffer serious injuries or experience sexual violence. This is where the gender argument about violence needs to stop. Men *are* victims of violence from women, and male victims deserve the same belief, sympathy and support as female victims. Their circumstances require specialised services and this should be available to any man who needs help. But supporting male victims should not require disproving women's experience, nor does it dilute the fact that women as a group are at a far greater risk of experiencing violence from their opposite-sex partner.

When media reporting perpetuates the myths listed at the start of this chapter, it is not only women who are harmed.

A 2017 study showed how media reports that assume men commit violence because they're angry (the 'just snapped' trope) can reinforce the myth that men are emotionally one-dimensional and 'real men' have no emotions other than anger or lust.

> This framing of male perpetrators is problematic for non-abusive men because it restricts their ability to display fear. In other words, a male victim may feel unable to display fear, even if he is scared, and instead pretend as if the abuse does not bother him.

Adult male victims of sexual violence

One of the myths mentioned earlier is that men are always keen for sex and therefore would never say no when it's offered. By this logic, pressure or coercion of men is not an issue in heterosexual sex, and, because men are usually physically larger and stronger than women, it's more difficult to understand how that coercion could take place. Because of this, men might feel discouraged from reporting sexual violence from women, and these factors could affect their ability to recognise it as violence. Research on this is, again, conflicting and complicated. Underreporting of sexual violence is as high for men as it is for women. Evidence from the U.K. suggests that men who do report sexual violence to the police receive very poor responses, particularly gay men, who suffer homophobic reactions as well as the disbelief and lack of support experienced by heterosexual men.

A research paper by Lara Stemple called 'Sexual Victimization Perpetrated by Women: Federal data reveal surprising prevalence' was given a lot of media attention all over the world in late 2016. Reports on it were published under headlines such as 'Female sex predators: Why there are more of them than you think' and repeated the paper's claim that women commit sexual violence against men as often as men do against women. Unfortunately, the paper's author had fallen into the trap of misusing data in an effort to validate the rare victims of women's sexual assault by attempting to prove they offend at the same rate as men. It would have been a far more credible piece of research if it had presented the data accurately to show that male victims of female sexual violence are rare but do exist and therefore are in need of support services. The paper used a single statistic from the American Centre for Disease Control's National Intimate Partner and Sexual Violence Survey that appeared to show a similar level of women reporting rape as men who were 'made to penetrate' a female offender over a single year. The premise, that rape does not only apply to men forcing vaginal penetration upon women, is a sound one. It fits with recent reforms to sexual assault laws in Australia and the United Kingdom. But Stemple's use of the data was problematic in the same way that men's rights activists misused the Personal Safety Survey. Focusing on a single data item, without viewing it in context of the entire dataset, can be misleading, particularly when that data is incongruent with similar data taken over a wider period. While it is true that the CDC's twelve-month prevalence of men reporting 'forced to penetrate' was the same as the twelve-month prevalence of women reporting rape, the lifetime reports were significantly different. The CDC's analysis of the perpetrator data reports:

[F]or male victims, the sex of the perpetrator varied by the specific form of violence examined. Male rape victims predominantly had male perpetrators, but other forms of sexual violence experienced by men were either perpetrated predominantly by women (i.e., being made to penetrate and sexual coercion) or split more evenly among male and female perpetrators (i.e., unwanted sexual contact and noncontact unwanted sexual experiences).

Dr Stemple also manipulated Bureau of Justice Statistics to make it appear that sexual violence by women against men was a significant proportion of reported sexual assaults in America. Again, when you drill down into the data she's using, less than 9 per cent of rapes and sexual assaults in America between 2010 and 2013 were committed by female-only perpetrators. So, she's right that women do commit sexual violence but misguided in her attempt to inflate it.

MEN'S VIOLENCE AGAINST MEN

Like women, men are at far greater risk of violence from other men than from women. Although homicide is relatively rare in Australia, it is useful data to look at because it doesn't suffer any underreporting and the perpetrators are thoroughly investigated. The relatively low homicide rate does mean we need to look at data over a long period of time to smooth out the outliers. For example, when Peter Miles shot his wife, Cynda, their daughter, Katrina Miles, and her four children in 2018, six people were added to the average yearly murder rate of around thirty people per year, an increase of 20 per cent. Detailed examination of data from the last fourteen years gives a robust picture of how gendered the most serious violence is.

As reported in the New South Wales Coroner's Court domestic homicide report, 17 per cent of male victims of intimate partner homicide were killed by male partners, a hugely disproportionate amount given that less than one per cent of couples in Australia are same sex couples. Across all the other categories of adult victims of domestic violence homicides, which include immediate family, new partners and extended kin among others, men were around 90 per cent of the killers of both women and other men. They made up 65 per cent of the people who killed children. Outside domestic homicide, according to Australian Bureau of Statistic data, men were more than 80 per cent of the victims and nearly 90 per cent of the killers in all homicides across Australia in the last five to ten years.

Across all crime statistics, such as police reports, self-report surveys and crime victimisation data, men consistently comprise more than half the victims of and over 85 per cent of the offenders in physical assaults. Outside Australia, these results are broadly replicated by data from Statistics Canada, the U.K. Office for National Statistics and the American Center for Disease Control. America has a much higher rate of violence, particularly in homicide, but the gender balances are roughly the same.

VICTIMS BECOMING OFFENDERS

It's been well documented that abuse and neglect during childhood is frequently linked to anxiety, depression, low income, poor education, unstable personal relationships and, most significantly, violence in adulthood. The reality of this is not, however, a simple correlation that all people who have been abused will become abusers themselves. Many abusers were abused but the reverse is not true: most people who were abused as children do *not* go on to commit abuse against others as adults, although they are far more likely to suffer depression, anxiety and substance abuse problems. The most common correlation between childhood experience and adult violence is the gender of the offender and acceptance of stereotypes about gender roles and myths about violence.

We might look to smoking for an analogy here. There's a clear link between smoking and lung cancer, but only around 20 per cent of long-term, heavy smokers will contract the disease. Their risk is much higher than people who have never smoked (less than one per cent), former smokers (around 10 per cent) and lighter smokers (around 15 per cent). Lung cancer is the disease we most often think of in relation to smoking, but heart disease and stroke are in fact more common in smokers than lung cancer. Almost all smokers will suffer some health effects, but some develop them earlier and more severely than others. Contributing factors such as obesity, alcohol consumption and a sedentary lifestyle exponentially multiply the risk of cancer and early death in smokers, and each of those factors have their own separate risks. The effects of child abuse work the same way. Almost everyone who was abused in childhood will suffer some effects, but the risks involved are higher when the abuse was severe and ongoing, and higher still when there are other contributing factors, such as multiple types of abuse.

Another influence at work in adult effects of child abuse is epigenetic factors. In very simple terms, epigenetics is the relationship between genes and environment. For instance, if someone is born with a genetic predisposition to lung cancer and they start smoking, exposure to the carcinogens in cigarettes can switch on that gene and cause lung cancer. A smoker who does not have that gene can smoke and smoke and smoke and will probably not get lung cancer (leaving aside other health problems, of course). In the same way, childhood trauma can switch on genes in a person with a genetic predisposition to anxiety, depression and possibly even aggression. Not only does this affect the person who was traumatised, but also, once those genes have been switched on, they can also be passed on to children, even if the children themselves have never been exposed to trauma.

One single instance of abuse, in an otherwise supportive and loving childhood, is indisputably traumatic, but rarely has the same long-term effect as ongoing sexual abuse or a combination of neglect and multiple types of abuse. A 2015 study by the University of Washington attempted to understand how different kinds of abuse in childhood affect men's risk of perpetrating domestic violence, sexual violence, peer violence and sexual violence against children. Unsurprisingly, they found that men who had little or no experience of childhood abuse had better education, higher income, better mental health, lower incarceration and lower levels of domestic and peer violence. Men who had suffered physical and emotional abuse reported higher levels of ongoing abuse and were more likely to perpetrate domestic abuse than any other group. Incarceration rates and depression were lowest for men who had never been abused, higher for victims of emotional and physical abuse, higher still for victims of emotional and sexual abuse and highest of all for multiple-abuse victims. Interestingly, there was little difference between any of the groups (including the men who had not been abused) in their risk of committing sexual assault as adults and, of the three groups who had been abused, victims of multiple abuse had the lowest rates of perpetrating any kind of violence in adulthood. In other words, it is true that trauma in childhood can lead to men becoming abusive as adults, but most of the men who had been abused were not violent. It's a risk factor but not a cause. And there was no link found in this study between abused boys and adult men who rape adult women.

The biggest risk factor for children who have been abused and then go on to commit abuse in adulthood is gender. Most Australian and international research has found that while girls are more likely to be sexually abused than boys, both girls and boys suffer physical and emotional abuse at around the same rates. Boys, however, are overwhelmingly more likely to commit violence as adults than girls.

Researchers at the University of New South Wales conducted a review of credible studies on adult victims of child sexual abuse to establish whether there was any common link between experiences of abuse and perpetration of abuse in adulthood. The research found some tentative connection between abuse that 'represent[s] experiences of power (for the abuser) and powerlessness (for the victim)', but not enough to explain the differences between men's and women's experiences and perpetration of violence. This suggests there is some other factor interacting with the abuse that affects men who've been abused and does not have the same impact on women. I believe this other factor is the construct of masculinity in society, and how it affects men's view of themselves, the power they feel they should have, the power they believe they do have, and the things they've been taught. It also impacts the way some men feel they need to redress any perceived imbalance in such power.

Another question the University of New South Wales researchers looked at was whether there was any explanation for why men are so much more likely to commit abuse and violence than women. They certainly found that this was true, but could not establish a robust causal link. Other research has shown that the reasons are complex and cannot be explained by hormones or inherent gender-linked characteristics. It is both sexist and simplistic to assume that men are just naturally more violent than women. The notion that psychological differences between men and women are hardwired into our brains by hormones or evolutionary imperatives has also been debunked. Dr Cordelia Fine's *Testosterone Rex*, which won the prestigious Royal Society prize for science book of the year, thoroughly pulled apart the effects of inherent gender indicators and learned behaviour: 'Even quite marked sex differences in the brain may have little consequence for behaviour. Beyond the genitals, sex is surprisingly dynamic, and not just open to influence from gender constructions, but reliant on them.'

The underlying driver in violence is not male hormones or 'wiring', but power – and the need to experience that power both in how we see ourselves and how we see our place in the world. Torrey Orton, a Melbourne-based psychologist with more than twenty years' experience, agrees with Dr Fine's conclusions: 'We are also at the losing edge of a historical downturn in our power, the rage gets extra urging, often outside of consciousness. People in powerful positions are anxious about their power. This is expressed in attacks on anyone deemed critical of the powerful.'

The acquisition of power is also a never-ending process. Men who achieve any level of power quickly become accustomed to it. It becomes the status quo, and the need for power can be fulfilled only by acquiring more. The dual threat of seeing more powerful men ahead of them and the potential loss of power to women coming up behind creates a constant level of uncertainty and fear. The roots of violence lie in that uncertainty. From the moment they're born, men are taught they have an inherent right to power – all the myths they learn from babyhood, that boys are tough and strong and aggressive and have a right to anger, that girls are gentle and pretty and compliant, that domestic labour is women's responsibility and that men are dominant, violent, protective providers. Even in the most progressive and balanced of families, little boys see these lessons play out in the books they read and the movies they watch and the media constantly feeding into their subconscious.

The combination of a natural assumption of power and the fear of losing it means men are under pressure to constantly prove to themselves and the world that they still maintain this power. Violence committed against a less powerful person is one way to prove it. The victim's inability to fight back is integral to this kind of display. As QUT Law professor Dr Michael Flood points out:

> The rate of violence committed by men reflects very longstanding dominant traits of masculinity that come from how we socialise men and boys to dominate, take risks and refrain from empathy. These traits play themselves out in both violent and non-violent crimes. This issue must be considered in the context of class and ethnicity as well as gender. Men who are socially disadvantaged can feel they have little status or access to socially legitimate forms of power. Research tells us that crimes like joy riding, public violence and dealing drugs is a way to display manhood, particularly in front of other men.

Myths about masculinity are both the cause and effect of men's violence against women, children and each other.

Power in relationships

A pernicious form of sexism, which academics call 'hostile sexism', is where men have an antagonistic and aggressive perception that women are unfairly taking over men's social power. A 2018 study of the effect of this on intimate relationships found that men who demonstrate hostile sexism are more likely to underestimate the power they have in their own intimate relationships (a view not shared by their partners). The study found that this combination of hostile sexism and perceived lack of power frequently predicts aggressive behaviour like threats, yelling and derogatory comments. It makes logical sense: a man who thinks all women are out to get men and believes his wife or girlfriend has more control over the relationship than him will respond by putting her down and scaring her to regain what he believes is his rightful place of power. In lay terms, he's a jerk.

Given what we know about ongoing abuse being based on a need for power and control, it makes sense that the men who are abusive are often men who feel they lack power and control over their own lives or that they need to maintain power and control over their women to prove their masculinity.

Men's rights activists

Men are three times more likely to die from suicide than women. On average, around forty-one men lose their lives in this way in Australia each week. It's a tragedy that deserves far more attention than it gets. In addition to the murder and assault rates discussed above, men are twice as likely to die from cancer and drug overdoses, and three times more likely to die in car accidents. A staggering 92 per cent of Australian prison inmates are men. Men are twice as likely to suffer from problem gambling addictions, and while mental illness rates among the incarcerated is similar in men and women, men are significantly more likely to suffer substance abuse.

Given these figures, it's both sad and bewildering that men's rights activists are almost entirely focused on gaining recognition for male victims of domestic and sexual violence – the only areas in which men are underrepresented as victims. Men's rights activism inadequately addresses the real problems facing male victims, and the movement is nothing more than part of the long history of men fighting against the women's liberation movement.

The sentiments of the men's rights activists are not new. One such example comes from an article in a nineteenth-century American magazine *Putnam's Monthly*, the precursor to the modern publication *The Atlantic*. The article, published in 1856, bemoaned the changes women were making to American society:

> The husband cannot lay a finger on his wife by way of chastisement, except at the risk of being complained of for assault and battery, and perhaps, sued for divorce, and (which is worse than either) of being pronounced by his neighbours as a brutal fellow.

In 1908, Ernest Belfort Bax, known today as the father of the men's rights movement, wrote *The Legal Subjugation of Men*. He was enraged by legislative changes forced on England by the suffragettes and advocated for 'the abolition of modern female privilege'. He was particularly incensed by 'the malice of persons, always women, who practically get up the [rape] cases or provoke them' and described a fourteen-year-old girl who reported her father's sexual abuse of her and her eleven-year-old sister to police as 'one of the most virulent little minxes I ever saw'. More than a hundred years later, the only thing that's changed is the idiom. Men's rights activists are still dedicated to trying to prove that women lie about domestic violence and rape, and railing against laws that require men to contribute to the financial support of their own children.

Their activism is only focused on men's rights and masculinity in reaction to feminism or discourse about men's violence against women. In this way, it is not a movement on behalf of men, but rather a movement against women's rights.

If men's rights activists were truly advocating for men, they would be rolling out opinion pieces and news reports and interviews with grassroots organisers, and they would be interested in exploring the causes and effects of the real problems men face. If they were truly advocating for the rights of men, we'd see demands for government inquiries and substantial funding for research to find solutions to male suicide, violence, early death and substance abuse. These men who purport to be so dedicated to the cause would, if they were truly working as activists, give up careers and time to start volunteer-run refuges for the thousands of men at risk from these problems – just as women have done for decades. But men's rights activists are not the ones who do this work.

One of the only grassroots services for men in Australia, the Men's Shed, is a small but laudable and highly effective project. It provides a community, reduces isolation, and gives men a space to talk and find comfort and support when they need it. And nothing on the Men's Shed website or programs talks about women. It focuses only on issues of men's health and wellbeing. Perhaps this is why it is so effective.

This chapter has explored how myths about masculinity damage men, making them more likely to be the victim as well as the perpetrator of violence. When feminists speak of destroying the patriarchy it is, in many ways, about destroying the effects of these myths. These myths about masculinity feed back into myths about men's violence against women, about sexual abuse of children and about rape. They fuel the arguments by so-called men's rights activists and to this end cause even more harm to actual and potential male victims.

Chapter 8
Victims, perpetrators and the people who support them

A little bit of rape is good for a man's soul.

Norman Mailer, to an audience at the
University of California at Berkeley, 1972

The previous four chapters explored how myths about men's violence manifest in the media's reporting on the perpetrators and victims of violence. Identifying and undoing the biases produced by these myths is part of the central focus of Fixed It. When we start to uncover the truth about invisible perpetrators and blameable victims, we can see that the effect of this approach to reporting reaches far beyond idiotic headlines. It shapes the way we respond to victims and perpetrators in a community and legal sense, and it affects the services and support we offer them. Most dangerously of all, it allows perpetrators to justify their actions and perceive broad community support for the violent choices they made.

Myths about perpetrators and survivors

- Women and children who have genuinely been abused will always be believed and supported by friends, family and community.
- Survivors may cry sometimes but if they show any other effects, such as using alcohol or drugs, this is a sign of their own weakness not a result of PTSD-related trauma.
- Perpetrators of violence are either 'sick' or provoked to the point that they had no choice but to commit the violence.
- Everyone who finds out that a friend or family member has committed violence will immediately step in to prevent it happening again.

Media reporting of men's violence against women and community acceptance of myths about this type of violence are interrelated. There is considerable research suggesting that media reporting can reinforce the myths that blame victims and excuse perpetrators, but it can also be a positive influence on the public's understanding of violence. It's difficult to know whether the reporting has to change in order to change attitudes or the attitudes have to change first in order to influence the way violence is reported. It is likely the answer is a mix of the two. Activism, academic research, pressure from people working on the front lines in crisis support and prevention, amplifying the voices of survivors and support from politicians all combine to effect social change. These concerted efforts help push back against ignorant and inaccurate reporting of men's violence against women, while also increasing public curiosity and demand for more accurate reporting. The success of Australian writers such as Clementine Ford, Jess Hill, Nina Funnell, Miki Perkins, Julia Baird, Hayley Gleeson and Sherele Moody, who have each developed expertise, skill and large audiences for their writing on men's violence against women, proves to publishers that this work is valued by readers and encourages them to look for a wider variety of perspectives and knowledge.

Despite all the doom and gloom of the last few chapters, there has been some improvement in the Australian media over the last ten years. It's interesting that there has also been a similar improvement in self-reported community attitudes and understanding of men's violence against women over the same period. Again, it's difficult to untangle the chickens and eggs here, but it's implausible that there is no connection between changing attitudes and changing media.

Though there have been small improvements, we still have a problem with deeply entrenched subconscious beliefs, biases people might not even recognise they have but which still impact the way they think about victims, survivors and perpetrators of men's violence against women. The effects of this don't only play out in social media and the worst of the un-moderated comments sections; they have far more sinister effects on the lives of people who've suffered violence.

COMMUNITY ATTITUDES

The feminist agenda is not about equal rights for women. It is about a socialist, anti-family political movement that encourages women to leave their husbands, kill their children, practice witchcraft, destroy capitalism and become lesbians.

Pat Robertson (Televangelist)

The National Community Attitudes towards Violence against Women Survey, or NCAS, has been measuring the way Australians under-stand and think about men's violence against women every four years since 2009. The 2017 NCAS survey of 17 500 people aged sixteen and over shows some encouraging results, but it's worth remembering that these are self-reported attitudes. The survey is a good indication of how people think and is more robust in measuring change over time, but it is not uncommon for people answering surveys to report attitudes they think are acceptable rather than what they truly believe or would act on in everyday life, and we see this reflected in the survey results over the years. That even this has changed over time is encouraging.

The survey found that while there remains a wide gap between the way men and women understand men's violence against women, overall understanding has improved since 2009, and most of that change has happened in the past four years. Feminists and activists have been working towards these changes for many decades, but it is interesting to note that the most significant change in attitudes (2013–2017) coincided with a series of events that had a huge impact on the way mainstream media reported men's violence against women during that time.

As well as the encouraging results, there were also some concerning responses in the recent survey. These showed only small shifts in the overall support for gender equality, which hovered at around 64 to 66 per cent across all three iterations of the survey. Research from all over the world has shown that one of the most critical factors in reducing men's violence against women is intrinsic support for gender quality and a concurrent rejection of traditional gender roles.

Far more concerning is that Australians' belief that women are more likely to be the victims of intimate partner violence has dropped from 86 per cent in 1995 to 64 per cent in 2017. Belief that women were more likely to suffer physical harm from partner violence has also declined and fewer than half of Australians recognise that levels of fear from domestic violence are worse for women. These beliefs stand in direct opposition to the evidence collected by research from the ABS, Australia's National Research Organisation for Women's Safety, the World Health Organization and numerous other Australian and international peer-reviewed academic research projects.

While most people (over 80 per cent) showed some understanding of the difficulty women experience in leaving abusive relationships, 30 per cent still agreed that 'a female victim who does not leave an abusive partner is partly responsible for the abuse continuing'. Other results were also worrying. More than 40 per cent of people agreed that 'women going through custody battles often make up or exaggerate claims of domestic violence in order to improve their case' and that 'it is common for sexual assault accusations to be used as a way of getting back at men'. More than 30 per cent of Australians surveyed believe that 'rape results from men being unable to control their need for sex' and 28 per cent believe that, when sexually aroused, 'men may be unaware a woman does not want to have sex'. Thankfully, these attitudes are not the majority, but when you consider that three out of every ten people in Australia (the rates are higher for men) think rape happens because men can't control themselves and aren't capable of considering their partner when they're aroused, it becomes a lot more concerning.

The results from the Australian survey are roughly consistent with results from similar international surveys. The 2017 National Council of Women of New Zealand found mostly positive responses to gender equality questions, but 30 per cent of people still believe that 'false rape accusations are common' and that improving gender equality would not improve the rates of sexual and domestic violence or suicide rates. The 'Scottish Social Attitudes Survey 2014: Attitudes to violence against women in Scotland' found that while the vast majority of people in Scotland believe sexual and domestic violence is wrong, their attitudes change if they are presented with a scenario where the woman 'provoked' the violence, for example if she was unfaithful, and they profess a much lower rate of taking rape seriously if it occurred in a marriage rather than between strangers. A YouGov survey in 2018 found almost a quarter of people in Britain thought that in most cases it isn't rape if non-consensual sex occurs within a long-term relationship.

The results in all these surveys consistently showed that men, older people, people with strong religious views and people with traditional views on gender stereotypes (and there was a lot of crossover in those groups) were the most likely to be unsupportive of gender equality and show high levels of mistrust of women's reports of the violence they've experienced.

Another consistent finding across all these surveys was the difference in the way men and women understand consent and accountability. Men are less likely than women to understand that rape can occur without physical violence (i.e. using fear, pressure or coercion). Men are also more likely to excuse rape, or not believe it is rape, if a woman is drunk, flirtatious or in a relationship with the rapist.

It is dangerous for women who have experienced violence from men to live in communities where people might blame them for the violence someone else chose to enact against them. Crisis and support services need funding and government support to offer effective help to the hundreds of thousands of women who need it. They need to connect to police and courts, banks and welfare agencies, doctors and mental health workers, schools and work, housing and utility services, and they need to know those institutions will support them. An Australian woman told me her story of trying to escape her abusive husband and it's a sadly typical example of the dangers and barriers women face when they try to leave violent men.

Jenny* tried to leave her abusive husband, Andrew*, four times before she was finally able to escape. The first time she tried to leave was

---

* Jenny and Andrew's names and some identifying details have been changed to protect her life and the lives of her children.

in the 1990s. Services for women in violent families were much more difficult to find, and she found her attempts blocked by basic logistical obstacles. Because she was still married, she quite simply could not get a lease, electricity supply, medical care, new schools for her kids or bank accounts in her own name without risking him finding her address. The organisations either required a co-signature from her then husband, or would make her new address available to him.

I was like a rat in a maze. Every time I ran down another alley I'd hit a wall. When we were married he'd always insisted on putting everything in his name – lease, bills, bank accounts, cars, insurance, everything. At first I didn't realise that it mattered and later I was too scared of him to do anything about it. So the first time I tried to leave I had no rental record, no credit, no money of my own and whenever I tried to get anything they'd either want to check with him to verify my identity or they'd want to put things in both our names. Schools wouldn't take the kids without both of us filling in the forms, even though I had police reports and had started divorce papers. Landlords wanted references and they'd tell me they 'couldn't promise' that he wouldn't find out about the application. If I told them I was in danger from him I wouldn't get a lease. I could see it on their faces: I was 'trouble'. If I didn't tell them they'd ring him for a goddamn reference. It was unbelievable. I had a job but when I tried to buy a car they wouldn't give me finance without his signature because we were still married. I paid the extra fee to get a silent phone number but one of the times we moved out he got our address from the electricity company. Another time it was through the husband of one of my friends. That bloke had always believed Andrew when he told people I was treating him badly and going to take the kids off him, so he felt sorry for him and said he was just trying to help him out. Every time I went back to Andrew it would all start again but he kept promising he wouldn't hurt me again and he'd get so angry when I said no. It sounds crazy but I felt like I'd be safer if I moved back in with him and kept him happy than if I stayed where I was when he was so furious and could turn up any time he liked.

Over time, as services for women fleeing violence slowly improved, Jenny was finally able to escape. With the help of police, intervention orders and one of the very few domestic violence support services available at the time, she got a lease and moved to a new home with her children. Both Jenny and the police believed she had done everything she needed to do to make sure Andrew couldn't find her new address. They were wrong. Police are still not sure exactly how he found out where she was living. He won't say but Jenny thinks it's possible he simply followed her home from work.

He tried it lots of times. I'd see his car across the street or catch it in my rear-view mirror. Every time I saw him, I'd drive straight to the police station. Sometimes they'd be great; sometimes they'd carry on like I was just a pain in the arse. It all depended on who was on the counter when I got there. Maybe he borrowed someone else's car one night cause I was always really careful. I never ever stopped watching for him.

Despite multiple breaches of intervention orders, like waiting outside her work and following her home, ringing her and threatening to kill her, telling their children she was a manipulative bitch who didn't really love them, that she was just doing things for them to make him look bad, and stalking her when she went out with friends, Andrew was never imprisoned. He had multiple court appearances that ended in fines, intervention orders, good behaviour bonds, suspended sentences and stern warnings. This went on for nearly a year until one night he came to Jenny's home with a knife, kicked in her door and tried to kill her. One of her children, then only twelve years old, was quick enough to hide under furniture with a phone, call the police and stay on the phone so they could hear Jenny scream as she was being cut. Jenny had deliberately chosen a house close to a police station, a decision that probably saved her life that night because two carloads of police arrived in time to stop him before he killed her. Jenny was hospitalised with multiple stab wounds and Andrew was charged, convicted and imprisoned for attempted murder. The child who hid in the house that night, listening to his mother being stabbed, remains deeply traumatised.

Andrew is due for release soon, so Jenny has changed jobs and left everyone at her old workplace with a detailed description of him and how to respond if he turns up. She calls it her 'death-cheat-sheet'. It's a document she's assembled with photos of him and all the history, convictions and current court orders, as well as police contact details for anyone who hears from him. She's handed the death-cheat-sheet to all the people he might contact if he tries to find her or her children again. So far this has included: her children's schools and workplaces, parents of children's schoolfriends, her eldest child's partner, their parents and siblings, local police, family violence services, banks, utilities, her landlord, the bond agency, doctors, sporting clubs, social media, friends, family and extended networks, dentists, road toll organisations, Centrelink, eBay, the electoral roll, the tax office, superannuation accounts, lawyers, loyalty card companies, the car registration organisation, the local council and the local vet. She's not sure if she's covered every option and she knows it's a huge number of people who all have to be constantly vigilant about his manipulations and detailed knowledge of her life and habits.

If any one person at any of those places slips up, even once, and he is able to find her, she firmly believes he will kill her.

> It's a lot better these days but you still get people, you know, rolling their eyes and thinking I'm making a big drama of it all. Or they think I'm just being a bitch and not letting him see his kids. That's why I did the death-cheat-sheet. Seeing the attempted murder conviction in black and white makes a difference, even to the blokes who feel a bit sorry for him because they think, 'Oh, poor bugger, he just wants to see his kids.' The big organisations, they all have those privacy regulations, but he knows my date of birth and all kinds of other details and he has the marriage certificate. Most people aren't going to check whether a husband has tried to kill his wife if he pretends he's just trying to pay her phone bill or something like that. He's smart – that's what scares me.

It should be unlikely he'd be able to fool any of the large organisations now: they almost all have accounts for people like Jenny flagged to prevent exactly the situation that scares her. But she is one persuasive conversation, one person who believes women lie about domestic violence, one sympathetic interaction away from someone giving her address to the man who abused her, stalked her and eventually tried to kill her. He's got a four out of ten chance of finding her, according to the National Community Attitudes Survey. Damn right she should be scared.

VICTIMS AND PERPETRATORS

The people who buy into and benefit most from myths about violence and gender roles are, of course, the perpetrators of violence. Victims of abuse are also often convinced that these myths are true and apply very specifically to them and their behaviour. There's a complex interaction that goes on here. Violent men frequently seek out people who are vulnerable and manipulate those vulnerabilities to keep them afraid and powerless. Essentially, they groom their victims to accept the blame for the steadily increasing violence and control they endure. A 2006 report by UNICEF found that there's a high crossover between women who grew up in violent households or were the victims of abuse in childhood and women who are in abusive relationships as adults. Unsurprisingly, studies have found there's also a strong correlation between men who grew up in violent or controlling households, men who were subjected to abuse as children, and men who later become abusive in their adult relationships. It doesn't always work this way, of course. Many people who experienced violence in childhood are able to reject those role models in adulthood and live kind, empathetic lives, but it almost never works the other way. People who grew up with kindness, empathy and positive attitudes to gender equality rarely go on to become abusers.

One of the most comprehensive and robust reports on domestic and family violence in the world is produced by the New South Wales Coroner's Court. The report provides top level data on the number of domestic violence homicides and then drills down into intricate details, using court transcripts, police reports, arrest records, post mortem and toxicology reports, media articles and inquest findings to establish the interaction between gender, age, race, family history and justice system activities in domestic homicides. It also integrates Australian and international evidence-based research with findings from the New South Wales data. Each report interrogates data from the most recent year and builds on all the previous reports to look at changes over time and smooth out spikes in data caused by atypical homicides. The result is fourteen years of strongly credible information on domestic homicide that proves conclusively that it is highly gendered. Almost all men who kill their partners (male or female) had a history of abusing them. None of the women who killed their partners were the abusers in the relationship but most of them were the victims of abuse by the man they killed.

The report highlights the role the media plays in reinforcing attitudes to 'diminish perpetrator accountability, inappropriately blame victims, and reinforce problematic stereotypes around violence'. It cites several examples of egregious reporting on domestic homicide, two of which are reproduced below.

> For instance, the day following the alleged murder of a woman by her husband, a prominent Australian newspaper published an article which included the headline that the murderer 'suspected affair and trawled wife's phone before fatal stabbing'. The article described how the husband searched his wife's phone, and that 'an argument ensued escalating to the allegedly fatal point where [the perpetrator] is accused of grabbing a kitchen knife and stabbing [the victim] in the chest'. The article proceeded to quote statements from the perpetrator's legal representative, namely that 'the deceased was having an affair, he found out about it and the relationship came to a tragic end'. While it is acknowledged that murders are a crime of particular social interest, when an individual is murdered their voice ceases to be heard, and the perpetrator's voice often becomes the only account of the crime until the case is ventilated in court, or through reports such as those of this Team. The Team acknowledges that journalists are placed in a difficult position of having to report stories of public interest quickly, on limited facts, and have other challenges which may arise for them in the context of reporting about this violence.

However, the Team is of the perspective that framing stories in this way reduces perpetrator accountability and blames the victim for their death. Further, it is inappropriate to passively describe such a case as 'coming to a tragic end' when a victim was killed by a perpetrator.

. . . an abuser murdered his estranged wife after decades of subjecting her to extreme domestic violence. After murdering her he killed himself. The coronial finding described the case as a 'great human tragedy', which was a phrase subsequently reflected in media reporting around the case. Other media reports concerning this case did not attribute the murder to the perpetrator, rather talking about the victim having 'died', or being 'dead', without acknowledging that the perpetrator had strangled his victim before shooting himself. Articles also described the 'relationship' between the homicide perpetrator and victim as being 'marred by domestic violence' – mutualising the violence when the facts clearly indicate that the homicide perpetrator had been the primary domestic violence aggressor throughout the relationship.

The reports include case histories from homicides committed in the previous year. The most recent report provided fifty-five case summaries with details of family background, alcohol and substance abuse history, previous patterns of violence in the relationship and details of how and when the victims were killed. Taking all the dry data and showing how it translates into real lives makes for eviscerating reading and demonstrates over and over again how often a history of violence and abuse is present for so many perpetrators and, frequently, although not as commonly, for victims. This is not an excuse, because there are no excuses for violence, but it is, in part, an explanation, and reinforces the need to alter our perspective on violence and debunk the myths that support it.

A 2016 study of attrition rates in domestic violence reports in the U.K. found that victims of intimate terrorism often think of the abuse as a series of unrelated incidents. They might go to police to seek help at a particular moment where they are in danger but do not see the abuse as a cyclical process. In other words, they've bought into the idea that this kind of violence is just an isolated incident that occurred in response to a specific circumstance and believe that it won't happen again. This is often why they retract statements or police reports in the immediate aftermath of the violence. Their abuser has explained why it happened: 'you made me mad', 'I just lost control', 'I thought you were cheating', 'I had too much to drink', etc. The victim believes the excuse, often accepts the blame for her abuser's violence and agrees to work with him to 'fix the relationship' rather than seeing his behaviour as a pattern of abuse designed to keep her powerless and unable to leave. This is not to blame victims for staying with abusers, but to explain how abusers perpetuate myths about violence and control and manipulate the victim so she believes the violence is her fault. Our earlier case study, Jenny, described it this way:

> Every time he hurt me, he'd get so upset afterwards. He'd cry and he'd promise he'd never do it again. Then he'd say things like, 'I can't believe you want to throw our entire life away over just one thing. I did one thing wrong why can't you forgive me?' and I'd think, yeah, we've got kids and a life and history, I can't waste all that by giving up now. So I'd stay.

A fascinating study from the University of Virginia in 1984 demonstrates how rapists perpetuate myths to diminish their own responsibility for their crimes and shift the blame to their victims. Despite its age, the research remains relevant and has successfully stood up to scrutiny for more than thirty years. Experienced sexual offence researchers Diana Scully and Joseph Marolla conducted in-depth interviews with 114 men incarcerated in Virginia after being convicted of raping at least one adult woman. The researchers spent an average of more than four hours talking to each of the men about the crimes for which they'd been convicted and then compared their perception of it to police records, evidence presented in court, medical records and victim testimony. Eighteen of the men who had denied their crimes in court admitted them to the researchers. There were no cases of men who pleaded guilty but later told researchers they were actually innocent. Despite their conviction at trial, 83 per cent of the men interviewed did not view themselves as rapists. They found the rapists fit into one of three categories: 'admitters', those who acknowledged they had raped their victims (but this did not necessarily mean they saw themselves as rapists), and two types of 'deniers': those who claimed they had never had any sexual contact with their victims, and those who admitted to sex but denied that it was rape. The men who believe the rapes they committed were actually consensual sex often relied on rape myths to prove to themselves that their victims were 'asking for it'. These cases included men who were convicted of rape using weapons or breaking into women's houses to rape them.

The study found the admitters' accounts were basically the same as the trial evidence, though the rapist slightly altered facts to diminish the level of violence in the rape. Deniers, on the other hand, claimed a very different version of events from proven facts. Weapons were used in nearly 70 per cent of their rapes but only 6 per cent acknowledged the weapon was used to threaten or intimidate their victim. Most of them claimed the victim had either only suffered minor injuries or that they weren't injured at all. Deniers all blamed the victim for the rape they themselves had committed.

One myth was that of women as seductress, i.e., that women flirt and tease until men are so provoked they have no choice but to rape them. One man, who broke into a woman's home and raped her at knifepoint, still had no difficulty claiming she voluntarily removed her clothes and seduced him. Sixty-five per cent of the deniers interviewed believed in this myth.

Another myth, that women say yes when they mean no, was found to be believed by the interviewees. While the men admitted their victims struggled initially, this group claimed the resistance was pretence. In over two thirds of these cases there was a weapon involved. One of them told the researchers, 'She semi-struggled but deep down inside I think she felt it was a fantasy come true.' Another man, who used a bayonet to threaten his victim, said, 'At the time I didn't think it was rape, I just asked nicely and she didn't resist.' This belief was found among 34 per cent of the denier group and 24 per cent of the admitters.

Yet another common myth was that most women eventually relax and enjoy it. Sixty-nine per cent of deniers and 20 per cent of admitters believed this, the study revealed. Many of the rapists from both groups claimed their victims ended up enjoying the rape, sometimes to an immense degree. A man who broke into his victim's house said, 'She felt really proud after sex with me.' Another one who hid in his victim's closet and attacked her in her sleep said, 'Once we got into it, she was okay.'

A large percentage of the deniers groups believed that nice girls don't get raped (78 per cent of deniers and 22 per cent of admitters). That is, a woman with a 'bad' reputation or whose behaviour, clothes or speech is overtly sexual is asking for it, and therefore couldn't have been saying no. A man who abducted his victim from the street at knifepoint claimed she was hitchhiking and said, 'We knew she was a damn whore and whether she screwed one or fifty guys didn't matter.'

Eighty-four per cent of the deniers groups believed their victim was guilty of minor wrongdoing: 'I pulled a knife on her and I hit her as hard as I would hit a man. But I shouldn't be in prison for what I did. I shouldn't have all this time for going to bed with a broad.' In other words, while this rapist admitted the violence was wrong, he still insisted the rape was justified. 'I'm guilty of sex and delinquency of a minor, but not rape,' was the excuse of another man, who forcibly abducted an underage girl from a party and raped her.

The deniers claim they're not guilty of rape because their victim was the one to blame. Admitters, on the other hand, acknowledge their guilt, but claim they were not really responsible for the rape because there were external factors that 'made them do it'.

The study found that perpetrators from all groups blamed alcohol and drugs for their actions. 'Straight, I don't have the guts to rape,' said one. Another said, 'It brought out what was already in there but in such intensity, it was uncontrollable.' Deniers, who still don't think they did anything wrong and therefore don't need an excuse for their own behaviour, were more likely to blame the victim's substance intake.

Emotional problems were an excuse offered by none of the deniers, but 80 per cent of admitters. A common myth is that anxiety, depression, childhood trauma, etc. can cause a man who would otherwise be a good person to become a rapist. 'Being a rapist is not part of my personality.' The vast majority of admitters blamed their action on the betrayal of a partner putting them into such a state of rage they 'didn't know what I was doing'. They portrayed themselves as being temporarily 'sick' and therefore not responsible for what they did.

There is a lot of (graphic) detail from that study, but it's a stark representation of how violent men believe those myths about rape. These beliefs help them excuse and minimise their behaviour, even blame their victims. The men who were interviewed truly believed what they were saying, and most of them remained consistent in their version of what happened both in the initial police interviews and in the researcher interviews, which took place years after their conviction. This study demonstrates how abusers find it so easy to persuade victims to blame themselves. The most convincing lies are the ones told by someone who believes the lie to be truth.

Mitchell Peggie was convicted of raping a 21-year-old woman, which he did less than a week after being acquitted on another rape trial. In 2014 yet another woman accused him of sexually assaulting her. She told *The Courier-Mail* that he handcuffed her, grabbed her breasts and tried to put his hands down her pants. She says he told her he thought she was a 'kinky kind of girl' and when she demanded that he uncuff her, he said she was being a tease. The woman, who says she did not report the incident to police, also claims Peggie told her she'd brought it on herself.

Peggie, a former law student, who was described as initially coming across as 'nice' and 'charming', said in the trial where he was convicted that his victim had repeatedly told him in text messages before their meeting she was not going to have sex with him, but he thought she was 'playing coy'. He also told police that 'I did pin her wrists [but] not in a forcible "I was trying to molest her" way. She makes it out like I was trying to rape her, and that was not at all the case.' He claimed the reason she refused to kiss him on the lips was 'because she was doing the whole tease thing'.

This is why the media's endorsement of myths about rape and violence is so dangerous. It normalises those beliefs, giving substance to even the most disprovable of them. When violent men see these myths of violence given implicit legitimacy in mainstream news it reinforces their ability to excuse their own actions. It also reinforces their belief that *everyone* thinks as they do about women and violence and therefore their actions are 'normal'. Worse, it predisposes victims to believe they are to blame.

Chapter 9

Injustice in the justice system

Australia, New Zealand and the U.K. have all been making strong attempts to change the way victims of men's violence against women and children are treated in the justice system. But so far, these reforms have made little difference to the way rape victims are treated in court or to the conviction rate of rape trials. There have been some improvements in some jurisdictions on police response to domestic violence victims, but it remains patchy and inconsistent.

MYTHS ABOUT THE JUSTICE SYSTEM

- Genuine victims will always report to police and when they do so they will get the help they need.
- Juries, judges and criminal trials are always objective and free from bias.
- Every man tried for rape or domestic violence charges who is acquitted was falsely accused.

People such as Rosie Batty and Joy Rowley tried time and time again to get police to take action to protect them, and were failed by systemic problems inside the police force and by individual police who did not believe their stories. Even when the women were believed, the police didn't have the information or the power to take action that could have saved lives.

POLICE

Women who go to police pleading for help get very mixed results. There are, without doubt, wonderful individuals in the police forces who understand all the complexities of family violence and will do everything in their power to keep victims safe. They put in hours of overtime, sometimes unpaid, to get a perpetrator processed or a victim to a safe place. They reach out across networks of support services they only know because they've put years of work into building them all up. They vigilantly watch over survivors and have an astounding memory for perpetrators who constantly try to fool them by changing cars and wearing dark glasses, hats or hoodies to throw them off. These are the police you get sometimes. And then you get the ones who can't be bothered with more paperwork. The ones who didn't believe her the first time she called and are even less inclined to believe her the tenth time. The ones who don't understand the court system and turn away when they see victims fall through the cracks because it's just too much effort to do anything about it. The ones who end up trying to answer unanswerable questions in a coroner's inquest because the woman they didn't believe was murdered by a man they once called 'that poor bloke'.

Police are the gatekeepers between victims and the justice system. If they don't believe victims or if they don't think a report is worth investigating, it stops right there. A victim who reaches out to the police for help can only hope they get one of the officers who does think their report is worth investigating.

Waiting on the other side of the police is the rest of the legal system. Like the police force, the legal system is not an independent, unbiased machine where human failings are removed and replaced with the perfectly balanced scales of justice. The legal system is made up of people. Police, defence lawyers, prosecutors, judges and juries are all people from our community. Most of those groups are still highly male-dominated and, at senior levels, still made up of conservative older men – the very group most likely to mistrust women's reports of violence and believe that women provoke men into committing violence against them.

As we examine police responses to men's violence against women, it's also worth remembering that police who deal with sexual and domestic violence can suffer from vicarious trauma. This can have an impact on how they respond to victims. A 2017 study by the American Psychological Association indicated that some police in sexual assault teams had significant levels of compassion fatigue, secondary traumatic stress, and burnout. This was found to be detrimental to their ability to empathise with victims. Most police forces now recognise this and try to provide counselling and support, but the training and culture that emphasises being in control and in charge of any difficult situation can equally make it difficult for people working in police forces to admit to feeling overwhelmed or out of control. It's a complex situation that will take a long period of cultural change to overcome, and in the meantime both police and victims will continue to suffer.

Even for police who are not carrying secondary trauma, high rates of belief in rape myths cause problems for victims trying to report rape and domestic violence. A 2010 in-depth study published in the *Journal of Interpersonal Violence* comprised interviews with forty-nine Los Angeles detectives specialising in sexual assault cases and revealed the complexities of how widely accepted rape myths can complicate reporting to police. The researchers found that while most detectives acknowledged rape myths as false, this wasn't always reflected in the way they treated victims or responded to their stories. They also acknowledged that rape myths often affect the way victims will report what happened to them, one detective saying, 'They're afraid that if they divulge some part of the story that may make them look bad . . . they're afraid to tell. It will hurt their case or we'll pass judgment on them in some way, so they don't tell that part of the story. But, then when it comes out, it makes it look like they're not being completely truthful and it hurts their case eventually.' Interestingly, all the detectives involved in the study said that while date-rape drugs like Rohypnol were big media stories, they were almost unheard of in actual police investigations. They all said alcohol was the drug most likely to be used by sexual predators to incapacitate their victims, and while most (but not all) of them understood this didn't mean a rape *didn't* occur, they did report that victims would try to minimise the amount they'd had to drink because they were afraid they wouldn't be believed if they admitted to being drunk when the rape happened. Again, the problem with this was that it was relatively easy to establish how much victims had actually been drinking, via witnesses or credit card transactions, and the discrepancy between the initial report to police and the evidence presented at trial was frequently used by defence lawyers to discredit victims.

Despite the understanding of rape myths that all detectives claimed to have, a highly significant result to come from the study was their perceptions of false reports – buying into the myth that women lie about rape to punish men who've wronged them or protect themselves from the consequences of consensual sex. Keeping in mind the research quoted earlier, which puts the real level of false rape reports at somewhere between 2 and 8 per cent, over 55 per cent of the detectives with less than seven years' experience in sexual assault investigation said somewhere between 40 and 80 per cent of reported rapes were false reports.

The estimated level of false reports dropped with more experience. Nearly two thirds of police with more than eight years' experience correctly placed the rates of false reports at under 10 per cent. While it's encouraging that there's evidence that police learn to trust women eventually, it's dangerous that it takes more than eight years for them to learn this lesson. Victims who report their rape to relatively inexperienced police and see signs of not being believed may fall into the trap of trying to make their story more believable by leaving out or changing some of the details, which in turn reinforces police's reasons for thinking women lie about rape. It's a cycle that starts and ends with rape myths and is one of the many reasons it is so crucial to changing how everyone thinks about the victims and perpetrators of rape.

A 2016 study by Saint Xavier University in Chicago analysed 544 cases of sexual assault reported to a Midwestern police department. They found that despite most police again claiming to understand that the 'real rape' myth is false, victims were more likely to continue participating after initial reports to police if their assaults reflected the 'real rape' scenario. It's difficult to know whether this is due to victims already blaming themselves and therefore not believing they had the right to demand a police response, or whether they were genuinely picking up on cues that police were doubting their stories. Whatever the reason, several studies across Australia and the U.K. show that victims are more likely to continue with reports where they feel believed and supported by police and victims services.

In a U.K. study of 400 rapes reported to police in 2010 and 2011 nearly 80 per cent of the reports did not result in charges, more than two thirds due to 'insufficient evidence'. Almost all the other cases did not go ahead because the victim withdrew support for the charges and, of those, almost half were where the victim and offender were in an intimate relationship.

An Australian study had similar findings. Of 850 rapes reported to Victoria Police between 2000 and 2003, only 15 per cent of reports resulted in charges being laid. Rape victims who were most likely to see charges laid were male victims; physically injured; medically examined; not influenced by alcohol or drugs at the time of the offence; subject to other offences alongside the rape; and raped by offenders well known to police for previous sexual offending. In other words, all the things we know are not true of most rape victims. Cases that did not result in charges were typically more likely to involve younger victims; victims who were acquainted with or who had a cursory relationship with the offender; and victims who had consumed alcohol or other drugs around the time of the offence. Otherwise known as the most likely rape scenarios and the ones most subject to rape myths.

While much of this is discussing rape, it's important to remember that the most likely person to rape is a male intimate partner, and that the crossover of sexual violence and domestic violence is extremely high. When we talk about rape victims and survivors we are also, often, talking about people who have been subjected to violence from partners and family members.

PROSECUTORS

The attrition rate of rape investigations is not just about police not believing victims. There's a complex interaction that goes on between police, prosecutors and survivors about whether to go ahead with charges and a possible trial. Survivors can decide they don't want to take things any further. Sometimes this is due to pressure from the perpetrator, particularly if he is an intimate partner or close to family and friends of the survivor. It can also be a decision made with help from police and prosecutors where survivors start to understand the potential trauma that could result from going ahead with a trial. Sometimes police and prosecutors have to help them make that decision by ensuring they are fully informed about how long it will take for the trial to be heard and exactly what tactics defence lawyers will use to discredit survivors in court. If police or prosecutors think a trial is going to be particularly traumatic for the victim, or they know about evidence that will be used against victims in a way that could cause serious harm (such as evidence of mental illness or behaviour that will be twisted to make it look like the victim lied about or 'provoked' the violence) they have an obligation to warn them. On the other hand, a great deal of unfair pressure can sometimes be put on survivors to proceed with a trial because it is supposedly their responsibility to make sure the perpetrator does not have the opportunity to rape again. There is an implied suggestion here that if he does, it will be their fault. It is *never* their fault. One of the most repeated sentences I use in Fixed It is: The only thing that causes rape or murder is a person's decision to rape or murder another person. No one else is responsible for the choices made by a rapist or a murderer.

Research has repeatedly shown that rape myths are consistently wielded at trial to distance the case from the 'real rape' stereotype (another myth in itself), and to discredit the victim.

When survivors can make an informed choice about how to proceed with the legal events, it can be powerful and liberating. But survivors don't always get to make the choice. If police or prosecutors believe the survivor's story but don't think they have enough evidence to get a conviction, they will almost always refuse to go ahead with a trial. This is partly to save the court's time and taxpayers' money, but also to spare the victim the trauma of a trial that ends in exonerating their abuser.

In such cases, police and prosecutors may be right about the chances of getting a conviction, but this can still be traumatising for survivors who have already been subjected to violence that rendered them powerless. To then be told they also have no power to demand retribution or acknowledgement from their abuser is another kind of trauma that adds to the whole experience.

Assuming a reported rape goes to trial, the chances of a conviction are still much lower than for any other violent crime. Part of this is due to the nature of the crime, in that it almost never happens in front of witnesses, but this alone would not be enough to secure an acquittal. Some states in Australia, such as New South Wales and Queensland, still apply a subjective test, that is, did this particular perpetrator in this particular rape know there was no consent? Victoria recently changed their legislation to an objective test, which means the prosecution needs to prove that a reasonable person would know under the circumstances that there was no consent. This is where rape myths come to the foreground of rape trials. Is she a 'good woman' who would not consent to sex with this man and would not lie about it if she did? Is he an 'evil monster' who would force himself on a woman who made it clear she did not consent? If there is reasonable doubt about either of these things, and if the jury is made up of people who believe rape myths, the accused is likely to be acquitted.

It wasn't until 1997 that Queensland removed the requirement for judges to warn juries that they could not rely on victim's testimony unless it was corroborated by other evidence. And it wasn't until three years later that they stopped allowing perpetrators to represent themselves and cross examine their victims in court. Consider also the defence of 'mistake of fact', which says that a person who makes an honest and reasonable mistake about the facts should only be criminally liable to the extent that they would have been if the belief were true. In other words, if someone genuinely believed their underage victim was consenting, they can only be charged with sex with a minor; they cannot be charged with rape. This was the defence that in 2005 acquitted a 21-year-old man who crept into a thirteen-year-old girl's bedroom while she was asleep and raped her on four separate occasions. She struggled, tried to push him off, kneed him in the gut and tried to reach a metal bar she kept in her room to beat him off. Despite this evidence, and a jury conviction on at least one of the rapes, he was acquitted on appeal using the 'mistake of fact' defence. It is staggering to think anyone could believe that an adult who sneaks into a sleeping child's bed has made an 'honest and reasonable mistake' about her consent. Nevertheless, two of the three Queensland Supreme Court Judges in 2007 accepted this argument, vacated the rape conviction and substituted it with the 'lesser' offence of 'unlawful carnal knowledge'. He was freed on the basis of time already served (two years).

This is just one of the hundreds of stories of rapists acquitted or freed because judges and juries found that it was honest and reasonable for a man to ignore, not hear, not understand or not care about the physical and verbal defences their victim put up against their rape. New South Wales has a similar history, the most well-known recent one being Luke Lazarus's trial, conviction, appeal and counter appeal that left him in a grey area where both his conviction and appeal were overturned but no further hearings took place. His defence was that he didn't know a scared eighteen-year-old girl was too overwhelmed and afraid of his threatening stance and tone to fight him off. The appeal judge recognised the victim didn't consent but acquitted Lazarus of knowing that to be true.

Even trials that do reach a conviction are well recognised as being re-traumatising for survivors. Former One Nation advisor Sean Black was convicted in 2018 for raping his wife, Tanya, in 2007. Tanya's description of her experience during the trial was harrowing. She said it was almost as traumatic as the rape itself, she sat through twelve hours of gruelling cross examination that left her vomiting and suffering panic attacks. She said the defence lawyer was screaming and yelling at her and that she felt the duration of the cross examination was designed to wear her down. She felt like she was the one on trial. Sean Black did not testify at all.

JURIES

Research on whether the gender of jurors makes a difference to the verdict in rape is mixed. Some studies show women are more likely than men to sympathise with victims, others show they are less likely to do so. Possibly this is more due to the difficulty of doing intensive studies of juries and jury deliberations in real-life trials, particularly in Australia, which has strict rules against enquiring into jury deliberations.

Mock trials are a useful tool to delve into the way jurors interact witheach other and the evidence they've seen but they must be viewed with the understanding that the fact that mock jurors all know the trial is not real might have some impact on their reactions. However, an Australian Institute of Criminology study of mock rape trials in Australia showed how strongly rape myths influence jurors' perception of rape victim credibility. Two hundred and ten members of the public were assigned to eighteen rape trials where the only difference in the evidence they saw was whether the victim testified in court, by CCTV or on pre-recorded video (how she gave her evidence had no effect on jurors' perceptions of her credibility).

Examples which arose regularly and worked against the complainant included:

1. The complainant flirted and danced with the defendant (some degree of encouragement).
2. She did not scream or shout for help (why not?).
3. There was no evidence of injury and no medical evidence to support her claim (surely there would be evidence of injury or DNA).
4. The complainant went back to the party afterwards; she did not leave immediately (she would leave).
5. The complainant composed herself and pretended nothing had happened (why would she pretend nothing had happened?).

6. She continued to work with the defendant for two weeks after the incident (a rape victim could not continue to work with the person who had raped her).
7. The complainant did not report the incident to police for two weeks (why did she delay in reporting the rape?).

These issues were cited by many of the mock jurors as reasons for doubting the victim's credibility and 74 per cent of them favoured a not guilty verdict. The study also found that 'allegiance to rape myths' were significantly associated with being male, having a lower income, and holding conservative political views.

A review of rape trials by Sarah Zydervelt, Rachel Zajac and others in Australia and New Zealand titled 'Lawyers' Strategies for Cross-Examining Rape Complainants: Have We Moved Beyond the 1950s?' compared the way victims were cross examined in the 1950s, before all the law reform in both countries, with the way they were cross examined in similar trials between 1996 and 2011. The study reported that rape myths were still the underlying basis for defence cross examination of victims and said:

Our overarching finding is that, relative to 50 years ago, defence lawyers who question rape complainants are merely pursuing the same goals in slightly different ways. In essence, little has changed. Even after significant reforms to policy and law, complainants still find cross-examination to be distressing and demeaning and our data show that this sentiment is understandable given the tactics employed.

One fascinating study by Wendy Larcombe from the University of Melbourne examined how perceptions of an 'ideal' rape victim as 'virtuous' (read: 'virgin' or 'middle-class mother') are disrupted somewhat if we look at successful rape complaints. Larcombe's analysis of complainant characteristics in a limited sample of 'successful' rape trials in Victoria found, for example, that

> The 'successful rape complainant' is not necessarily one with an unblemished sexual history. Rather, she has a strong sense of herself and takes overt offence at (rather than being taken by surprise or accepting as all too familiar) alternative and derogatory constructions of her character and credibility. She will need to be reasonably familiar with and experienced in managing power-loaded situations so that she can be polite but not compliant, co-operative but not submissive. She is not prone to exaggeration or embellishment but seems to talk straight. She answers questions quickly and precisely and speaks fairly frankly and without shame about sexual acts and activities. Clearly, these attitudinal and linguistic qualities will be related to class, race, age, ability, and cultural background. What is interesting is that the axes of inclusion/exclusion here may not replicate exactly other patterns of discrimination and privilege. For example, the necessity for linguistic skill in evading put-downs and the requirement for voiced resistance will favour a complainant who is not too 'polite', too compliant or too shy. Class, age, and cultural/ ethnic background will obviously play a part here, as will physical and linguistic dis/ability. The necessity to talk frankly about sexual acts will similarly disadvantage certain groups of complainants on the basis of age, class and cultural/ethnic background. But, interestingly, on these bases the 'middle-class woman at home alone when the miscreant breaks in' will not necessarily make the best prosecution witness either. Indeed, we could predict that successful rape complainants in Australia are more likely working-class, young, able-bodied, non-Aboriginal, English-speaking women.

While that study is now more than twenty-five years old, as Larcombe
pointed out, race is often an issue for the victim. It's also an issue for perpetrators. Research conducted by the University of Queensland in 2016
found that while white people in Australia might not necessarily think
that white men are more or less likely to be guilty of rape, they are more
likely to perceive men of colour as being guilty. This dark underbelly of
racism is connected to the monster myth, where white people believe
men of colour are somehow different from white men, more dangerous, more violent, always looking to come and rape 'our women'. Like all
other rape myths, this is utter bullshit. Race plays no part in the decision
to rape. Rape happens when men believe they are entitled to women's
bodies and this has nothing to do with the colour of their skin.

As in rape law reform, most states have made concerted efforts to
change the way child abuse cases were prosecuted. In the 1950s, for
example, children under ten were only allowed to testify in court if
the child could prove they understood what it meant to 'swear to tell the
truth' for example, showing they knew that lying would mean they went
to hell. Again, as with rape trials, judges had to tell juries they could not
rely on the child's evidence without corroboration and perpetrators were
allowed to cross examine their witnesses in court. Reforms over the last
twenty years have changed all those requirements and put stricter rules
on what questions can be asked in cross examination, but again, as in
rape trials, it has made little difference. As with the comparative studies
of historical and recent rape trials, studies have been conducted on child
abuse trials from the 1950s and compared to similar trials from the last
ten years. One such study, by Rachel Zajac and others, compared sixty-
five trials from each time period and reported:

Our findings do not support the view that law reforms have
improved the way in which lawyers cross examine child sexual abuse

complainants, or even that child cross examinations have 'always been like this.' Instead, our data suggests that, despite the reforms, cross-examination has changed for the worse. Instead of a targeted selection of strategies, lawyers now use every strategy available to them with nearly every complainant.

While the legal fraternity might like to fondly imagine that juries are able and willing to discard all personal prejudices as long as they are instructed to do so by a judge, research has shown that this is just not true. One study, published in the journal of the Society of Legal Scholars, showed that juries can ignore, misinterpret or misapply judicial instructions and are 'reluctant to jettison their more natural inclinations . . . on the basis of narrative constructions grounded in "common sense" and "personal experience".' Research by the Australian Institute of Family Studies found juries in rape trials 'pay more atten-tion to evidence of character and conduct than they do to substantive evidence of rape'.

It's interesting that the debate about allowing women to sit on juries didn't fully resolve across all states in Australia until the 1990s. Some states allowed women on juries (under very limited circumstances) as early as the 1920s. Aboriginal women were of course barred by not being allowed on the electoral role until the 1960s. As late as 1953, con-cern was raised about the kinds of cases that women jurors would hear and the potential impact it would have on jury deliberations. The then WA Minister for Justice argued in state parliament that:

There are cases of sodomy and lesbianism which are very embarrass-ing. A modest woman hearing such cases would be so embarrassed a true verdict would not be returned. Her observations and her judgment would be clouded, and her presence would probably be embarrassing to those with whom she was sitting on the jury and would make the situation extremely difficult, especially in the jury room. A full and frank discussion of such a case would be difficult . . . It would be extremely embarrassing when sexual cases were being heard. It would be very embarrassing for one to meet at some social function a woman with whom one had been associated as a juror when dealing with such a case. I would feel she had deteriorated to a great extent.

While most of the research quoted so far specifically focuses on rape trials, this doesn't mean it's not relevant to domestic and family abuse. The largest group of offenders in rape cases are intimate partners of the victims. They are also the rapists least likely to be reported to police, which means many women dealing with violent partners in the court system are facing a man who raped them as well as abusing them in other, more visible ways. Most domestic and family violence that ends up in court in Australia goes to the Magistrates Court, which is where intervention orders are issued; 'minor' assault charges are heard along with other non-indictable offences such as stalking, harassment and verbal assault, and results of financial abuse such as unpaid fines and debts accumulated under a victim's name by their abuser. Many states in Australia are working towards specialist family violence Magistrates Courts, but this is still in the early stages. While it's working reasonably well in places like Melbourne, regional areas and some other states are slower to respond to domestic and family violence, and are still putting victims and perpetrators in a courtroom at the same time, assuming that victims who don't show up at court have no further need of protection (rather than the far more frequent explanation that they have been terrorised into staying home), and hearing ongoing abuse as individual instances in separate cases.

Where women are forced to bring domestic and family violence matters to the Family Court, they face many of the same barriers that rape
victims face in County and Supreme courts. When judges and court
advisers assume women and children lie about abuse to demonise men,
it belittles and dehumanises them. Additionally, they have to face what
research for the *Journal of Psychiatry, Psychology and Law* described as
'fear of the ex-partner and having to confront him at hearings, constantly
reliving the relationship via affidavit, and the insensitivity of some legal
professionals to the difficulties experienced by women confronted with
these experiences'.

Add to that the fact that many survivors of domestic and family
violence can easily have cases being heard or be responding to several
different courts at the same time, as with one survivor (who will remain
unnamed), who told me:

> I had the results of the weapons and assault charges from the County
> Court, orders from the Family Court and we were still fighting for
> permanent intervention orders in the Magistrates Court and they
> all had to be separate but related and wait on each other and honest
> to god there were even times when I reckon my lawyer couldn't
> make sense of it all. I didn't have a prayer.

This woman's abuser was gaming the system and using his wealth to
give him access to court-appointed intimidation of his ex-partner. At the
time of writing, she has been involved in at least one ongoing court case
with him for fifteen years.

JUDGES
Judges are thought – by themselves and most of society – to be entirely
free from the prejudices and biases that affect the rest of us. Such moral

objectivity is thought to be a requirement of the job, but studies have shown that they are not infallible. One study of judges' sentences and remarks for comparable domestic murders in Victoria and New South Wales between 2002 and 2010 looked at the difference between sentences and commentary on murders where women killed their male partners and where men killed their female partners. They found a distinct difference in the sentencing: women were given an average of nearly twenty-five years and men an average of twenty years. The longest sentence for a woman was thirty-six years; for a man it was twenty-three years.

The research also found gender differences in the sentencing remarks. This is where judges sum up the evidence and explain their reasoning for the sentences they've imposed. Positive comments on men, both murderers and victims, were common: they were described as being 'a good provider', 'a hardworking member of the community', 'popular in your workplace', 'an honest, hardworking family man' and 'well respected'. They found no such positive comments about the female murderers and almost none about the female victims.

There were no negative evaluations of the men who killed women, but the women who killed men were repeatedly described as 'wicked', 'heartless', 'callous' and 'extremely manipulative'. Men who killed women were often given excuses such as depression, loss of control and dysfunctional background, but none of the women who killed were ever granted these excuses. In almost all the cases where men killed women, judges commented that the reason for the murder was that the victim was leaving or about to leave the man who killed her, or had been unfaithful to him. In one case, the victim-blaming was so blatant the judge actually said to a murderer, 'Your wife was the source of the conflict.' Even when men had murdered another person as well, or attacked police with weapons, they were given excuses for their behaviour.

Needless to say, none of the male victims of women was blamed for his own murder, nor were the female murderers allowed any of the diminished responsibility given to men. One explanation for this discrepancy could be the rarity of women killing their male partners – researchers could only find five cases involving female murderers that fit their criteria of intimate partner murder (rather than manslaughter). Maybe it's true that, in the very few cases where women kill their male partners, they are indeed cold-blooded killers. However, this doesn't stand up to the in-depth review by the New South Wales Coroner's Court Death Review Team, which found that between 2000 and 2014, there was not one single case of a woman killing her male partner without a significant history of her having been the victim of his abuse.

The most likely explanation is that even judges are subject to the expression of subconscious violence myths, where women who kill are deviants because they both break the law and go against patriarchal requirements, that is, remaining gentle and nurturing simply because they are women. Men who kill their partners have broken the law but they have not breached any masculine taboos. In fact, such violence is reinforced and endorsed by myths about masculinity and violence, and that makes these men easy objects of sympathy and understanding.

Research from Finland analysed the media coverage of Rosemary West's trial over her collusion with Fred West to commit multiple rapes and murders in what the media dubbed the House of Horrors murders.

The research noted some interesting trends in the reporting. Rose West's failure to be a good mother made her easy to demonise, noting that 'mothers are expected to die for children, not to condone, instigate and participate in their abuse and murder'. Her sexuality and supposedly 'voracious' libido reinforced 'male fears and concern over women's uncontrolled/uncontrollable sexuality'. The researchers also noted the duality of reporting on women in the Rose West case – as much as Rose West was demonised for not adhering to expected female stereo-types, victims were either valorised or blamed for venturing 'outside the boundaries of male protection or family control'.

Part III
Representation, Misrepresentation and No Representation

Chapter 10
The politics of gender

The myths used by political powerbrokers to keep women and other disadvantaged groups out of the power structures that govern economic and social policy are inextricably linked to the myths that excuse and enable more visible forms of violence because they are based on the same gender and racial stereotypes. Those stereotypes form the basis for the myth that white men are the only people who can be trusted with power. Media coverage of politics subtly legitimises and reinforces those myths, both to the people in power and the people who vote to put them there.

MYTHS ABOUT WOMEN IN POLITICS
- Women have the same opportunities as men to succeed in politics.
- Political candidates are chosen and judged on merit.
- Women are too emotional to handle political life.
- Men are far more logical and objective than women.
- Women with children can't give their full attention to their job.
- Women without children can't understand family life.
- Men's views and time are unaffected by having children.

When the First Minister of Scotland and the Prime Minister of the United Kingdom met to discuss Britain's exit from the European Union they probably had a few things to talk about. Small things such as the legal, political and financial ramifications of Brexit and the continued unification of the United Kingdom. These issues will have a huge impact on the lives of all people living in the U.K. They need to know about it and understand its effects. But one of the most read newspapers in the country decided that the most important issue to explain to their readers was that the leaders involved were women. Y'know, women. The collection of body parts that has no other purpose than to appeal to men.

'NEVER MIND BREXIT, WHO WON LEGS-IT' ran the headline in huge font down the left-hand side of *The Daily Mail*'s front cover. On the right-hand side was a photo of Theresa May and Nicola Sturgeon, with their legs *right there*, joining their feet to their hips, as women's legs are wont to do when their owners are after attention. The article that followed this headline, entitled 'Finest weapons at their command? Those pins!' discussed the political significance of Nicola Sturgeon's clothes and 'shapely shanks'. The nail polish worn by 'vicar's daughter' Theresa May got its own paragraph. And then there was this: 'But what stands out here are the legs – and the vast expanse on show. There is no doubt that both women consider their pins to be the finest weapon in their physical arsenal. Consequently, both have been unleashed.'

The headline and article made a glaring statement to women that no matter how successful you are or how much power you have, your achievements can always be dismantled by a public reminder that how women look matters far more than anything they can do.

The Legs-it piece was a particularly egregious example of how women in politics are constantly and insidiously undermined by political journalists, most of whom are men. The techniques are the same all over the

world: measure a woman against outdated but persistent gender stereotypes, find all the ways she doesn't conform to them and then label her a
failure, either as a woman and or as a leader. It's extraordinarily effective
and has never been limited to any one country or side of the ideological
divide.

HISTORY

Human history is the story of men in power. Kings, emperors and
presidents have almost always been men. In the days when power was
inherited, many countries had laws in place barring women from the line
of succession. Men could inherit thrones from their mothers even when
the mother was not permitted to rule. Henry VII's dubious claim to the
English throne came through his mother but she was never considered
as a replacement for the Yorkist kings. The role of women in monarchies was to bear sons to kings to continue the line of rule. A woman who
could not provide male heirs was a political and personal failure.

But most cultures have at least one female ruler in their past.
Boudicca. Cleopatra. Elizabeth I. Catherine the Great. The Queen of
Sheba. Maria Theresa of Austria. Wu Zetian, Empress of China. Queen
Victoria. All those women gained power only because a combination of
birth and circumstance removed all the male alternatives. If they held
onto that power it was usually due to a magnificent combination of skill
and force of personality.

While few women have ever been allowed to hold official positions of power, it would be naïve to think women have never had any
influence over politics. Some very strong and capable women have led
nations and directed the course of human history. The vast majority of
them, however, were working behind the scenes. Their unofficial grasp
on power was solely dependent on the men they advised, persuaded or
manipulated.

Borte Ujin ruled Genghis Khan's empire in his many absences. Theodora of Byzantium was the brains behind Emperor Justinian of Rome. Eleanor of Aquitaine influenced the politics of twelfth-century Western Europe with political acumen, alliances and a strong bond with her son, Richard the Lionheart. Isabella of France was instrumental in deposing her husband Edward II of England, arguably one of the worst kings England ever had. Catherine de Medici, wife of Henry II of France and mother of three kings, retained significant power over French politics for decades after her husband's death. Joan of Arc gave Charles de Valois his throne. Empress Dowager Cixi effectively ruled China for forty-seven years. Kosem Sultan ruled the Ottoman Empire as regent for her sons. Madame de Pompadour was Louis XV's unofficial prime minister for years. Nana Asma'u, daughter and sister of the Sultans of Sokoto, guided her brother's rule and was pivotal in expanding women's education in West Africa. Eva Perón was so adored by the *descamisados* of Argentina that even now her memory overshadows her presidential husband's. Eleanor Roosevelt's political activism and popularity propelled her husband into the presidency.

The common thread running through the stories of all these women is the threat they posed to men. That threat specifically came from their gender, not their actions. Men who held power behind the scenes, and there were many of them, may have been disparaged or even taken down. But they were not attacked on the basis of their gender. These men were collateral damage in political battles or superseded by men with better connections and more power. Gendered attacks, however, were almost always used to bring women down.

Eleanor of Aquitaine was accused of having an incestuous affair with her uncle and was imprisoned by her husband for the 'unwomanly' crime of supporting her sons in their rebellion against him. Catherine de Medici was called a witch because surely only the dark arts could explain how a woman held power for so long. Eva Perón was dismissed as a prostitute and it was her sexual attraction, not her valuable political acumen and advice, that explained her hold over Juan Perón. Washington gossip labelled Eleanor Roosevelt a lesbian and at the same time accused her of affairs with men. Elizabeth I was presumed to be sleeping with several of the men in her court and decried as unwomanly for her refusal to marry, while Queen Victoria was reviled for mourning her husband too deeply.

Women in official positions of power have become more common in the twenty-first century but they are still the exception. Australia has had a total of eleven women serve as heads of government – one out of the twenty-nine prime ministers, six of the 252 premiers and four of the nineteen chief ministers of a territory. The United Kingdom has had more than seventy prime ministers in the last 300 years. Only two of them have been women. The United States has never had a female president and in May 2017 only six of the fifty states had a female governor.

Even now, when men hold positions of power, it is perceived to be the natural state of things. Men don't have to prove their right to hold power; all they need to do is convince people they deserve it more than the next man. Women who aspire to political leadership must constantly prove that they have a right to even want such a position. Their ability to do their job is automatically suspect; in white able-bodied straight men it is assumed.

POLITICAL JOURNALISM

The rise of democracy coincided with journalism's increase in power. In politics, journalism serves as a link between people seeking power (candidates) and the people who will allow them to have it (voters). Journalism is how most voters find out information and form perceptions of candidates. Government policies are complicated, and most people aren't interested in the complexities of foreign affairs or macroeconomic theory. They vote on gut instincts and how they feel about a candidate. Are they likeable? Trustworthy? Strong? Principled? Do they have similar values to me? Every candidate has a team of experts whose job is to influence the media in how they are portrayed. But journalism is the push back on this, and the reporting on politicians is what provides the general public with information on which they can base voting decisions.

Politics and political journalism have always had an uneasy relationship. The fourth estate likes to think of itself as holding the powerful to account. In truth, it is just as often a tool with which the powerful prop up their claim to power and diminish their opponents. All too often certain publications pursue an ideological agenda that gives them an allegiance to a particular party or person rather than the purpose of their profession.

Some journalists do provide knowledgeable analysis and information for an audience who want details and nuance, but too many political journalists become so enmeshed in political culture they lose sight of the world outside politics. This can be particularly noxious when they lose themselves in the privileged boys' club of the political class.

Political journalism, like politics itself, is very much a man's job. Research from all over the world has shown that most journalists who report on politics are men. While this has been slowly changing over the last decade the women who stand out in political journalism are as rare as the women who stand out in politics.

In Australia, the 2016 Women In Media report found over three quarters of political journalists were men. There are now some outstanding female journalists in leadership positions in Australia but they have had to fight a toxically sexist culture to get there.

Karen Middleton, long-time member of the Canberra Press Gallery, wrote a detailed account for *The Saturday Paper* of what she called 'extremely common' predatory behaviour by politicians, media executives and interview subjects.

I was about [21 years old] and working in the press gallery in Old Parliament House when an MP with an octopus reputation popped his head around the door of our tiny office and noted the new recruit. I'd pushed back my chair and had my feet against the desktop, with legs outstretched. It was the only way to make enough room to properly read a broadsheet newspaper.

Remarking that he had not met the newest member of the bureau, the MP quickly stepped into the minuscule room and started running his hand up my stockings, with a sleazy 'And who have we here?'

I froze. In a flash, his hand had reached the hem of my skirt and was not slowing. My fiery Irish-Australian bureau chief, the very fine journalist Paul Malone, flew around the filing cabinet from where he'd been sitting out of view. 'Don't you touch my staff!' he barked, as the MP backed away out the door. Needless to say, I was grateful for the intervention.

Middleton went on to describe numerous other encounters with members of parliament and male journalists. Many of these encounters were brazen, occurring in front of other men she had to work with. The culture of the press gallery normalised sexually demeaning women, especially young women.

The litany of groping and inappropriate comments Karen Middleton described, the blacklist of elected members of parliament young female journalists were warned to avoid and the blatantly sexist culture where grabbing a woman's breasts was greeted with 'bellowing laughter from the group' is revolting. That it was not just one incident or a single individual's experience is apparent in the Women In Media report, which found that half the women currently working in media have experienced sexual harassment, bullying and intimidation. Similar results were found at a global level by the International Women's Media Foundation. Sixty-five per cent of women had experienced intimidation, threats or abuse, and 46 per cent had been sexually harassed.

These figures suggest that journalism is more toxic for women than other male-dominated cultures of defence and police. We don't see this reflected in the news, however – because, while the ADF and Police reports make for front page news, journalists are unlikely to report on their own harassment.

Despite an almost even gender split in journalism, a survey of the four most read newspapers in the U.K. found three quarters of opinion articles and two thirds of all articles in the news and business sections of the newspapers were by men. Women In Journalism research found that in June and July 2016 only 20 per cent of front-page stories in daily newspapers were written by women. Stories with female by-lines tended to relate to health, the royal family and television programs, while men's by-lines dominated the coverage of the election, the London Bridge terror attack, and Grenfell Tower. Remember the 'soft' vs 'hard' news identified in Chapter 2? This is a telling example of how that works in practice.

In late October 2017, the so called 'spreadsheets of shame' hit the media. Thirty-six U.K. members of parliament were named and accused of sexual harassment and sexual assault. Researchers from the Trades Union Congress and the Everyday Sexism Project found that 52 per cent of women had experienced unwanted behaviour at work including groping, sexual advances and inappropriate jokes. Female journalists created an industry support group called The Second Source for women who have been subjected to harassment at work.

American journalism suffers many of the same issues. News reports covering the 2016 U.S. election were dominated by men. Research by the Women in Media Center found over 70 per cent of the analysts on U.S. cable news stations were men and nearly 86 per cent of analysts on Fox News prime-time shows were men. In a tight race between one of the most underqualified men and the first ever woman to run for the presidency, the reporting was gendered, partisan and at times wildly unhinged on both sides. It is also interesting to note how many of the men hounding Clinton were later the subject of multiple sexual assault and harassment allegations in the #MeToo campaign.

What are little girls made of?

So, what happens when a male-dominated toxic media reports on a male-dominated toxic political class just as women are starting to break through the barriers long raised against their entry? A toxic mess of reporting that concentrates on women's appearance over their abilities and plays into all the myths about women being over-emotional, untrustworthy, weak and silly.

An easy way to prove a woman is unfit for public office is to measure her against the traditional expectations of womanhood. If she can be portrayed as pretty, feminine, compliant, sweet or nurturing she is a failure as a leader. If she is strong, ambitious, resolute and powerful, she is a failure as a woman. Either way she fails.

Women in public life are checked on their qualities as mothers and nurturers rather than whether they can do their jobs well. As Annabel Crabb wrote for the ABC in 2018, Scott Morrison and Josh Frydenberg are the first Prime Minister/Treasurer team in more than forty years who both have young children and yet they have never been asked how they're going to juggle their career with the demands of looking after primary school–age offspring. Jacinda Ardern, Kelly O'Dwyer and

Tanya Plibersek, on the other hand, are questioned about their juggling capabilities with monotonous regularity. Their physical appearances are endlessly monitored. Their likeability is determined by whether they can walk the wafer-thin line of being warm enough but not *too* warm. Likeable enough but not *too* likeable. Approachable enough but not *too* approachable. And the goal posts are constantly moving.

WIVES, MOTHERS AND GRANDMOTHERS

Who is going to do women's work if women are out there taking over men's jobs? It sounds like a question that belongs to our grandmother's generation, but men in politics are never asked about their ability to juggle a demanding schedule with raising their children. Making lunches and doing the school run is still the mother's job.

Australia's first female Prime Minister Julia Gillard was labelled 'deliberately barren' and 'unfit for leadership' by a sitting senator. She was 'wooden' and 'lacking in empathy', according to a former leader of her party. Her 'lifeless kitchen' and 'empty fruit bowl' were the subject of media speculation. As later Deputy Prime Minister Tanya Plibersek once said, 'So many of the criticisms of Julia Gillard were about the fact that she was unmarried and childless. But on the flip side, if she'd been exactly who she was, only married and a working mother, the criticisms about neglecting her children would have been just as strong . . . possibly, they would have come from the same people.'

When Mitt Romney was running for President of the United States, he had eighteen grandchildren. This fact was mentioned in a few articles about him, but the tone was often congratulatory and never accusatory. It was somehow extra proof of his virility. No one questioned his ability to fulfil the obligations of the presidency because he should be home caring for his grandkids. Hillary Clinton had one child and one grandchild when she was running for president. *Time* magazine published a discussion of the problems Clinton would face running for president after the birth of her first grandchild under the headline: 'The Pros and Cons of "President Grandma".' The article concluded that being a grandmother was going to be a problem for Clinton: 'The image of a blue-haired granny is a tried-and-true American stereotype, and one that is antithetical to the image of the commander-in-chief with his finger on the button.'

Overemotional and illogical

When then President Barack Obama made a historic visit to Australia, one of the most read news sites in the country reported it under the headline, 'The Audacity of Grope: Julia and Barack's special relationship'.

The first paragraph set the tone of the entire nauseating article: 'They are a touching pair and touchy pairing. Their hands, like disembodied life forms, seek out the other's shoulders, backs and, quite possibly, bottoms. When such targets are out of reach, digits settle on forearms or the nearest available body part.'

Obama was characterised by his 'American teeth', Gillard by her schoolgirl blushes and her triumph at finally capturing the attention of the 'football captain' after dreamy nights spent plotting in her bedroom.

The article went on for another 800 words about Gillard's 'coquettishness' and Obama's 'charisma'. It effectively demeaned Gillard's successful efforts to improve Australia–U.S. relations to a girlish giggle and a hair flip.

Playing the 'gender card'

If there was one thing that should have been different about Gillard's prime ministership, it should have been that Australia's first female prime minister should have been a flag bearer for women.

'We expected more of Gillard', Peter Hartcher,
Sydney Morning Herald, 2012

Throughout Gillard's prime ministership, journalists in the conservative press thundered about Gillard's manipulative use of gender politics for her own ends. When she gave her now famous misogyny speech in parliament in 2012, even the liberal media were critical of her. One such article in the *Sydney Morning Herald* ascribed the resounding support from women all over the world to their failure to understand 'the context'.

Three million views on YouTube says they were wrong. The speech was a clarion call, a recognition of women's constant reality of subtle or overt put-downs and the breaking point when it all just gets too much to take in silent submission. It's not surprising a male-dominated media were unable to understand this, less surprising that they resented it and even less surprising that they were so frustrated by their inability to enforce their views on all the women who so vocally supported the speech.

Five years after that speech Gladys Berejiklian became the second female Premier of New South Wales. Powerful conservative radio commentator Alan Jones, who once famously expressed his exasperation with women in power 'destroying the joint', called a radio show from his hospital bed to say that although 'Gladys Berejiklian is a nice person, she is not across these issues in a million light-years'. It was a perfect example of how men who fear women put them down. She's 'nice' (sweet and gentle, therefore not leadership material) but incapable of fulfilling her position. Berejiklian had two postgraduate qualifications, fourteen years in parliament, twelve years in portfolio positions, three years as deputy leader of the NSW Liberal Party and nearly two years as NSW Treasurer. No one would suggest a man with that resume was not 'across the issues', but the yardstick for women is very different.

Women who aren't 'nice' are unfeminine. *The New York Times* published a story about Elizabeth Warren, describing her as 'imperious' and a 'scold'. And it's not only men who reinforce this. MSNBC's Mika

Brzezinski described her in 2017 as 'shrill' and 'almost unhinged'. This is relatively well-trodden ground. None of these words would ever be used to describe a man. Men can be passionate, which makes them dedicated and principled, but women are emotional and therefore illogical and not to be trusted.

U.K. Labour MP Angela Eagle was once told to 'calm down, dear' by then Prime Minister David Cameron, during a heated exchange in parliament. A male journalist later asked her, 'Shouldn't you be able to control those emotions when you're under great stress?' This is a question that would never be asked of men in the notoriously acrimonious U.K. parliament.

Strength in male leaders is a positive. In women, this trait is interpreted as being cold or hard, so they are constantly walking the fine line between too soft to lead and too hard to appeal to voters. There is a relentless drip of commentary in the media reminding voters that women are not suited for leadership. This is so normalised it can be difficult to recognise it as objectionable.

The Telegraph, in one of many comment pieces about U.K. Prime Minister Theresa May's leadership, wrote, 'There are some areas that need work. Her inscrutability means she can come across as cold. Boris might not be everyone's cup of tea – some Tory MPs see him more as a jar of Marmite – but he pumps hands, slaps backs and makes people laugh. Mrs May is in no danger of being mistaken for a stand-up comedian.' According to the journalist, a woman who has enough gravitas to not be mistaken for a comedian is a problem.

During the 2016 leadership challenge in the U.K., a BBC journalist commented that 'May and Leadsom may both be women, but they have quite different views.' There was some eye-rolling from women on Twitter and a few comment pieces in the feminist press but mainstream media largely ignored it. Why wouldn't they? Women *are* all the same.

Too pretty or not pretty enough?

Research by U.S. antisexism group Name It, Change It showed that any mention of a female political candidate's appearance, whether it's positive, negative or neutral, will significantly diminish her standing. It has no effect on how people perceive male candidates. This group also researched how sexist language about women influences how qualified they are deemed to be for their positions. Phrases such as 'ice queen' or 'mean girl' have an immediate negative impact on people's perception of the woman. She becomes less likeable and less trustworthy.

Interestingly, when the woman, or even someone else, responds directly to the comments and points out that commentary on someone's appearance has no place in political debate, the effect is almost completely reversed. The difficulty with this is that most female politicians would have to waste far too much time better spent on actually doing their jobs if they pushed back on every idiotic media article about the shoes, hair or nails.

Julia Gillard's tenure as Prime Minister was peppered with commentary about her appearance. Her clothes, her hair, her face, her voice, her figure, even her ears were subjected to constant scrutiny, most of it derogatory. One of the leading online news outlets in the country ran an article titled: 'Prime Minister Julia Gillard's ears distract from federal election campaign'. The opening line of the article read: '"HECK, there must be a surgeon who can help," worried one voter yesterday in a web debate over Julia Gillard's pendulous earlobes.'

Only in a bizarre parallel universe could anyone imagine the shape of a *male* prime minister's ears becoming front-page news or a credible reason to question his ability.

The *International Business Times* published an article about Theresa May in July 2016. She'd just been elected Prime Minister of England and was preparing to move in to Number 10. This is what they had to say:

Before even stepping into the top job, May distanced herself from the homogenised style of the female politician with success, eschewing the simple skirt suit and matching accessories that the likes of Nicola Sturgeon, Angela Merkel and short-lived rival Andrea Leadsome rely on and refused to bow to the pressures upon women in power to simplify their dress sense in order to be taken seriously.

The article analysed May's leadership abilities, potential and history on the basis of her shoes and style. It quoted Nick Clegg describing her as an 'ice maiden', and compared her sartorial choices to Hillary Clinton's clothing. The entire article reduced her political and professional achievements to nothing more than being a successful clotheshorse.

The Evening Standard managed an astounding comparison between David Cameron's navy suits and Theresa May's shoes, reporting: 'As David Cameron took down his ornaments and packed away his navy suits, May had to carefully gather together one of the most talked-about shoe wardrobes of this decade. And we all know shoes don't take kindly to a suitcase.'

The BBC published a list of 'Seven notable things about the U.K.'s next prime minister'. Among such gems as the facts that she likes hot chips and was orphaned in her twenties, was number four, shoes: Mrs May is known for her love of shoes (leopard skin being a favoured design). To commemorate her rise to Prime Minister, *The Sun* newspaper featured a mocked-up picture of one of her stilettos stamping on the heads of her male colleagues in the Conservative Party.

Hillary Clinton's appearance was also the subject of constant debate. As she once famously said, 'If I want to knock a story off the front page, I just change my hairstyle.'

White House correspondent Glenn Thrush habitually disparaged Clinton's appearance. He described photos of her as 'dour' and endlessly reported on the state of her pants suits. She was 'chilled-out in an aqua-blue suit that suggested marine tranquillity' or 'wearing her "closer outfit," an arctic white pantsuit'. He was disgusted by her pursuit of power but didn't think to question the same ambition in male candidates. This man, who wrote many articles disparaging Hillary Clinton's ambition, skills and personality, was later accused by several young female journalists of groping and lunging at them. An article in *Vox* alleged Thrush had a history of gossiping about the women who had turned him down, telling colleagues that young women were coming on to him and claiming that he had been a gentleman and courteously declined their invitations. Then, in very gentlemanly fashion, he allegedly told all their male colleagues about it the next day.

Mark Halperin dismissed the allegations of sexual assault and harassment against Donald Trump as 'nothing illegal'. He took a little logic detour and suggested Trump should 'celebrate' the allegations because they couldn't be proven and were therefore a win for him. He was accused by five different women of groping, unwanted kissing and propositioning employees for sex.

Matt Lauer was widely criticised after he chaired a live prime-time debate between Trump and Clinton. He talked over her, interrupted her and contradicted her but did almost nothing to fact check Trump or rein him in when he blustered too long. Lauer was later fired from NBC after sexual assault allegations and his co-anchors read out an internal memo on air, which stated there was 'reason to believe this may not have been an isolated incident'.

Roger Ailes, who founded Fox News with Rupert Murdoch, was the proud creator of a network that hated what its journalists called the 'liberal media' and 'political correctness', resigned after numerous women who had worked with him over twenty years alleged he sexually harassed them.

Bill O'Reilly was one of Fox News's most prominent commentators. He was fired after several prominent women at the network accused him of sexual harassment. One of the allegations, allegedly settled for an astounding $32 million, came from Lis Wiehl. She was a Fox News legal analyst who appeared on O'Reilly's show for more than fifteen years. She accused O'Reilly of repeatedly harassing her and forcing her into a sexually abusive relationship.

Leon Wieseltier, former editor of *The New Republic* and long-time writer for *The Atlantic*, often expressed his contempt for Hillary Clinton. In one example, he said she was 'like some hellish housewife who has seen something that she really, really wants and won't stop nagging you about it until finally you say, fine, take it, be the damn president, just leave me alone'. In 2017 he made a formal apology after several women accused him of sexual harassment and inappropriate advances.

These are some of the men who were directing the media's narrative of the 2016 U.S. election. Given their backgrounds, it's hardly surprising that the twenty women who accused Donald Trump of sexual harassment got short shrifted. Even less surprising is that Hillary Clinton, the first woman to seriously challenge the male stranglehold on the presidency, was painted as an overweeningly ambitious harpy, dishonest, unlikeable and incompetent.

The summary of all these stories is the persistent belief that power is the province of men. If a woman has power she has taken it not from a man but from men collectively. A man who wins power has taken it from one man, his opponent. A woman takes it from all men because power has always belonged to them.

A woman who demonstrates driving ambition and lust for power is by definition unwomanly because power has always belonged to men.

She is leaving her own domain and intruding into their territory. The threat this represents to the status quo is real to those men who have always benefited from it. Their unspoken collusion in punishing women for this threat plays out across all forms of journalism. We see it in the prominence given to men like Bill O'Reilly, Alan Jones and Piers Morgan, who blatantly dislike and fear women. When we, as readers, accept without question the narratives of journalists who concentrate on female politician's physical beauty (or perceived lack of it) and their willingness (or otherwise) to conform to womanly roles of nurturing, comforting and submitting, we help reproduce the myths that lie beneath these narratives.

That women persist in the face of the tremendous forces against them is a remarkable testament to the strength and determination of individuals and collective movements.

Chapter 11

The politics of 'women's issues'

When Kelly O'Dwyer, then Minister for Women, Jobs and Industrial Relations, announced she was quitting politics after the 2019 election, the ABC and *The Guardian* both reported it as a 'shock resignation', and they, along with most other mainstream publications, commented on the effect this would have on the election given the dearth of women left in the Coalition government. There were hints about the resignation being due to the overthrowing of Turnbull in 2018 or O'Dwyer's looming likelihood of losing her seat in 2019, but very few journalists picked up on the fact that the federal Minister for Women and Jobs had said she was resigning from her job because she was unable to manage the demands of her professional life and her family life. If the government minister responsible for addressing this issue has to quit herself because of it, how could anyone believe their government is interested in changing the status quo? It's difficult to understand why this angle was not the lead on almost every media report on her resignation, until you go back and have another look at the statistics in Chapter 2, and realise that it probably didn't occur to most of the journalists who reported on it. It's telling that one of the few journalists to write about this was a woman – Linda Reynolds at the

Sydney Morning Herald – and she did so by including memoir and her observations of the personal lives of women around her.

All the prejudices and barriers women face in politics have a real-world effect on the way women and the issues that directly affect them are dealt with by government.

The myths about 'women's issues'

> Real equality is when a female mediocre fool gets the same job that
> a male mediocre fool has now.
>
> Amanda Vanstone, *On Merit*, Paula Matthewson, 2019

Theresa May's shoes and Julia Gillard's earlobes. It's a little bit vomit-inducing when you see it all in one place like that. However much sexism these women have encountered in their work and through the media, they are hardly disadvantaged in comparison to most other women in the world. They're not at risk of homelessness or being forced to take soul-destroying work to keep food on the table. But the sexism levelled against them does have a flow-on effect to women in different socioeconomic circumstances.

Myths about women's representation

- Representation doesn't matter, we just need the right person for the job.
- Women in politics are only there to pursue a feminist agenda.
- Women voters only care about women's issues.
- Childcare, domestic violence, the gender pay gap and reproductive rights are women's issues.

Representation

The effects of sexism in politics go much further than any one individual. Politics is not just populist theatre or an ideological battleground.

It's where our elected representatives create and legislate the policies that determine how public money is collected and spent, and what social issues take priority in government activities. These decisions affect every person in the community, and when the priorities of taxation and spending drift too far from the needs of people living in the community, governments are failing their constituents. I'm not suggesting that only a person from a particular group is able to develop policy or legislation that includes that group, but perspective matters. When the perspective of a government is dominated by well-educated wealthy straight white men, the priorities of people outside that demographic slips away, not so much ignored as forgotten or misunderstood.

In 2010 Tony Abbott, as Leader of the Opposition, said during a press statement: 'What the housewives of Australia need to understand as they do the ironing is that if they get it done commercially it's going to go up in price, and their own power bills when they switch the iron on are going to go up.'

Abbott was fighting a strong campaign against carbon reduction in Australia's energy industry and focused on convincing middle Australia that a price on carbon would drastically increase their energy bills. But in doing so he revealed his world view, in which ironing is done by women and most women are housewives. But this not representative of the way most Australian women perceive themselves. The impression Abbott tried to give was that he understood and supported women who wanted to stay at home to care for husbands and children, but women whose lives or ambitions were vastly different from this were incomprehensible to him and therefore not necessary to include in his development of government policy. He was (and remains) deeply conservative and far more driven by ideology than facts. Ideological constructs, however, bear little resemblance to complex realities. Family life for many people looks nothing like the idealised, romanticised haven prescribed by those who promote 'family values' as the solution to social ills. Abbott's deeply entrenched conservatism made it difficult for him to understand how his government was not representing the general public in Australia or why this made him so unpopular. It was an indication of how Abbott valued women's contribution and viewed the allocation of power when his first cabinet included only one woman – Julie Bishop, who automatically got her cabinet seat after being voted into the deputy leader position by the Liberal Party. Jenny Macklin, who served as a cabinet minister under Kevin Rudd and Julia Gillard, told *The Guardian* at the time that she was deeply concerned about the lack of female voices in cabinet. She said the women in Rudd's and Gillard's cabinets were not just dealing with women's issues but that what they 'did bring to cabinet was an awareness of the different life experiences women have, and the priorities that women can hold'. While there's clearly a partisan element to her comments, her point holds true and was reiterated by Liberal MP Kelly O'Dwyer in her 2019 resignation speech when she said, 'Lack of representation is about government policy and the lives of people living in the electorate.'

The effect of this lack of women's representation was clearly demonstrated by the Abbott/Turnbull/Morrison governments when issues directly affecting women, such as funding for domestic violence crisis support and prevention, action on the gender pay gap and affordable, accessible child care (and the fact that this was presented as a women's issue, not a parents' issue) were demonstrably low priority.

WOMEN VOTERS AND WOMEN'S ISSUES

Getting women involved in politics is mostly up to political parties making sure they select and promote women within the party system, but it also requires that strong, driven, intelligent women are willing to become involved. Volunteering themselves as candidates is only one way to do this. Advocating for or advising candidates is another way. Agitating for policy outcomes and engaging in political debate are also powerful activities for women, particularly in small and rural communities. It is, however, difficult to encourage women to do this if they feel they will be shut out of the political process no matter what efforts they make. If they view government as something that is by men and for men, they won't see any reason or opportunity to get involved.

The U.K.'s YouGov program asked people over the age of eighteen to describe how they felt about participation in politics. Fifty per cent of men and 42 per cent of women agreed that being involved in politics was a good way to benefit groups that people care about, such as pensioners and the disabled. Just over 25 per cent of men and only 15 per cent of women agreed that involvement in politics was a good way to benefit themselves and their family. While these numbers demonstrate that both men and women lack faith that getting engaged in politics will make any substantial difference in their lives, there is a significant difference in how women view their ability to make a change in their own lives by engaging with government.

The 2019 Edelman Trust Barometer Global Report found significant differences all over the world in how much women say they trust governments and media. Trust scores for women in general are lower, notably in developed markets like the U.S., Germany, Australia, Japan, France and Canada. In their report on the gender gap in trust, Edelman noted that the persistent pay gap and lack of women in senior positions in business was a major factor in reinforcing women's belief that their abilities were not as highly valued as men's. The report also noted that, 'Engagement is a key factor in trust for women. As women are more engaged with news and information, their trust gap with men closes.'

It's difficult to trust institutions that appear to not trust you. When governments, media and other institutions don't trust women to function equally in their key roles, how can they expect women to trust that those institutions will see their concerns as important or act empatheti-cally on their behalf? And if women see that their voices are not heard why should they wear themselves out on attempts at what looks like futile engagement?

The evidence of this in Australia is quite clear. The Museum of Australian Democracy published an in-depth examination of how much Australians trust their government and democratic processes. The results were based on a 2018 survey of a representative sample of over one thou-sand people and twenty different focus groups. Satisfaction with the way democracy works in Australia had fallen from 86 per cent in 2007 to 41 per cent in 2018 and only 31 per cent trusted the federal government. The people least likely to be satisfied with democracy or to trust the gov-ernment were women and people on low incomes. Both women and men believe politics is the area of society where sexism is the most prevalent, although more women than men believe this. The three areas perceived to be the most sexist were politics, workplaces and the media, ahead of sport, advertising and social media. While around 20 per cent of people were found to dislike it when the media concentrated on personality rather than policy, the main objections to the political process were that politicians can't be held to account for broken promises and that they do not deal with the issues that matter. While men and women were pretty much the same in their dislike of these issues, women were twice as likely to report being unhappy that 'women are not well represented in power'.

TAXES AND SPENDING

In 2017 the Australian federal government announced it was creating a multi-billion dollar Home Affairs Office to address terrorism. The experiences in Europe over the preceding few years had shown terrorism to be a serious issue that required action and resources from governments all over the world. But around seventy Australian women are murdered each year, more than 80 per cent of them by men who claimed to love them. When Australia's National Research Organisation for Women's Safety (ANROWS) did a detailed analysis of the 2012 Personal Safety Survey, they found more than 2.9 million Australian women have experienced physical or sexual violence at the hands of a man known to them. This figure is almost certainly understated and does not include all the women who are emotionally and financially abused by men.

Compare this to figures looking at terrorism-related deaths. According to the Global Terrorism Database, six people were killed in terrorist incidents in Australia over the last twenty years. Three of those six were the perpetrators. While all these incidents were called terrorism by the media and the government, only one of the perpetrators was shown to have clear ties to terrorist groups. The other two did not, but were included because they were Muslim and claimed to be acting on behalf of Islam. A further ten people suffered injuries in events that were categorised as terrorist incidents.

By 2017, the Australian federal government was spending around $35 billion on national security and $160 million on domestic violence each year. If you divide that spending between the past twenty years' worth of victims of both terrorism and men's violence, it comes to $53 billion per person affected by terrorism and $55 per woman affected by male violence. While national security will always command a high level of resources from governments, the hugely disproportionate response to the harm caused by terrorism and the harm caused by domestic violence clearly demonstrates how the Australian government perceives threats of violence, and how it prioritises its victims.

GENDER PAY GAP

The gender pay gap debate in Australia can get surreal. In 2018, official government estimates put the pay gap at 21.3 per cent. If that were true it would be bad enough, but the reality is much worse. The gender pay gap is calculated by taking the average earnings of men and women in Australia and working out what the difference between them would be if every Australian were working full time, presenting the difference as a percentage of men's wages. The following examples use the 2018 Australian Bureau of Statistics Employee Earnings and Hours data to show how this works.

If Mary and John are both working full time and Mary earns $1516 per week while John earns $1811, John is earning $295 per week more than Mary. This difference is 16 per cent of John's salary and this figure gives us the gender pay gap. It makes sense at first glance, but this is not the full story of the official gender pay gap figures.

If Mary is working part time and earns $663 per week and John is working full time and earns $1742 per week, we don't base the gender pay gap figure on the difference between their two salaries. Instead, we calculate the full-time equivalent of Mary's salary (what her part time hourly rate would earn her if she was working full time) and compare Mary's *potential* salary of $1254 to John's full-time salary. This shows the gender pay gap is 28 per cent.

The official gender pay gap figure is derived by taking the full-time equivalent salary of all the Johns and Marys in Australia and calculating the difference as a percentage of all the Johns' salaries. The basis for this is the principle of comparing apples with apples so we calculate everyone's potential full-time salary and this gives us a fair comparison. The thing is that it doesn't, because the gender pay gap is not about potential earnings: it's about the difference between what men and women earn and the reasons there is such a difference. There's no reason to present it as a percentage of John's salary other than that's how it's always been done. As Jackie Woods of the Australian government's Workplace Gender Equality Agency said, 'It is a matter of convention in Australia and globally that gender pay gaps are calculated as a percentage of male earnings. The agency calculates gender pay gaps according to this convention so that our data is consistent with other research in the field.' Once again, men are the baseline against which we measure all women's experience.

More than half of all working women in Australia are working part time, whereas just over a quarter of men work part time. The Household, Income and Labour Dynamics in Australia (HILDA) report shows around 40 per cent of women are not in the workforce at all and are therefore excluded in the gender pay gap calculations. Only 25 per cent of men are not in the workforce. The main reason women are working part time, or not looking for work, is that they are caring for children or other family members (over 40 per cent; men citing similar reasons was around 6 per cent). The main reason men are working part time or not looking for work is that they are pursuing some form of education.

The expectation that women will take on the unpaid work of caring for children and family is a crucial component of the gender pay gap. That it is commonly erased from gender pay gap calculations seems to be based on the assumption that women choose this so it's not relevant to the pay gap. It's probably true that many women do choose to stay home to care for young children, but the choice seems to be predicated on social expectations, time pressures and perceptions of earning capacity and it is extremely relevant to the gendered nature of economic disadvantage.

The HILDA report in 2018 noted that 'the disproportionate involvement of women in unpaid work arguably limits their labour market availability and career options, and contributes to a persistent gender pay gap.'

Dr Judy Rose of Griffith University conducted extensive research on women who try to continue paid work after having children.

She found that women were consistently modifying their paid working hours to fit family schedules and calling on partners as 'helpers'
rather than equal participants in domestic labour. Her findings are
supported by the HILDA report, which found that women spend
more time on unpaid work when they live with a partner than when
they are single, and their amount of unpaid work increases dramati-
cally after they have children, whereas men tend to increase their paid
work and decrease their unpaid work when they have children. This
pattern peaks in the first few months after children are born and then
stabilises at women doing around 65 per cent of the unpaid labour in
a household for at least the first ten years of their child's life. Even if
women are working full time and their male partners are not working
at all, women still do half the unpaid work of the household. If both
partners are working full time, women do nearly two thirds of the
household labour.

Women spend far more time on unpaid work than men, and when
women have children, they give up far more paid work than men. The
long-term impact of this is demonstrated in HILDA and ABS data:
by the age of forty-five, the average superannuation balance for men is
more than double the amount accumulated by women. Child-rearing
and the division of household labour is central to this discrepancy, and
yet raising children is still viewed as women's choice or a natural outcome of gender. Women who stay with their partner their whole lives
might, if he permits, share the economic rewards of the paid work he was
able to undertake while she managed the unpaid work of their relationship. However, given that close to half the marriages in Australia end in
divorce after an average of twelve years, women cannot afford to assume
their financial future is secure.

There is room for individuals to take some responsibility for this
sort of situation. Women must maintain their financial literacy and

access to paid work, and men need to stop falling back on traditional gender roles (as they do after marriage and children, according again to HILDA data) and make a concerted effort to divide paid and unpaid work more equally in their relationships. Government policy might not be able to force this upon people but it can certainly help the women and men who try to achieve it. Encouraging flexible work arrangements for all working parents, not just mothers, and at all levels of the public service, would go a long way. Equally, discouraging the notion that overtime is proof of dedication and favouring productivity and ability to delegate, again at all levels of the public service, would greatly assist both men and women to work in harmony with demands of family rather than against it. This would require top-down cultural change of many government departments and it would not be easy or simple to achieve. It would, however, make the public service a highly desirable employer and force many large private corporations to follow its lead in an effort to attract valuable employees.

These are the kinds of changes that could only happen with full government backing and resources and they are unlikely to happen in governments who do not see changing gendered expectations of paid and unpaid work as a priority.

REPRESENTATION IN POLITICAL JOURNALISM

Diversity in media and politics is not about tokenism: it's about perspective. It's about the conversations in newsrooms and the various angles they toss around when they're nutting out a story. It's about the preconceptions and subconscious biases that dictate what stories are told, and how they are told. Is it just news for the women's pages or is it news? I don't believe this is just women's news. There are plenty of men who would like to spend more time caring for children or who would be happy to work part time so they can share the joys and responsibilities of raising children, were it not for the fear they would lose money or opportunities for promotion (and therefore both professional and personal status). Normalising this choice would do a lot to reduce the fear of its consequences. Again, government policy could address this and wider perceptive reporting could encourage it.

'Women's issues'

This happens in part because of the way political issues are categorised. Economy, foreign affairs, environment, welfare. And 'women's issues'. Women's issues are usually grouped together and presented, both by politicians and the media, as a broad spectrum of policies that are only relevant to women voters and women ministers. They usually consist of topics like funding for domestic violence services, the gender pay gap, childcare, reproductive rights and, in state politics, sexual assault law reform. When the cost of childcare is still framed as a women's issue, something that needs to be weighed only against a woman's potential income rather than joint income or future earnings, we are supporting and reinforcing the myth that caring for children is women's responsibility. When we frame domestic violence as a women's issue, we are ignoring the fact that the overwhelming majority of perpetrators of domestic violence are men: it is an issue for everyone, not just women. Similarly, sexual assault and rape are not just about the women victims, they are equally about the (mostly) men who commit these crimes. Enabling men to ignore their responsibility for addressing rape and domestic violence by framing it as a women's issue is playing in to all the violence myths decried in the Fixed It section. It is victim blaming at a policy level and it has to change if we are going to make any headway in reducing men's violence against women. The gender pay gap is an economic issue, a welfare issue, a productivity issue and a social issue before it's a women's issue and it needs to be addressed at all those levels. That these issues most directly affect women does not mean they are issues only for women.

It does not benefit men to have women disengaged or lacking representation in government and media reporting of it. A fair and functional society is less divisive, less polarised than one where half the people feel that they are left behind or shut out of opportunities that should be available to them. Merit is not a fair yardstick when one group is viewed as having inherent merit and another group has to perform giant leaps to prove they have it.

Chapter 12
Pop culture

This is what most girls are taught – that we should be slender and small. We should not take up space.

Roxane Gay, *Hunger*, 2017

As I mentioned in the Introduction, U.K. tabloid *The Sun*'s 2017 'shock' headline, 'RUDEY DENCH: Dame Judi Dench says she still has sexual desires at 82 – and still loves naughty knickers', was news! Can you imagine it? A woman still being sexual when she's old! Ew! And she's not just a little bit old like Sally Field, she's *properly* old, like Rupert Murdoch. And she still has sex! The very idea that a woman in her eighties could still experience a full range of human emotions was so bizarre it made headlines all over the world. As Helen Garner, writing about aging as a woman, observed in *The Monthly*:

Your face is lined and your hair is grey, so they think you are weak, deaf, helpless, ignorant and stupid . . . It is assumed that you have no opinions and no standards of behaviour, that nothing that happens in your vicinity is any of your business.

Ageism in pop culture is very strong and it's not hidden. The 'Last Fuckable Day' sketch from *Inside Amy Schumer* went viral in 2015 as women all over the world immediately recognised the truth it depicted. In the sketch, Amy Schumer stumbles upon Julia Louis-Dreyfus, Tina Fey and Patricia Arquette in a field where they've gathered to celebrate Louis-Dreyfus's 'last fuckable day'.

It's a funny but true depiction of Hollywood's view of women. Almost a year after the sketch was aired, Julia Louis-Dreyfus said she started to panic halfway through filming it.

> I started to feel unbelievably paranoid that I was making fun of myself, and wondering, was this really happening to me? Like, how meta is this moment in my life? I started to have a kind of soul-searching crisis in the middle of the day. And I didn't know [the other women] well enough to bring it up, so I was just trying to be a good sport even though I was dying a little bit on the inside.

One of Hollywood's most successful, skilled and attractive actors was genuinely terrified that she might be aging out of her industry at the age of fifty-five. Not something 76-year-old Harrison Ford, 57-year-old George Clooney, 56-year-old Tom Cruise or 55-year-old Brad Pitt would need to fear. These men still play leading parts and are apparently believably fuckable. They get cast alongside women twenty years younger than them. In the 1999 movie *Entrapment*, 69-year-old Sean Connery was the love interest for thirty-year-old Catherine Zeta-Jones. Nearly fourteen years later, not much had changed when 54-year-old Sean Penn was paired with 25-year-old Emma Stone in *Gangster Squad*. As leading men get older, the age of their co-stars stagnate. Tom Cruise hasn't had a love interest less than ten years younger than him since *Vanilla Sky* in 2001. The vast majority of Harrison Ford's leading ladies have been at least fifteen years younger than him and almost none of 56-year-old Johnny Depp's female co-stars have been older than twenty-five.

The too old to be 'fuckable' rule for women is just one of the rules only women must obey in the entertainment industry, and the real world as well. There are many others.

MYTHS ABOUT POP CULTURE
- Women over forty are not attractive, sexual or interesting.
- People only want to see women who are young, white, slim, conventionally pretty and able bodied. Every other woman is only relatable in niche markets or bit parts.
- Only women are interested in movies, books, sport, comedy or music produced by women.
- Men of any age, size, attractiveness and sexuality produce work that is relevant to everyone.
- When women claim they were abused by famous men, they are almost always lying to get attention and/or money.
- Women are weak, subservient sexual objects. Men are strong, aggressive and inherently prone to violence.

We cannot observe the way pop culture treats women without observing how pop culture treats non-white people. It is often assumed by producers of popular culture that women of colour are only of interest to other women of the same ethnic background.

The topic of racism in the entertainment industry deserves its own book, and is too broad to cover here, but to give a brief overview: according to a study by the University of Southern California's Annenberg Inclusion Initiative, sixty-four of the top 100 films in 2017 did not include one Latina character, sixty-five did not have any women of Asian background and forty-three did not include any black women.

Seventy-eight films had no female characters with a disability and ninety-four did not include LGBTQIA+ characters. The report calls it an 'epidemic of invisibility'. In American television in 2018, 68 per cent of broadcast, cable and streaming shows featured more male than female characters. Of the female speaking roles, Latinas were 7 per cent, black women were 19 per cent and Asian women were 6 per cent. Women were 27 per cent of all creators, directors, writers, producers, executive producers, editors and directors of photography working on broadcast network, cable and streaming programs. These figures have not significantly changed in the past ten years.

There is no commercial reason for this. Movies and TV shows with a wide range of women, are commercially successful. *Wonder Woman*, with Israeli lead actor Gal Gadot, was the highest grossing superhero origin film of all time, with a box office total of more than $820 million. Of the 350 top grossing films between 2014 and 2017, 105 were female-led. These were the films leading global box office revenue at every budget level, according to analysis from the Creative Artists Agency. Films that passed the Bechdel Test – where two named female characters have a conversation about something other than a man – made more revenue at the box office at every budget level than films that failed the test. Gender non-binary showrunner director and writer Jill Soloway's series *Transparent* provides unconventional representations of female desire and sexuality and features many queer and transgender characters. It won the 2015 Golden Globe Award for Best Television Series – Musical or Comedy, and the first three seasons had an approval rating on Rotten Tomatoes of over 98 per cent.

If the reason is not commercial, what is it? Part of it may be tradition, the old but-this-is-how-we've-always-done-it chestnut, but it seems feasible that men's dominance of the power structures (as writers, directors, producers) has the same effect in entertainment as it does in politics.

Their perception of the stories worth telling and the way they should be told is coloured by their collective perception of the world. If they are not the centre of the story they don't understand how the story is relevant.

The evidence of this is stark. In the top 100 grossing films of 2017, women were 24 per cent of sole protagonists, 37 per cent of major characters, and 34 per cent of all speaking characters. 2017 was also the year *Star Wars: The Last Jedi*, *Beauty and the Beast* and *Wonder Woman* were released, all of which had strong female leads and were highly commercially successful. The Strong Female Lead character can, however, be deceptive.

Lisa Annese is the CEO of the Diversity Council Australia. She spoke at an event in 2015 about what she called 'chicks up the front'. Many of us remember 1990s punk icon Kathleen Hanna's iconic call, 'girls to the front', asking men dominating the mosh pits to stand back and let women come forward, partly to stop sexual assault and harassment pushing women to the back of music gigs, and partly to help Hanna herself feel safe by filling the front of the audience with women. Lisa Annese's 'chicks up the front' is not that. She says she found the term when she was reading about the Vietnam War protests:

All the guys [were] marching in line, and then when the TV cameras turned up, they'd yell 'chicks up front'. What it meant was all the pretty girls get to the front of the crowd, then they'd increase the chance of making it on to the news. And it worked.

It's a strategy that still works today but in a completely twisted way. Chicks up front. It acts as an enabler and an authenticator for bad behaviour. Sometimes very bad male behaviour. Chicks up front is the reason Kyle doesn't lose his job, he has his chick up front every day, in the form of Jackie O. If we look at our parliament, our businesses, we always see women positioned up front, and that is an enabler. When people have this unconscious reaction, well if the woman's there, then it must be OK . . . you don't need to be female to be a feminist or a misogynist.

Rinko Kikuchi's fantastic character Mako Mori hid the fact that the rest of the *Pacific Rim* cast were almost all men, much as Idris Elba's character masked the overwhelming whiteness of the male cast. Sigourney Weaver's Ellen Ripley is the chick up the front of the *Alien* movies, likewise Linda Hamilton's Sarah Connor in the *Terminator* movies. It's also known as the four to one ratio. Sci-fi, action and super-hero movies 'work' roughly when you have four male characters for every one female character. Think of *Justice League*, where Gal Gadot is the chick up the front of Ben Affleck, Jason Momoa, Ezra Miller and Henry Cavill, and Ray Fisher is the African-American up the front. If we were to glance back at the politics chapter, Julie Bishop is the Liberal Party's 'chick up the front' to hide their abysmal distrust of women in power.

Don't let chicks up the front fool you.

BEAUTY MYTHS

When pop culture tells women that they are only attractive if they fit within the very narrow definitions that lie somewhere between 22-year-old Jennifer Lawrence and 24-year-old Scarlett Johansson, women are also told that being attractive by that definition is the only thing that makes them interesting. Outside that definition your story is of no interest to anyone. *You* are of no interest.

Jameela Jamil, one of the stars of TV show *The Good Place*, told *Allure* magazine in 2019 about her realisation that her career would always be judged on her appearance when she became the first woman to host *The Official Chart*, a huge streaming radio show in England. 'All that anyone cared about was that I'd gained weight. No one cared that I'd gotten this huge job and made this leap for a young woman, especially a young woman of color.'

Most of us do not live our lives by these definitions. No one is going to watch a Hollywood movie and suddenly decide they're not attractive enough to do their job. But the beauty myths so deeply embedded in pop culture add subtle pressures – an insidious reinforcement of the myth that a woman's worth is primarily judged in terms of her attractiveness to men. Most of us reject this myth, but it takes work. Even though I acknowledge the idiocy of erasing women over forty from public storytelling, I still notice the signs of aging on my own face and body: I don't like them or celebrate them. I wish I could. I know I should. But I don't. I still regret the loss of firm skin and taut muscles. Fat that sits not sags. This is the result of a lifetime of culture that says only youth is beautiful and beauty is the most valuable characteristic women have. Hollywood didn't create this myth, but it absolutely reinforces it.

Being slim is another requirement of the mainstream entertainment industry. Women who are bigger than a size 2 (size 6 in Australia and the U.K.) can play the 'fat' friend or the comedy sidekick, but if they're the romantic lead it's a niche product, the exception that proves the rule. Emma Thompson, whose long career and proven abilities as an actor put her in the fortunate position of being able to break rules, has no hesitation in condemning the pressure to be thin in Hollywood: 'The anorexia – there are so many kids, girls and boys now, and actresses who are very, very thin, who are into their 30s, simply don't eat . . . It's evil, what's happening, what's going on out there, and it's getting worse.'

What is a 'normal' body? Gwendoline Christie, who plays Brienne of Tarth in *Game of Thrones*, is 190 centimetres tall. Caitlyn Jenner is

188 centimetres. Sigourney Weaver is 183. Jada Pinkett Smith is 150; Carrie Fisher was 155. Which one of them has a 'normal' body, and who gets to decide what 'normal' is? Is it Scarlett Johansson's body? Or Emma Watson's? Because that's weird. The only person who looks like Scarlett Johansson is Scarlett Johansson. What about someone who's had a heart transplant, or someone who can run a marathon in two hours or someone whose knees hurt when they walk up stairs – do they have 'normal' bodies? The restraints and pressures on women in the public eye to conform to a particular body type is a misrepresentation of the reality of women's bodies – that there are as many types as there are women.

VIOLENCE IN POP CULTURE

Violence is a common feature in movies, TV, music and gaming, and its representation is rooted in the idea that men are violent and women are victims. A Western Michigan University study of 230 trailers for the top grossing movies between 1950 and 2015 found the portrayal of women as victims and men as perpetrators of violence was high and did not change over time. The paper's review of previous research found violence was depicted in three quarters of all movie trailers and rarely resulted in any consequences. Women depicted as 'promiscuous' (the moral connotations of which only apply to women) were more likely to be murdered; women who attempt to create their own identities outside of being a mother and wife were frequently punished; and sexualisation of women was common. The foregrounding of these myths in popular culture has consequences. As the study pointed out, when a person constantly repeats an action and sees other people doing it too, the action becomes a pattern. If these patterns are repeated by enough people, they become legitimised and institutionalised over time, forming social constructs we then think of as normal. Hollywood has so consistently portrayed women as weak, sexualised and subservient that this concept of women has become institutionalised in movies and TV.

ADVERTISING

It's probably not news to anyone that advertising is frequently based on overly sexualised images of women. One of the first recognisable cases of advertisers using women's bodies to sell products was in 1871, when Pearl Tobacco featured a naked woman on an advertising poster. The woman was not smoking a cigarette. In 1885 another tobacco manufacturer, W. Duke & Sons, started putting trading cards featuring attractive women in every cigarette packet, and became a leader in the tobacco industry at the time. Since then advertising has been replete with sexually objectified women. Think the 1981 TV ad by Calvin Klein, in which the camera trails lasciviously over 15-year-old Brooke Shields's spreadeagled legs, then draws back to show her face as she says, 'Want to know what gets between me and my Calvins? Nothing.'

In the 1970s, second-wave feminists vehemently objected to the way women were depicted in advertising, but it didn't have much effect until recent years, and in 2018 the U.K.'s Advertising Standards Authority banned advertisements that promote gender stereotypes or objectify women. The effects of this ruling will become clear over the next few years, and will be interesting to observe.

Once again, the data about advertising paints a stark picture of a male-dominated industry which does not welcome women in decision-making roles. Research published in 2018 by the U.K.'s *Marketing Week* found 93 per cent of ads are made by men, and only 12 per cent of creative directors in London are women. Eighty-four per cent of filmmakers in advertising (76 per cent of males and 87 per cent of females) think the ad industry is sexist and 73 per cent of female directors say they've witnessed sexism first hand while working in the sector. A 2016 survey reported in America's Statista, a database for market and consumer data, found 85 per cent of Americans have seen ads that portray women as 'dumb, helpless or incompetent' and 82 per cent have seen ads they find 'ridiculous in how they portray women'. A further 76 per cent have seen advertising 'they deem offensive to women'. A study published by the Geena Davis Institute on Gender in Media looked at over 2000 ads and found men were featured in ads twice as often as women and men in advertisements spanned across their twenties, thirties and forties, while women were almost universally in their twenties. Women were six times more likely to be dressed in 'sexually revealing' clothing, and men were 62 per cent more likely to be portrayed as someone 'smart' (like a doctor or a scientist).

As author Terry Pratchett wrote, 'Most books on witchcraft will tell you that witches work naked. This is because most books on witchcraft are written by men.'

In Australia, 2016 data collected by the Workplace Gender Equality Agency showed there were no women chairing boards of advertising companies. Only 20 per cent of full-time permanent CEOs or heads of business and 30 per cent of key management personnel were women. The statistics can be eye-wateringly boring to pore over, but such collections of data show that feminists are not simply a bunch of whinging killjoys when we talk about the cause and effect of shutting women out of power structures. The level of sexism and male narrative in popular culture is highly relevant to how women are perceived. It's the constant background noise of our lives and, going back to the point I made in the chapters on violence, it's because it is so constant that we stop noticing it. The things we don't notice are the most dangerous because they seep into our subconscious and reinforce the violence myths we've all grown up with.

#MeToo

I can't write about violence myths in popular culture without talking a bit about the #MeToo movement. The story of #MeToo is embedded in all the data about the entertainment industry I've just churned out. It's also worth mentioning that most of these examples come from outside Australia. Defamation law, particularly after the recent Geoffrey Rush case, makes it very risky for women in this country to talk publicly about harassment they have suffered.

#MeToo was started in 2006 by Tarana Burke, creator of Just Be Inc., a non-profit organisation to help young black girls who had suffered sexual harassment and assault. She was struggling to find resources for Just Be and started using the phrase Me Too to increase awareness and a sense of shared experience.

On 16 October 2017, in the wake of the *New York Times* reporting the first accusations of sexual harassment and assault against Harvey Weinstein, actress Alyssa Milano tweeted to her three million followers: 'Me Too. Suggested by a friend: If all the women who have been sexually harassed or assaulted wrote "Me Too" as a status, we might give people a sense of the magnitude of the problem.' The tweet went viral and spread to a range of social media platforms. According to CBS News it was shared on Facebook more than twelve million times in the first twenty-four hours.

Two days later, many women of colour pointed out that Alyssa Milano had taken a black woman's movement and turned it into a white woman's crusade without recognising how often the stories of women of colour are ignored or how much greater risk they have of sexual violence. In response, Milano reached out to Burke. She said she hadn't known about Burke's work on #MeToo and asked if they could collaborate. She also publicly credited Burke in an interview on *Good Morning America*. Burke told *The New York Times* that her first reaction was alarm that her life's work was going to be co-opted and used for a purpose that she had not intended, but that despite how often women of colour are ignored in feminist issues, #MeToo is about all women. '#MeToo is bigger than me and bigger than Alyssa Milano. Neither one of us should be centred in this work. This is about survivors,' Burke said.

The inevitable backlash started immediately and has got worse over time. A survey conducted for *The Economist* found that in the year following Alyssa Milano's #MeToo tweet, the number of American adults who believe false accusations are a bigger problem than unreported assaults increased from 13 per cent to 18 per cent. While men were more likely to hold this view than women, the biggest split was along political lines. By September 2018, the number of Trump voters who believed this had jumped from 20 per cent to 35 per cent. Over 60 per cent of them said men who sexually harassed women twenty years ago should not lose their jobs now. On the other side, only 15 per cent of Clinton voters agreed with this statement. *The Economist* ascribed this difference to the fight over Brett Kavanaugh's nomination to the Supreme Court and the wave of rage unleashed against Christine Blasey Ford when she gave evidence that he had attempted to rape her while they were in high school.

When Ford was interrogated at a Senate Judiciary Committee hearing, she was calm and polite, almost deferential, as if she knew that displaying any feelings while talking about trauma would have her labelled as an over-emotional woman and therefore not to be trusted. Kavanaugh yelled and wept, confident in his role as the outraged victim for whom any passion is proof of innocence.

Jia Tolentino, writing for *The New Yorker*, pointed out that 'men are borrowing the rhetoric of the structurally oppressed, and delivering it with a rage that is denied to all but the most powerful'.

A year after the #MeToo tweet, *The New York Times* published an analysis of the men brought down by the movement. At least 920 people had to come forward to bring down the 201 men who lost their jobs. (One third of those men were from news media, a quarter from government, and a fifth from entertainment and the arts.) In other words, it took an average of at least four allegations for one man to lose his job.

There were other problems with the #MeToo movement. Though it had amplified the voices of women who already had access to a public platform, it didn't do much for isolated black women working for minimum wage. Even the women who did have the required power and support needed so much more evidence before they were believed. The myth that women lie about men's violence is deeply entrenched and acts as a buffer against consequences for the men who commit violence against vulnerable women.

FIXING POP CULTURE HEADLINES

The Telegraph: ~~WOMEN MORE LIKELY TO LOSE INTEREST IN SEX IN LONG TERM RELATIONSHIPS~~
Fix: *MEN MORE LIKELY TO BECOME SEXUALLY UNDESIRABLE IN LONG-TERM RELATIONSHIPS*
What if women aren't actually the problem?

TMZ: ~~IT'S A BIT NIPPY OUT! RIHANNA SHOWS OFF HER NIPPLES . . . AGAIN!~~
Fix: *WOMAN GOES OUT, WEARS CLOTHES ON HER BODY*
A woman who is a successful singer goes out in public and, apparently, she had a body under her clothes. Weird, right?

Daily Mail: ~~HELENA BONHAM CARTER CUTS LONELY FIGURE AS SHE SPORTS MESSY BUNCHES TO GRAB COFFEE AFTER SHOPPING SPREE~~
Fix: *BREAKING: WOMAN GOES SHOPPING, HAS COFFEE. UPDATE AT 11*
A woman went shopping and had a coffee and the whole time she was doing that she had hair and appeared to be satisfied with her own company. You can see exactly why this made headlines, can't you?

TMZ: ~~GEORGE CLOONEY REPORTEDLY ENGAGED TO HOT SUCCESSFUL LAWYER~~
Fix: *AMAL ALAMUDDIN REPORTEDLY ENGAGED TO OK LOOKING, MOSTLY SUCCESSFUL ACTOR*
I think Clooney is punching above his weight here, but presumably Amal Alamuddin, a human rights lawyer with a very long and successful career, is more than capable of making her own life choices so good for them. I hope they have a lovely life.

Breitbart: ~~BIRTH CONTROL MAKES WOMEN UNATTRACTIVE AND CRAZY~~
Fix: *BREITBART IS SHIT AND NEEDS TO GET IN THE BIN*
Enough said.

Daily Mail: ~~UNVEILED: GAME OF THRONES' MAISIE WILLIAMS GOES BRALESS IN SHEER LACE DRESS AND QUIRKY HEADPIECE AT CHARITY MASQUERADE BALL~~
Fix: *GAME OF THRONES ACTOR MAISIE WILLIAMS HELPS RAISE THOUSANDS AT A SUMMER MASQUERADE BALL FOR NATIONAL SOCIETY FOR THE PREVENTION OF CRUELTY TO CHILDREN.*
Maisie Williams tweeted this fix. I can't top it.

Daily Mail: ~~UH OH . . . YOU CAN SPEND A FORTUNE TRYING TO LOOK YOUNG BUT THOSE DROOPY EARS WILL GIVE YOU AWAY (ARE YOU LISTENING, MADONNA)!~~
Fix: *HERE IS A LIST OF BULLSHIT REASONS WOMEN OVER 30 SHOULD HATE THEMSELVES*
A listicle of all the different parts of a woman's body (because aging isn't a thing in men) that age as you get older, with added extras recommending plastic surgery and sneering at women who have had plastic surgery.

Fox News: ~~JENNIFER GARNER ALMOST UNRECOGNISABLE IN MAKEUP-FREE SELFIE~~
Fix: *JENNIFER GARNER PUBLISHES SELFIE THAT LOOKS LIKE A SELFIE*
After spending a day with her three children Jennifer Garner had the temerity to post a selfie that was not about being sexually attractive – how is the tabloid media supposed to deal with this? Well, by writing an article about how important it is for women to spend a fortune and huge amounts of time on looking after their skin, of course!

The Hill: ~~HLN TO REVISIT THE MONICA LEWINSKY SCANDAL WITH TWO HOUR SPECIAL~~
Fix: *HLN TO REVISIT THE CLINTON IMPEACHMENT WITH TWO HOUR SPECIAL*
Another one where the subject of the sexist headline tweeted the correction and there's nothing left for me to do but nod.

The Washington Post: ~~KUMAIL NANJIANI OPENS UP ABOUT HIS WIFE'S ILLNESS, THE INSPIRATION FOR 'THE BIG SICK'~~
Fix: *KUMAIL NANJIANI OPENS UP ABOUT WIFE EMILY V. GORDON'S ILLNESS, WHICH INSPIRED THEM TO WRITE 'THE BIG SICK' TOGETHER*

Well, if a man was involved with creating a critically acclaimed movie, why would anyone assume a woman might have contributed something to it? And she doesn't need a name – she's clearly identified as being his wife. Like, does she want to exist as her own person or something? Weirdo.

Chapter 13
Sport

Richard Keys: Somebody better get down there and explain offside to her.
Andy Gray: Can you believe that? A female linesman. Women don't know the offside rule.

Richard Keys: Course they don't. I can guarantee you there will be a big one today. Kenny (Dalglish) will go potty. This isn't the first time, is it? Didn't we have one before? The game's gone mad. Did you hear charming [West Ham vice-chairwoman] Karren Brady this morning complaining about sexism? Do me a favour, love.

SKY TV commentary of Wolves–Liverpool game, 2011

One does not need to be an expert in sport to be able to notice the plethora of lazy or ignorant reporting in most sports news. Such as when Naomi Osaka won the Australian Open in 2019 and, at the press conference afterwards, a reporter asked her why she didn't smile when she won. Because women should always smile, right? They look so pretty when they smile, especially when they've just won a grand slam tournament and become the world number one player in women's tennis. It's a very important time to be pretty and pleasing.

Osaka is a professional athlete, not an activist or public speaker, so, rather than slam the reporter for being stupid and sexist, she answered the question. She explained the focus and competitive state she had to put herself in to win one of the most demanding tennis tournaments in the world, and how she doesn't immediately snap out of that mindset as soon as the game is over. 'I forgot to smile,' she said. It was a throwaway line at the end of a long explanation of how she had felt at the end of the match. Cue a slew of articles from *The Guardian*, *The Age*, *Yahoo Sport* and *Fox Sport*, screaming the 'I forgot to smile' quote at the front of every headline. Most of these articles did not even mention that she had won the Australian Open. The *Herald Sun* didn't include the lack of smile in their headline, but they made up for it with a series of sly digs at Serena Williams 'hijacking the moment' with 'histrionics' and being a 'sulking loser' for expressing frustration with sexism and racism at the 2018 US Open.

MYTHS IN SPORT JOURNALISM

- Men's sport is interesting to all sports fans.
- Women's sport is only interesting to friends and family of the players.
- Football, cricket and rugby are men's sports. Gymnastics, netball and cheerleading are women's sports.
- Boys will be boys, especially boys who play sport.
- Women lie about being raped by sports players because they want money and attention.
- Men's sporting careers are too important to damage by taking rape claims seriously.
- Women are only interesting athletes if they are conventionally attractive.

Professional sport is a highly commercialised industry. Men's sport dominates funding and media coverage, while women's sport is still trying to catch up to the huge opportunities of training from childhood, high salaries and public support men have had for decades in professional sport.

More than 90 per cent of sports coverage in Australian news focuses only on men's sport, and is written by male journalists, as demonstrated by the Women in Media report. This is a pattern found all over the world. The United Nations Educational Scientific and Cultural Organization's 2018 study of sports coverage found only 4 per cent of sports media content is dedicated to women's sport and only 12 per cent of sports news is presented by women.

Dozens of research studies have confirmed that most people see sport through a gendered lens: there are women's sports (gymnastics and netball) and men's sports (football and cricket). Tennis is one of the few likely to be seen as a sport for any gender, but it is still highly sexualised. A German study in 2017 found coverage and perceptions of female tennis players shows the popularity of female athletes depends on their physical attractiveness whereas male athletes are popular when they perform well.

There was a touch of the 'chicks up the front' phenomenon in the coverage of women's sport in Australia over 2018 and 2019. A few of the standout women were given coverage, but most sports journalism is still very much men reporting on men. Women like Ellyse Perry, Stephanie Gilmore, Ash Barty and Erin Phillips all performed outstandingly well last year. Their abilities and professionalism deserved far greater recognition than they were given. Sadly, many talented athletes made the news because of disgracefully sexist reactions as much as they did for their sporting prowess. A powerful photo of AFLW star Tayla Harris in midair after a glorious kick was removed by Channel Seven's social media channels because of all the offensive comments about her body and sexuality. Although they later returned the photo and apologised, the initial reaction shows how entrenched and vicious sexism in sport is accepted as inevitable by the people who report on it.

Men are frequently glorified for their achievements in sport. Well-known players become heroes and role models to other men. Many of these men use their public profile and hero status to reach out to young men and boys. Men such as Johnathan Thurston, Adam Goodes, Luke Ablett and Jimmy Bartel have all worked to change the lives of disadvantaged boys and young men.

Aboriginal sports stars have been subjected to horrific racism. Adam Goodes said he was 'gutted' after a thirteen-year-old girl called him 'an ape' at a football game in 2013. 'It's not the first time on a footy field that I've been referred to as a "monkey" or an "ape"; it was shattering,' he told reporters at the time. Nicky Winmar took an iconic defiant stand against racism in 1993 when, after a game in which he'd been subjected to relentless racist abuse, he lifted his jersey, pointed at his black skin and shouted, 'I'm black and I'm proud.' The moment was captured by a photographer from *The Age* and appeared on the front page of the newspaper the next day. More than twenty years later that image still resonates as a heroic moment for Aboriginal people. 'People forget that words have a big impact,' he said in a 2009 interview. 'They can lift a person or destroy a person. So that day I responded by saying to those people, and I still say it today: "I'm black and I'm proud."'

Unfortunately, not all male sports stars are like Jimmy Bartel or Adam Goodes. Sometimes they are more like Brock Turner. Deb Waterhouse-Watson's book *Athletes, Sexual Assault, and 'Trials by Media'* provides a forensic analysis of the way professional athletes are so frequently given immunity from the consequences of sexual violence by a media narrative that focuses public perception on blaming victims and valorising offenders. She found that, of the more than fifty-five cases of alleged rape committed by elite football staff and players in Australia since 1999, not one has been convicted. Pleading guilty to a lesser offence, however, was not uncommon. Stephen Milne, for example, avoided a rape conviction in 2014 by pleading guilty to indecent assault. He was given a $15,000 fine and released without conviction. The Victoria Police officers in charge of investigating the rape allegation against Milne later told Channel Nine News that they were subjected to constant threats and intimidation, from both inside and outside the police, in an attempt to get them to drop the investigation and close the case. An Office of Police Integrity investigation in 2012 confirmed that evidence had been removed from the case file and was still missing, and that some of the police investigating the case were personally involved with the football club. The allegation was made in 2004 and did not go to court until 2013. Milne was one of St Kilda's leading goal kickers until he retired in 2013.

Well-known sports stars can be so familiar to the fans that they feel like someone they know. Sports journalism is replete with interviews, feature pieces and personal stories about high-performing men in sport. They're real, humanised, well-liked and easy to empathise with – they become what Deb Waterhouse-Watson calls the 'personalised stranger'. It's then difficult for people to have empathy for a victim when allegations of sexual violence are reported in the media against a personalised stranger, especially when the victim is anonymous and silent. The media narrative of women sexually assaulted by sports stars reproduces the myths of Predatory Women, Gold Diggers, Women Scorned, Groupies and Party Girls, and this affects the public perception of the victim. These stories are often presented by reporters who are ex-footballers or who have long histories of reporting on sport and are therefore given 'insider' status; in other words, their narrative is credible because they have personal experience with the inner workings of the sports world that may not be available to the reader. Damien Foster's op ed for *The Age* in 2004 summed up how this works when he wrote, 'many young, attractive girls are very talented at getting the attention of young, impressionable footballers and milking the situation for the associated prestige', and went on to link this to footballers landing themselves in trouble when they are led astray by these predatory women and haven't learned 'diplomatic methods of saying goodbye'. He opined that women pursue football stars and think that if they have sex with them it will lead to a loving relationship, then, 'when the girl realises the total indifference with which she is being treated after intimacy, bitterness sets in and it lingers'.

The story told over and over again is that of the innocent young man, helpless in the face of a manipulative, predatory woman, who later 'cries rape' because she's bitter that she didn't land a football player boyfriend. Even though we cannot discount that this is possibly true in some cases, the data we looked at in Chapter 4 on false allegations of rape suggests that it is not the case in the majority of rape claims – even those made against sports stars.

Media reports also frequently quote officials and spokespeople from the sport or club about how distressed or hurt the player is by the accusations and linking their distress to the sport itself. Not only are innocent players harmed but the code itself is hurt (and therefore needs defending from) by accusations of rape. The victim is rarely humanised in this way, but from fans of the game, the club or the players are implicitly called upon to alleviate hurt done by an anonymous woman. As St Kilda coach Grant Thomas told *The Age* regarding the rape claim in 2004: 'As you'd expect [Milne and Montagna are] obviously very distressed about the whole thing.' The alleged perpetrator, especially when he is a famous sports star, gets publicly defended and protected in the manner that should be afforded to the victim.

*

The combination of hyper-masculine culture, cosy relationships with reporters, valorisation of stars and the tendency to close ranks against 'predatory' women permeates so much of male sport culture. This goes a long way towards explaining why there are so many allegations of rape and sexual assault against male sports players and so rarely any consequences for the offender.

In 2014, the NRL introduced serious penalties for any player who punched another player on the field. Despite the arguments at the time that the nature of the game led to players getting 'hotheaded', the immediate effect was a reduction in the number of on-field punches to almost zero. This proves that even NRL players can control violent impulses if they are afraid of the consequences. Before 2017 the NRL had not banned players who were convicted of domestic and sexual violence. The rationale given was something along the lines of not letting a 'mistake' derail someone's very important career in kicking balls between two sticks. After four players were charged with various violent crimes against women NRL CEO Todd Greenberg declared it was time to impose serious penalties, telling *The Daily Telegraph* in January 2019, 'I can't make it any clearer. If you are found guilty of these criminal offences there is no place in the game for you.' It will be interesting to see what effect this has. Given the policy is to issue more serious penalties, 'they'll be spending longer out of the game', but players convicted of criminal offences will not automatically be permanently banned.

FIXING THE SPORT HEADLINES

Huffington Post: ~~OLYMPIC ANALYST LAMENTS HOCKEY PLAYER'S 'UNFORTUNATE' DOMESTIC ABUSE INCIDENT. 'THIS GUY WAS A SPECIAL PLAYER, AND AN UNFORTUNATE INCIDENT LEFT THE LOS ANGELES KINGS WITHOUT A GREAT DEFENSEMAN.'~~

Fix: *MAN PLEADS GUILTY TO CHOKING AND ASSAULTING HIS WIFE. HIS HOCKEY TEAM DECIDED THEY WERE BETTER OFF WITHOUT HIM AND GOOD FOR THEM BECAUSE VIOLENCE IS NEVER OK.*

When a man hits and chokes his wife, the saddest thing about it is not that the sports team he used to play for might not win a game. If it's being discussed in sports commentary, perhaps a big 'Yay you!' for the teams who make it clear they will not give a platform, money or fame to men who are violent might be a better perspective than pity for the man who assaulted his wife. But that would require all sports journalists to think that way. It seems we're not there yet.

Herald Sun: ~~EX-TIGERS FOOTBALLER AARON JAMES MUST WATCH THE GRAND FINAL FROM BEHIND BARS~~
Fix: *AARON JAMES GUILTY ON MORE THAN 130 DOMESTIC VIOLENCE CHARGES SO HE'S IN PRISON NOW*

The article in the *Herald Sun* led with a paragraph describing how James 'put his head in his hands and groaned on hearing he'd spend the AFL Grand Final behind bars'. The second paragraph talked about how he wanted to watch his 'beloved Tigers' play but now he has to go to prison instead. The third paragraph described him as a 'hothead' and a 'real life Tony Soprano'. It's not until we get to the fifth paragraph that we finally learn why he's going to prison: 'he pleaded guilty to a swag of driving and domestic violence charges alongside a charge of trafficking methamphetamine.' How many charges are in a 'swag'? Worse is the fact that there is no mention in this article of the 133 charges of breaching intervention orders against his ex-wife, in which he was so intimidating she feared for her life. But sure, the real story here is how sad it is that he won't get to go to a football match.

Reuters: ~~DOMESTIC TROUBLE THREATENS INDIAN PACEMAN SHAMI'S CAREER~~

Fix: *SHAMI CHARGED WITH ATTEMPTED MURDER OF PARTNER*

Q: When did attempted murder become 'domestic trouble'? A: When the man charged is a professional sports player. Q: When did attempted murder become a threat to the man attempting the murder? A: When the man charged is a professional sports player. Q: When is this repulsive reporting of attempted murder ever sanctioned? A: When the man charged is a professional sports player.

ESPN: ~~REUBEN FOSTER TO MISS OFFSEASON PROGRAM TO TEND TO LEGAL ISSUES~~

Fix: *REUBEN FOSTER ALLEGEDLY PUNCHED GIRLFRIEND IN THE HEAD EIGHT TIMES*

So, this headline needs some new prepositions and a goddamn conscience.

Chicago Tribune: ~~WIFE OF BEARS LINEMAN MITCH UNREIN WINS BRONZE IN RIO~~

Fix: *COREY COGDELL WINS SECOND TRAP SHOOTING BRONZE IN RIO*

Look. Mitch Unrien didn't make it to the Olympic Games, but the woman he owns did and how great does that make him? It's also really important that you know what sport he plays but not so important that you know what sport she was playing when she won her two Olympic medals. Hooray for Mitch!

Korea Times: ~~BOYFRIEND A TALL ORDER FOR 192CM SOUTH KOREAN VOLLEYBALL STAR~~

Fix: *KIM YEON-KOUNG CAPTAINS VOLLEYBALL TEAM IN THE FINAL AT RIO OLYMPICS*

I wonder if the boyfriend is the biggest thing on the mind of the captain of a team that made it all the way to the finals at the Olympic Games. Of course it is. What else would she have to think about?

Mail Online: ~~HISTORIC MOMENT: SPRINTER IN HIJAB BECOMES THE FIRST WOMAN TO COMPETE FOR SAUDI ARABIA IN THE 100M . . . BUT STILL MANAGES TO FLASH A SLIVER OF FLESH AS SHE NARROWLY AVOIDS LAST PLACE IN OLYMPIC HEAT~~

Fix: *HISTORIC MOMENT AS KARIMAN ABULJADAYEL BECOMES THE FIRST WOMAN TO COMPETE FOR SAUDI ARABIA IN THE 100M.*

So the important things for you to know here is that she wears a hijab and her clothes move when she runs. These things are equally as important as her colossal achievement of being the first Saudi woman in the 100 metres race at the Olympic Games. Or, you know, her name, except that it sounds all so foreign, doesn't it? People don't want to read about women with foreign-sounding names because everyone who reads news is a white person.

The Sun: ~~SIX APPEAL RIO 2016: MICHELLE JENNEKE LOOKS ABS-OLUTELY FABULOUS AS SHE SHOWS OFF HER OLYMPIAN FIGURE IN A SKIMPY BIKINI~~

Fix: *OLYMPIAN MICHELLE JENNEKE POSTS TRAINING PHOTOS ON INSTAGRAM AND WEARS BATHERS IDK WHAT THIS STORY IS ABOUT*

Am I missing a sporting person's in-joke here? Is the 'six appeal' meant to reference a six-pack? Or is it an attempted pun on how New Zealanders pronounce 'sex'? Does someone need to tell *The Sun* that Australia and New Zealand are not, in fact, the same place? I read the article three times and I'm still not sure what it was about. Apparently, she is 'hot' and people take photos of her and while she's waiting for a race to start she jumps around to keep her muscles warmed up. Should someone tell *The Sun* that even I know athletes have to keep their muscles warmed up while they're waiting for a race to start? I don't know, this is just weird.

Chapter 14

Making change

I think every woman in our culture is a feminist. They may refuse to articulate it, but if you were to take any woman back forty years and say, 'Is this a world you want to live in?', they would say 'No'.

Helen Mirren, 2011

Writing this book has consumed most of the past year of my life. Preparing for it took almost ten years of learning about the causes, effects and expressions of violence and the realities of modern journalism. I've reviewed countless research papers, talked to hundreds of survivors and read thousands of news articles. Burying myself in this for so long has permanently changed how I see the world and the power structures that enable men's violence against women, and spending too much time in these trenches can make it difficult to see anything positive. Each week, as I read about another woman killed and the daily reports of assaults or rapes, it can feel like nothing has changed. On the bad days it feels like nothing ever will. But I've been doing this long enough to know that change is often about time. Very little changes in a day or a week, but the worm's-eye view is not the right perspective. The changes we need are structural, global and cultural, and that can take decades.

My mother can remember having milk bottles delivered to her house by a horse and cart when she was a child. These days she has to make sure her bag is big enough to fit her smartphone, her kindle and her iPad. That phone, by the way, has access to more information than Bill Clinton had access to when he was President of the United States. The world changes, whether we want it to or not. The changes in my mother's lifetime are testament to that. When she started working in IT an entire room was needed for storage space for the equipment to enable the use of just 32 kilobytes of data. The marriage bar (which said women in the public service had to stop work when they got married) was still in place. There was no equal pay legislation. No government assistance with childcare. Rape in marriage was not a crime when she first married and there was no government support for her unmarried friends who had children. The term 'domestic violence' did not exist, although the fact of it most certainly did. Journalists never reported on it, unless it was a particularly sensational murder, and police did not interfere in 'disputes' between husbands and wives. It was considered fair and reasonable to question a rape victim about her sexual history to prove she was promiscuous (a word that never applies to men) and therefore unrapeable. Judges routinely warned juries not to put too much weight on evidence from women and children in rape trials unless they had corroborating witnesses. Aboriginal and Torres Strait Islanders were not even citizens, let alone equals. Homosexual acts (if you were a man) were a crime in most Australian states, and transgender people were 'perverts' not even mentioned in polite company.

In a single lifetime all these things have changed, at least in legislation if not in practice, and received the broad public support legal changes need to become law. It's not easy to hold on to the long view when women are being killed every week, but it is the only way to hold on to hope.

This book is mostly about the way the media reports men's violence against women and it hasn't been a pretty picture. However, despite all the terrible examples I've included, there is reason to hope the book will one day become a curio, interesting only because of its description of what used to be rather than what is.

In 2016 the Australian Press Council issued guidelines on reporting domestic and family violence. They are guidelines, not requirements, and they're broad, even a little vague sometimes. For examples, the guidelines state that 'publications should consider the unintended consequences' of interviewing survivors without providing any information about what these could be. This might be a useful reminder for journalists and editors experienced in reporting on domestic violence, but would not be much help for someone who has never interviewed a survivor. This person might not understand how vulnerable the survivor can be and how publishing details of their abuse, or worse, getting those details wrong, can traumatise or even put lives in danger. However, while there is definitely room for improvement, the fact that the guidelines exist and do provide some information on the basics of reporting family violence is no small thing. It sets a baseline and gives grounds for official censure of the worst reporting, something that would have been unimaginable even ten years ago.

The improvement we need has not been left to chance. Our Watch was established by the Australian Federal Government in June 2013 as part of the National Plan to Reduce Violence Against Women and their Children 2010–2022. Its purpose is to drive change in culture, behaviours and power imbalances underpin men's violence against women and children. From the beginning Our Watch understood the power the media has in setting and changing public understanding of men's violence against women and they have consistently worked to improve Australian media's understanding and reporting on this issue. In March 2019 they released their guidelines on reporting violence against women and their children. It's a much longer, more detailed and far more useful document than the Australian Press Council guidelines. Although it has the same problem of being aspirational rather than enforceable, it adds to the weight of the Press Council guidelines and expands the information available to journalists. Our Watch also works with Australia's National Research Organisation for Women's Safety Limited (ANROWS) to commission and publish on research men's violence against women, providing resources and fact sheets for journalists looking for definitions and statistics to give context to reporting on individual instances of violence. These things are not an instant fix, but they are the stepping stones to changing the way violence is reported and understood by the media, which has a flow on effect of changing the way it is understood by the public.

Australia is not alone in making these changes. In the U.K. in 2016 a group of feminist campaigners created an organisation called Level Up. A collaboration of academics, survivors and their families, journalists, and domestic violence experts put together a list of guidelines for how the media should report on domestic violence. The list includes ensuring accountability for domestic violence is assigned to perpetrators, requires accuracy in terminology (naming the crime as 'domestic violence' not a 'tragedy'), avoiding sensationalism and eschewing stock images that perpetuate myths about domestic violence. In April 2019 the two main press regulators in the U.K., IPSO and IMPRESS, endorsed Level Up's guidelines. Similar resources and guidelines exist in New Zealand and Canada, as well as global resources provided by the United Nations and the World Health Organization.

The collective weight of all this work gives us strong evidence to make a case for change and a much wider acceptance of the need for it. It's not just hairy feminists on the fringe demanding these changes now, the demands are mainstream and backed by public institutions.

Even in the few years I've been doing the work on Fixed It I've seen changes in the response to bad reporting on men's violence against women. Social media allows audiences to react in real time and the pushback is getting stronger and being taken much more seriously. A great example of this is the 'good guy' narrative in reporting of men who kill their partners and children before killing themselves. As covered in Chapter 5, this narrative was so thoroughly entrenched in media reports of these crimes that it was almost impossible to find a report that didn't include a quote about how a man who killed women and children was a 'lovely', 'caring' or 'good' man. Journalists mostly dismissed or ignored the people who objected to this kind of reporting. If they did respond at all it was often about defending their reports as 'accurate'. In 2018, after Peter Miles killed his wife, Cynda, his daughter, Katrina, and his four grandchildren, Taye, Rylan, Ayre and Kayden, in Margaret River, ABC's *Media Watch* ran a segment on the way murder–suicides were reported by Australian media. *Media Watch* host Paul Barclay gave numerous examples of the 'good guy' trope and provided expert commentary from Domestic Violence Victoria CEO, Fiona McCormack and Walkley Award–winning journalist and academic Margaret Simons. They pointed out that domestic violence is usually hidden from family and neighbours, so comments from such people on the type of person the killer is are not meaningful. They also made the point that giving this kind of commentary without context of the systemic nature of family violence reinforces the idea that this kind of violence is an isolated incident and hides the underlying sense of entitlement that means men who commit these crimes view women and children as commodities to be controlled rather than people in their own right. It's worth noting that the first case after the *Media Watch* segment of a man killing his children was when John Edwards shot his two teenage children then himself. Not only was there no 'good guy' reporting in the coverage of Edwards' murders, but also *The Daily Telegraph*'s front page showed a photo of Edwards with the word 'Coward' in large font underneath it. Above it the headline read 'Ice cold father's meticulous plan to stay and slay his own children'. It was a horrific crime and ended in the children's mother's suicide six months later. There's nothing good about this story. But at least the media reporting showed that some of the messages about how to report it were getting through.

I would never claim sole responsibility for this. Change never happens because of a single person. It comes from a collection of people, a slowly coalescing chorus that eventually overwhelms complacent silence. Fixed It has undoubtedly been one of the voices demanding change in the way the media reports men's violence against women, but it would not have had any effect if it had been the only one. The changes I've just described are evidence that those collective voices are being heard. From the Fixed It vantage point, some of the changes I see are vastly encouraging (such as the *Media Watch* story and the subsequent change in 'good guy' reporting). Others are bewildering. A couple of publications that used make regular appearance in Fixed It posts no longer put all their crime stories outside their paywall, but now lock up everything. Perhaps it's just easier to hide than to change. Then there are the on-the-fly headline changes at ABC because they have nowhere to hide but don't seem to want to learn.

Fixed It is a passion, maybe almost an obsession for me, because once you see something you can't unsee it. Another reason to keep it going is the response from people who support Fixed It. Some of them even support it financially, but many more do so with social media shares and commentary. There are hundreds of people with smaller-reach social media accounts who do their own headline fixes because I didn't have the time or strength to do another one. Someone had to, so they did, and the audience grows. I get many responses to the work I do but the one that tells me Fixed It is necessary and worth the time and heartache is this: 'I hadn't noticed it before, but now I see it everywhere.'

The changes we've seen to women's legal and social status is the result of a thousand small steps by feminists, scholars, and activists. In March 2019, after Harsh Narde murdered Preethi Reddy and then died in a car accident, ABC News released an article about her murder under the headline 'Suitcase murder suspect's family were on the lookout for potential brides'. Not long after the article came out, Tarang Chawla tweeted, 'Come on @ABCNews, be better. The suitcase was not murdered. A woman was. And her name is Preethi Reddy. #PreethiReddy #NotOneMoreNiki @JaneTribune #FixedIt'. Less than an hour later the ABC changed the headline to read 'Preethi Reddy murder suspect's family were on the lookout for potential brides'. In an ideal world, no media organisation would need to be reminded that a murder victim is a person not a sensationalised headline, but until we become an ideal world, the fact that an activist like Tarang can catch this so quickly and the ABC responded almost immediately is, at the very least, a good start.

Tarang Chawla has reason to understand the horrors of domestic violence homicides. His sister Nikita Chawla was murdered by her partner in 2015. After her murder Tarang became an activist and educator on men's violence against women. He was the Young Australian of the Year finalist in Victoria in 2017, has won many other awards, and is an advocate to the Victorian State Government for victim's rights. It's terrible that he had to go through this tragic loss to become such a staunch advocate for preventing domestic violence. But as we know, around seventy families every year suffer the same loss and few of them are able to pursue a public life of activism – which is not in the least a criticism of them. No one who has been bereaved or traumatised has an obligation to do anything more than care for themselves and the people they love.

But those few remarkable people who can turn rage and grief into conviction and passion for change have an effect on the public no one else can match. Rosie Batty. Ann O'Neil. Tarang Chawla. Phil Cleary. Someone murdered a person they loved and all of them have dedicated themselves to pushing for structural change by showing that these structural problems have real victims. Rosie, Ann, Tarang and Phil, among others, made that happen. They turned the statistics into real people and energised empathy into public support for change.

The 2019 federal election in Australia, which gave government to a party that appears to embody its perception of merit in the privileged straight white man, made it more difficult to hold onto hope for change. The analysis on how and why that election result happened will go on for years but it's unlikely to be attributable to a single cause. A mixture of presidential politics, fear of change, entrenched distrust in government, lack of engagement, corruption, unethical journalism and personal interests trumping public good were all on display. But the basic fact, that the so called progressive side of politics was not able to connect to the majority of the country, is starkly unavoidable. The unedifying prospect of watching the overconfidence of mediocre white men play out on the political stage for another three years might be cause for despondence but not despair.

Change is inevitable. As you read these pages the world is changing. If it is to change for the better, we all need to become a part of something that will happen with us or without us. The potential for change is in every conversation we have with someone who hasn't yet made up their mind, every interaction we have with a child still learning about the world and their place in it, every idea we express and every small action we take. Change doesn't require that we all believe the same thing or act for the same cause or get it right every single time. It doesn't mean we have to fight every fight and win every battle.

It just takes time, effort and hope. The sructural restraints that limit individual opportunities will always fall in the face of collective action and individual will – not immediately but always eventually, there is change. And that is how we fix it.

Notes

All online source URLs were correct at time of printing.

Page **Introduction**

3   **The opening lines of a story about her murder** Nino Bucci and Jared Lynch, 'St Kilda prostitute brutally murdered', *The Age*, 23 July 2013.

5   **Then, in September 2015** Chris McMahon, 'Townsville police say selfie could have led to alleged stabbing murder', News.com.au, 28 September 2015.

10   **An in-depth study of crime statistics** Jane Gilmore, 'No, women aren't as likely to commit violence as men', *The Age*, 19 November 2017.

11   **The Mates Over Merit report** Media, Entertainment and Arts Alliance 'Mates Over Merit: The Women in Media Report', MEAA, 2017. meaa.org/download/mates-over-merit-full-report/

13   **ABC: Child abuse linked to arts school**: Kathleen Calderwood and Riley Stuart, 'Child abuse linked to arts school included raping 4yo boy, police allege', *ABC News*, 26 July 2018.

Chapter 1

21   **It is part of the business of a newspaper** Arthur Lawrence, *Journalism as a Profession*, Hodder & Stoughton, London, 1903, pp 184–185.

21 **In May 2017 Carter Wilkerson** Elena Cresci, 'How one teen's plea for free nuggets became one of the biggest tweets ever', *The Guardian*, 10 April 2017.

22 **One of the best definitions of journalism I've heard** Media, Entertainment and Arts Alliance, 'Journalist Code of Ethics', meaa.org/meaa-code-of-ethics/

23 **Take another example of news versus 'newsworthy'** Rod McPhee, 'Dame Judi Dench says she still has sexual desires at 82 – and still loves naughty knickers', *The Sun*, 5 September 2017.

25 **In 2013 Los Angeles Superior Court** Erika Aguilar, 'Court reporters disappear from courtrooms because of budget cuts', KPCC, 10 January 2013.

25 **In 2015 Yahoo7 journalist Krystal Johnson** Supreme Court of Victoria, Judgment handed down In DPP V Krystal Johnson & Yahoo!7 Pty Ltd, published 17 February 2017. supremecourt.vic.gov.au/news/judgment-handed-down-in-dpp-v-krystal-johnson-yahoo7-pty-ltd

29 **A slightly different feature piece** Jessie Smith, 'Christchurch: Why avoiding terror laws might be best for victims', *Sydney Morning Herald*, 21 March 2019.

30 **On 16 September** Chris Cillizza, 'The volcanic temper of Donald Trump', CNN online, 27 September 2017.

Chapter 2

34 **Bill Kovach and Tom Rosenstiel are among** Bill Kovach and Tom Rosenstiel, *The Elements of Journalism: What newspeople should know and the public should expect*, Three Rivers Press, New York, 2007.

36 **Why are women only** Claudine Ko, 'Whiskey Tango Foxtrot: why Tina Fey turned my life as a war reporter into a comedy', *The Guardian* [US], 28 March 2016.

37 **Gender skews in journalism have been** See, for example, Louise North, 'The gendered newsroom: embodied subjectivity in the changing world of media', PhD thesis, University of Tasmania, 2006.

37 **Not only are around 70 per cent** Women in Media, 'Mates Over Merit: The Women in Media Report', 2016. meaa.org/download/mates-over-merit-full-report

38 **Her research has found** statistics quoted here come from Louise North, '"Blokey" Newsrooms Still a Battleground for Female Journalists', *Australian Journalism Review*, vol. 34, no. 2, 2012b.

38 **According to the 2016 Census** These stats were found at abs.gov.au/census

38 **This data is collected** Quick Facts, United States Census, 2018, census. gov/quickfacts/fact/table/US/PST045218

39 **Research I conducted** Jane Gilmore, *Journalism, Gender and Memoir: how gender and changing journalistic values influence the use of memoir in journalism*, University of Melbourne unpublished thesis, 2018.

40 **To give it some context** *Review into the Treatment of Women in the Australian Defence Force*, Australian Human Rights Commission, 2012. defencereview.humanrights.gov.au/report-review-treatment-women-australian-defence-force

41 **And 40 per cent of women** *Independent Review into Sex Discrimination and Sexual Harassment, Including Predatory Behaviour*, in Victoria Police, Victorian Equal Opportunity and Human Rights Commission, 2015. humanrightscommission.vic.gov.au/index. php/component/k2/item/1056-independent-review-into-sex-discrimination-and-sexual-harassment-including-predatory-behaviour-in-victoria-police

42 *The Guardian*, **for example** Sam Jones and Simone Whey, 'Beyoncé hits Grammys for six', *The Guardian*, 1 February 2010.

46 **A 2018 study by the International Federation of Journalists**: IFJ, 'IFJ global survey shows massive impact of online abuse on women journalists', 23 November 2018. ifj.org/media-centre/news/detail/article/ifj-global-survey-shows-massive-impact-of-online-abuse-on-women-journalists.html

49 **One evening I was** Karen Middleton, 'Sexual Harassment in Politics', *The Saturday Paper*, 15 October 2016.

Chapter 3

51 **No black woman writer** bell hooks, *Remembered Rapture: The Writer at Work*, Picador, New York, 1999.

51 **This clamour for** Eliza Lynn Linton, *The Wild Women As Politicians*, Henry S. King & Co., Brighton, U.K., 1891, p82.

55 **When I learnt, however** Dale Spender, *Women of Ideas and What Men*

Have Done to Them: From Aphra Behn to Adrienne Rich, Routledge & Kegan Paul, Pandora Press, London, 1982, page 4.

57 **There is no** bell books, *Bone Black: Memories of Girlhood*, Holt Paperbacks, New York, 1996, page xiii.

60 **The most constructive thing**, Spender, *Man Made Language*, Pandora Press, Ontario, Canada.

61 **Nina Funnell was sexually assaulted** personal interview with the author, 19 February 2017 and 2018. An earlier version of this was published at Jane Gilmore, 'Terrifying truth about rape convictions: "It shatters your belief that the world is a safe place"', News.com.au, 23 February 2017.

Part II

77 **Toxic masculinity is** The Good Men Project, 'What Is Toxic Masculinity?', 2018. goodmenproject.com/featured-content/what-is-toxic-masculinity-cmtt/

Chapter 4

81 **Jason Bosland, Deputy Director of the Centre** personal interview with the author, 1 February 2019.

82 **According to the Victorian Solicitor-General's Office** Victorian Government Solicitor's Office, 'Managing the Risk of Sub Judice Contempt', 2015. vgso.vic.gov.au/node/331#tendency

88 **Because false accusations of rape** One research paper that outlines this difficulty is Liz Wall and Cindy Tarczon, 'True or false? The contested terrain of false allegations', The Australian Institute of Family Studies, *ACSSA Research Summary* No. 4 – November 2013. aifs.gov.au/publications/true-or-false-contested-terrain-false-allegations/export

88 **almost never have serious consequences** Sandra Newman, 'What kind of person makes false rape accusations?', *Quartz*, 11 May 2017.

88 **If you apply all those numbers** 'Recorded crime – Victims, Australia, 2017', Australian Bureau of Statistics, 2018 abs.gov.au/AUSSTATS/abs@.nsf/DetailsPage/4510.02017?OpenDocument

89 *The Sun* **reported it under the headline**, Richard Wheatstone, '"17 MONTHS OF HELL" Man, 29, accused of raping a "10-out-of-10 drunk" woman on night out is cleared', *The Sun*, 5 January 2018.

89   **The National Community Attitudes to Violence against Women study** published by Australia's National Research Organisation for Women's Safety, 2017. ncas.anrows.org.au

90   **A study by Boston University** Nicholas Groth, Ann Wolbert Burgess, Lynda Lytle Holmstrom, 'Rape: Power, anger and sexuality', *The American Journal of Psychiatry* vol. 134, issue 11, November 1977, pp. 1239–1243.

90   **A 1984 paper by Virginia University** Diana Scully and Joseph Marolla, 'Convicted Rapists' Vocabulary of Motive: Excuses and justifications', *Social Problem*, vol. 31 issue 5, June 1984, pp. 530–544.

90   **Another study by Marquette University** Kristine Chapleau, 'Power, Sex, and Rape Myth Acceptance: Testing two models of rape proclivity', *The Journal of Sex Research* January vol. 74 issue 1, pp. 66–78.

91   **During the successful trial** Vanda Carson, 'Brisbane student who claims she was raped grilled about why she wore "sexy lingerie",' *The Courier-Mail*, 9 August 2016.

91   **All of this was reported** Alexandra Patrikios, 'Man pleads not guilty to churchyard rape', News.com.au, 9 August 2016; 'Alleged rapist bragged about penis before cathedral assault, court hears', 9 News online, 9 August 2016; 'Guilty Brisbane churchyard rapist met victim on dating site: court', *Brisbane Times*, 12 August 2016.

92   **I felt so alone** Anon, 'I wasn't his first, but I will make sure I'm his last', SBS *Insight*, 27 February 2018.

97   **As Sally Tonkin, then CEO of St Kilda Gatehouse Sally Tonkin,** 'She's Someone: Humanising women involved in street-based sex work', TEDx St Kilda, published 25 June 2015. youtube.com/watch?v=ti9o18VlPc0

99   **The trauma of colonisation** National Voice for our Children (SNAICC), National Family Violence Prevention Legal Services Forum (NFVPLS) and National Aboriginal and Torres Strait Islander Legal Services (NATSILS), 'Strong Families, Safe Kids: Family violence response and prevention for Aboriginal and Torres Strait Islander children and families', September 2017.

100   *The Courier-Mail* **never issued an apology** Kate Kyriacou, Thomas Chamberlin, 'Killer chef Marcus Volke worked as sex worker

before murdering wife at Teneriffe, *The Courier-Mail*, 8 October 2014.

101 **In Georgia, United States** Joe Kovac Jr, 'Macon man who raped mentally disabled woman gets 25 years for "savage, inhumane" act', *Macon Telegraph*, 9 April 2018.

Chapter 5

103 **One woman a week is killed** Australia's National Research Organisation for Women's Safety, *Violence against women: Accurate use of key statistics* (ANROWS Insights 05/2018). Sydney, NSW: ANROWS.

112 *Kidspot,* **under the headline** Madeline Hoskin, 'Davidson Family Tragedy: Was Mum struggling to cope?' *Kidspot*, 18 October 2016.

114 **A man murders four people** Linnea Dunne, 'Rest In Peace, Invisible Woman', 31 August 2016. linneadunne.com/2016/08/31/rest-in-peace-invisible-woman/

116 **The ethical duty of a journalist** Loni Cooper, 'But he's such a good guy . . .', *Uncovered*, 2 May 2016. uncovered.org.au/hes-such-good-guy

117 **Monash University researcher Gary Dickson's study** Gary Dickson, 'Don't Be a Fuckwit': Media reporting of men's public violence against men', Melbourne University unpublished thesis, 2016.

Chapter 6

124 **A study conducted for the Australian Royal Commission** Jane Goodman-Delahunty, Annie Cossins and Natalie Martschuk, 'Jury Reasoning in Joint and Separate Trials of Institutional Child Sexual Abuse: an empirical study', Royal Commission into Institutional Responses to Child Sexual Abuse, Sydney, May 2016.

125 **In the U.K., the Criminal Injuries Compensation Authority (CICA)** Owen Bowcott and Kevin Rawlinson, 'Government "denying sexually abused children compensation"', *The Guardian*, 18 July 2017.

125 '**In my experience** Dino Nocivelli, 'The Catholic church must stop blaming victims: children cannot consent to sex', *The Guardian*, 24 August 2017.

126 **Research by the U.S. Crimes Against Children Research
     Centre estimates** *Child Sexual Abuse Statistics*, National
     Center for Victims of Crime, 2011. victimsofcrime.org/media/
     reporting-on-child-sexual-abuse/child-sexual-abuse-statistics

129 **I've spent many** Claire Martin and Will Zwar, 'Former Belmont Scout
     leader Neville Budge guilty of 24 indecent assault charges', *Geelong
     Advertiser*, 30 June 2017.

132 **'I really felt** 'Dublin man jailed for "sexual defilement" of daughter',
     The Irish Times, 13 February 2014.

133 **Research on the effects of child sexual abuse** For more about the
     history of research in this area, see D. Scott and S. Swain, *Confronting
     cruelty: Historical perspectives on child protection in Australia*. Carlton:
     Melbourne University Press, 2002.

133 **An Australian study of twins** S. Dinwiddie, A. C. Heath et al., 'Early
     sexual abuse and lifetime psychopathology: A co-twin-control study',
     Psychological Medicine, vol. 30 issue 1, 2000, 41–52.

135 **Reports of priests** Thomas C. Fox, 'What they knew in 1985',
     National Catholic Reporter, 17 May 2002 and Michael Rezendes
     (prepared with Matt Carroll, Sacha Pfeiffer and Walter
     V. Robinson), 'Church allowed abuse by priest for years', *Boston Globe*,
     6 January 2002.

Chapter 7

140 **Part of the reason** One in Three, 'Is Men's Intimate Partner Violence
     (IPV) More Severe, And More Likely To Inflict Severe Injury?', 2009.
     oneinthree.com.au/faqs/

140 **Research on male victims** Suzanne C. Swann, Laura J. Gambone, et al.,
     'A Review of Research on Women's Use of Violence With Male Intimate
     Partners', *Violence Vict.*, vol. 23 issue 3, 2008, pp. 301–314. ncbi.nlm.
     nih.gov/pmc/articles/PMC2968709/ and J. A. Scarduzio, K. E. Carlyle,
     et al., '"Maybe She Was Provoked": Exploring Gender Stereotypes About
     Male and Female Perpetrators of Intimate Partner Violence', *Violence
     Against Women*, January, vol. 23 issue 1, 2017, pp. 89–113. ncbi.nlm.nih.
     gov/pubmed/27020376

144 **This framing of** Scarduzio, Carlyle, ibid.

144 **Research on this is, again,** S. W. Masho and L. Anderson, 'Sexual
     Assault In Men: A population-based study of Virginia', *Violence Vict.,*
     vol. 24 issue 1, 2009, pp. 98–110 and Michelle Lowe and Paul Rogers,
     'The Scope of Male Rape: A selective review of research, policy and
     practice', *Aggression and Violent Behaviour,* vol. 35, 2017, pp. 38–43.

144 **Evidence from the U.K.** Elizabeth Bates, 'Hidden Victims: men and
     their experience of domestic violence' in *5th National Conference on Male
     Victims of Domestic Abuse: Surviving Domestic Abuse: Experiences, Services
     and Solutions,* 21 November 2017, London, U.K. (Unpublished) insight.
     cumbria.ac.uk/id/eprint/3463/

144 **A research paper by Lara Stemple** Lara Stemple, 'Sexual Victimization
     Perpetrated by Women: Federal data reveal surprising prevalence',
     Aggression and Violent Behaviour, vol. 34, May 2017, pp. 302–311.

144 **'Female sex predators:** Debra Killalea, 'Female sex predators: why
     there are more of them than you think', News.com.au, 1 December 2016.

145 **The paper used a single statistic** Centers for Disease Control and
     Prevention, 'The National Intimate Partner and Sexual Violence Survey',
     page last reviewed 19 September 2018. cdc.gov/violenceprevention/
     datasources/nisvs/index.html

145 **[F]or male victims** American Centre for Disease Control, 'Prevalence
     and Characteristics of Sexual Violence, Stalking, and Intimate Partner
     Violence Victimization', 2014.

147 **America has a much higher** *Intentional homicides (per 100,000 people),*
     The World Bank, data.worldbank.org/indicator/vc.ihr.psrc.p5

148 **A 2015 study** Kelly Cue Davis, N. Tatiana Masters et al., 'How
     Childhood Maltreatment Profiles of Male Victims Predict Adult
     Perpetration and Psychosocial Functioning', *Journal of Interpersonal
     Violence,* vol. 33 issue 6, 2015, pp. 915–937.

149 **Researchers at the University of New South Wales** M. Plummer and
     A. Cossins, 'The Cycle of Abuse: When Victims Become Offenders'
     Trauma Violence Abuse, July 2018, vol. 19 issue 3, pp. 286–304.

150 **Dr Cordelia Fine's** Cordelia Fine, *Testosterone Rex: Myths of Sex, Science,
     and Society,* W.W. Norton & Co., New York, 2018.

151 **The rate of violence** Dr Michael Flood, phone interview with the
     author, October 2017.

152 **A 2018 study of the effect** Emily J. Cross, Nickola C. Overall, et al.,
     'An Interdependence Account of Sexism and Power: Men's Hostile
     Sexism, Biased Perceptions of Low Power, and Relationship Aggression',
     Journal of Personality and Social Psychology, 26 November 2018.

153 **The husband cannot** 'A Word For Men's Rights.' *Putnam's Monthly,*
     A Magazine of Literature, Science, and Art, vol. II, February 1856,
     no. XXXVIII, p. 208.

Chapter 8

157 **The feminist agenda** This statement was included in a fundraising
     letter sent out under Robertson's name to supporters of the Christian
     Coalition in 1992, seeking to rally opposition to a proposed Iowa state
     Equal Rights Amendment. It was reported by Associated Press on
     26 August 1992.

157 **The National Community Attitudes towards Violence against**
     Women Survey Summary report 'Are we there yet? Australians' attitudes
     towards violence against women & gender equality', ANROWS, 2017.

165 **A 2006 report by UNICEF** 'Behind Closed Doors: The Impact of
     Domestic Violence on Children', UNICEF, 2001.

165 **Unsurprisingly, studies have found there's also a strong** Kelly Cue
     Davis, N. Tatiana Masters, op. cit.

166 **For instance, the day** NSW Domestic Violence Death Review Team
     Report, 2015–2017, Sydney, 2017.

168 **A fascinating study** Diana Scully and Joseph Marolla, op. cit.

172 **She told** *The Courier-Mail* Thomas Chamberlin, 'Brisbane woman
     allegedly groped, handcuffed by Mitchell Peggie, convicted rapist',
     The Courier-Mail, 20 August 2016.

Chapter 9

176 **A 2017 study** D. Turgoose, N. Glover, et al., 'Empathy, compassion
     fatigue, and burnout in police officers working with rape victims'
     Traumatology, vol. 23 issue 2, 2007, pp. 205–213.

176 **A 2010 in-depth study** R. M. Venema, 'Police officer schema of sexual
     assault reports: Real rape, ambiguous cases, and false reports', *Journal of*
     Interpersonal Violence, vol. 31 issue 5, 2006, pp. 872–899.

178 **A 2016 study by Saint Xavier University** M. Alderden, L. Long, 'Sexual
     Assault Victim Participation in Police Investigations and Prosecution',
     Violence Vict., vol. 31 issue 5, 2016, pp. 819–836.

178 **In a UK study of 400 rapes** Genevieve F. Water House, Ali Reynolds,
     Vincent Egan, 'Myths and legends: The reality of rape offences reported
     to a UK police force', *The European Journal of Psychology Applied to Legal
     Context*, vol. 8 issue 1, 2016, pp. 1–10.

179 **An Australian study had similar findings** Dr Melanie Heenan and
     Suellen Murray, *Study of Reported Rapes in Victoria 2000–2003*, Statewide
     Steering Committee to Reduce Sexual Assault, 2006.

183 **Some studies show** A. L.-T. Choo, 0000-0002-4122-8963 and J.
     Hunter. (2018). 'Gender Discrimination and Juries in the 20th Century:
     Judging women judging men', *International Journal of Evidence and Proof*,
     vol. 22 issue 3, 2018, pp. 192–217.

183 **However, an Australian** Natalie Taylor and Jacqueline Joudo Larson,
     'The Impact of Pre-recorded Video and Closed Circuit Television
     Testimony by Adult Sexual Assault Complainants on Jury Decision-
     making: An experimental study', *Research and Public Policy Series
     No. 68*, Canberra, Australian Institute of Criminology, Canberra,
     2005.

184 **Our overarching finding** Sarah Zydervelt, Rachel Zajac, et al., 'Lawyers'
     Strategies For Cross-Examining Rape Complainants: Have we moved
     beyond the 1950s?', *The British Journal of Criminology*, vol. 57 issue 3,
     1 May 2017, pp. 551–569.

185 **The 'successful rape complainant'** Wendy Larcombe 'The "Ideal"
     Victim v Successful Rape Complainants: Not what you might expect',
     Feminist Legal Studies, vol. 10 issue 2, May 2002, pp. 131–148.

186 **Our findings do not** Rachel Zajac, Nina Westera and Andy Kaladelfos,
     'A Historical Comparison of Australian Lawyers' Strategies for
     Cross-examining Child Sexual Abuse Complainants', *Child Abuse &
     Neglect*, issue 72, October 2017, pp. 236–246.

187 **There are cases of** WA Hansard, Legislative Assembly, 14 October 1953,
     p. 1060 and 1061.

190 **One study of judges' sentences** Guy Hall, Marion Whittle and
     Courtney Field, 'Themes in Judges' Sentencing Remarks for Male and

Female Domestic Murderers', *Psychiatry, Psychology and Law*, vol. 23, 2016, issue 3, pp. 395–412.

191   **Research from Finland** Eileen Berrington and Päivi Honkatukia, 'An Evil Monster and a Poor Thing: Female Violence in the Media', *Journal of Scandinavian Studies in Criminology and Crime Prevention*, vol. 3 issue 1, 2002, pp. 50–72.

Chapter 10

196   **'NEVER MIND BREXIT** *The Daily Mail* front cover of print edition, 20 March 2007.

200   **Karen Middleton, long-time member** Karen Middleton, 'Sexual harassment in politics', *The Saturday Paper*, 15 October 2016.

202   **In late October 2017** Jill Lawless, 'U.K. politicians look to end "locker room" culture as fallout continues over "spreadsheet of shame"', The Associated Press, 2 November 2017.

202   **Researchers from the Trades Union Congress** Alice Ross, 'Half of women in UK have been sexually harassed at work, study finds', *The Guardian*, 10 August 2016.

203   **Research by the *Women in Media Center*** '#whotalks – Cable/news analysts & gender in 2016 presidential election project totals', Women's Media Center, 7 December 2016. womensmediacenter.com/reports/whotalks-cable-news-analysts-gender-in-2016-presidential-election-project-t

203   **As Annabel Crabb wrote** Annabel Crabb, 'Google "Scott Morrison" and "children" and "juggle". The result may surprise you', ABC News, 19 September 2018.

204   **As later Deputy Prime Minister** quoted in Annabel Crabb, *The Wife Drought*, [Kindle edition] Penguin Random House Australia, Sydney, 2015.

204   ***Time* magazine published** Jay Newton-Small 'The Pros and Cons of "President Grandma"', *Time* [online], 29 September 2014.

205   **'They are a touching** Patrick Carlyon and Owen Vaughan, 'THE AUDACITY OF GROPE: Julia and Barack's special relationship', News.com.au, 17 November 2011.

205   **If there was one thing** Peter Hartcher, 'We expected more of Gillard', *Sydney Morning Herald*, 10 October 2012.

206 **Throughout Gillard's prime ministership** See for example Denis
     Shanahan, 'The PM will rue yet another bad call', *The Australian*,
     10 October 2012.

206 **'Gladys Berejiklian is a nice person** Liz Burke, 'Alan Jones slams incoming
     NSW premier Gladys Berejiklian', News.com.au, 20 January 2017.

206 *The New York Times* **published** Jennifer Steinhauer, 'Elizabeth Warren
     endorses Clinton and goes taunt-for-taunt with Trump', 9 June 2016.

206 **MSNBC's Mika Brezinski** Matt Wilstein, 'Mika Brzezinski Turns
     on Elizabeth Warren: "I'm Getting Tired of This Act"', *Daily Beast*,
     29 November 2016.

207 *The Telegraph,* **in one of** Lucy Denyer, 'Who should be the next PM?
     Theresa May gets my vote', *The Telegraph*, 28 June 2016.

208 **One of the leading** anon., 'Prime Minister Julia Gillard's ears distract
     from federal election campaign', *The Daily Telegraph*, 27 July 2010.

209 **Before even stepping** Alice Cuffe, 'Theresa May's shoes are almost as
     important to her power as her politics', *International Business Times*,
     12 July 2016.

209 **'As David Cameron took** Charlie Teather, 'Theresa May's most
     memorable looks from parliament's most talked about shoe closet as she
     heads to 10 Downing Street', *The Evening Standard*, 13 July 2016.

209 **Mrs May is known** BBC News, 'Theresa May: Seven notable things
     about the UK's next prime minister', BBC, 12 July 2016.

209 **If I want to knock** Annie Karni, 'Hillary's hair: She's in on the joke',
     Politico, 28 May 2015.

210 **Matt Lauer was widely criticised** Laura Cohn, 'Why the internet is
     outraged about Matt Lauer's interview with Hillary Clinton', *Fortune*,
     8 September 2016.

211 **Leon Wieseltier, former editor** Maureen Dowd, 'The Nepotism Tango',
     The New York Times, 30 September 2007.

Chapter 11

214 'Real equality is when Amanda Vanstone on Paula Matthewson, *On
     Merit*, Melbourne University Press, Melbourne, 2019 (cover endorsement).

216 **'did bring to cabinet** Jenny Macklin, 'The panel: why is there only one
     woman in Tony Abbott's cabinet?', *The Guardian*, 16 September 2013.

217 **'Engagement is a key factor** Carol Potter, *Women Trust Less*, Edelman, 21 January 2019. edelman.com/research/women-trust-less

218 **The Museum of Australian Democracy** Gerry Stoker, Mark Evans and Max Halupka, 'Trust and democracy in Australia', *The Museum of Australian Democracy*, December 2018.

219 **Compare this to** *Global Terrorism Database*, start.umd.edu/gtd/search/ Results.aspx?chart=country&search=australia.

220 **'It is a** phone interview with the author, May 2016.

221 **Dr Judy Rose of Griffith University** Dr Judy Rose, '"Never enough hours in the day": Employed mothers' perceptions of time pressure', *Australian Journal of Social Issues*, vol. 52 issue 2, June 2017, pp. 116–130.

Chapter 12

226 **Your face is lined** Helen Garner, 'The Insults of Age', *The Monthly*, May 2015.

227 **I started to feel** Lacey Rose, 'Julia Louis-Dreyfus reveals awkward fan letter from Hillary and her panic on that "Last F— Day"', *Hollywood Reporter*, 20 April 2016.

230 **All the guys [were]** Lisa Annese, Positions of Strength speech, Soapbox event, 3 November 2015. Attended and recorded by the author.

231 **'All that anyone cared** Brennan Kilbane, 'The importance of challenging mainstream beauty standards, *Allure*, 12 February 2019.

233 **A Western Michigan University study** Brooke S. O'Neil, 'Approved for All Audiences: A Longitudinal Content Analysis of the Portrayal of Women in Movie Trailers', unpublished master's thesis, Western Michigan University, August 2016. scholarworks.wmich.edu/masters_theses/715/

234 **Research published in 2018** Erin Lyons, 'Sexism, price deflation, social media spend: 5 killer stats to start your week', *Marketing Week*, 3 September 2018.

235 **A 2016 survey** 'Data on sexism in advertising in the United States as of July 2016', *Statista*, 2019. statista.com/statistics/628166/ sexism-advertising-usa/

235 **A study published by the Geena Davis** 'Unpacking Gender Bias in

Advertising', J. Walter Thompson Worldwide, 21 June 2017. jwt.com/en/news/unpacking-gender-bias-in-advertising

235 **As author Terry Pratchett** Terry Pratchett, *Good Omens: The Nice and Accurate Prophecies of Agnes Nutter, Witch*, Transworld Publishers Ltd, London, 2010.

235 **In Australia** by 2018 this increased to 3 per cent; CEO heads of business increased to 30 per cent and key management personnel rose to 33 per cent. WGEA Data Explorer, Advertising Services. data.wgea.gov.au/industries/43#governing_bodies_content

236 **According to CBS News** 'More than 12M "Me Too" Facebook posts, comments, reactions in 24 hours', *CBS News*, 17 October 17 2017.

236 **Burke told *The New York Times*** Sandra E. Garcia, 'The woman who created #MeToo long before hashtags', *The New York Times*, 20 October 2017.

237 **A survey conducted for *The Economist*** 'Measuring the #MeToo backlash', *The Economist*, 20 October 2018.

237 **'Men are borrowing** Jia Tolentino, 'One year of #MeToo: what women's speech is still not allowed to do, *The New Yorker*, 10 October 2018.

238 **A year after the #MeToo tweet** Audrey Carlsen, Maya Salam, et al., '#MeToo Brought Down 201 Powerful Men. Nearly Half of Their Replacements Are Women', *The New York Times*, 29 October 2018.

Chapter 13

242 **Richard Keys: Somebody better get down** 'Football pundits caught ridiculing female linesman on air, *Sydney Morning Herald*, 24 January 2011.

243 **The *Herald Sun* didn't include** Leo Schink, 'Only tears of joy this time for Osaka', *Herald Sun*, 26 January 2019.

244 **More than 90 per cent** Women in Media, *Mates Over Merit: The Women in Media Report*, 2017. meaa.org/download/mates-over-merit-full-report/

244 **The United Nations Educations Scientific and Cultural Organisation** 'UNESCO calls for fairer media coverage of sportswomen', UNESCO, 8 February 2018. en.unesco.org/news/unesco-calls-fairer-media-coverage-sportswomen

244 **Dozens of research studies** Jeffery Sobal and Michelle Milgrim, 'Gendertyping Sports: Social representations of masculine, feminine,

and neither-gendered sports among US university students', *Journal of Gender Studies*, vol. 28 issue 1, 2019. 29–44; Mélissa Plaza, Julie Boiché, et al., 'Sport = Male . . . But Not All Sports: Investigating the gender stereotypes of sport activities at the explicit and implicit levels', *Sex Roles*, February 2017, vol. 76 issue 3–4, pp. 202–217; François Ruchaud, Aïna Chalabaev and Paul Fontayne, 'Social Judgment, Sport and Gender: A cognitive asymmetry?', *Movement & Sport Sciences* 2017, pp. 43–50; John K. Gotwals and April K. Hadley, 'Explaining Sport-based Moral Behaviour Among Adolescent Athletes: The interactive roles of perfectionism and gender', *Sport Psychology*, vol. 49 no. 1, 2017.

244 **A German study in 2017** Mara Konjer, Michael Mutz and Henk Erik Meier, 'Talent Alone Does Not Suffice: Erotic capital, media visibility and global popularity among professional male and female tennis players', *Journal of Gender Studies*, vol. 28 issue 1, 2019, pp. 3–17.

244 **A powerful photo** Simone Fox Koob, 'Footy star Tayla Harris calls for change after photo removed due to "derogatory" comments', *The Age*, 20 March 2019.

245 **Adam Goodes said he was 'gutted'** Adrian Crawford, 'Adam Goodes "gutted" by racial slur but wants AFL fan educated', ABC News, 27 May 2013.

245 **Nicky Winmar took an iconic** Al Paton 'Nicky Winmar remembers the day he lifted his jumper and pointed to the colour of his skin', News.com.au, 18 April 2013.

245 **Deb Waterhouse-Watson's book** Deb Waterhouse-Watson, *Athletes, Sexual Assault, and 'Trials by Media' Narrative immunity*, New York, Routledge, 2013.

247 **Damien Foster's op ed** Damian Foster, 'When an elite footballer has sex with a girl . . .', *The Age*, 12 March 2004.

247 **As St Kilda coach Grant Thomas** AAP, 'Saints close ranks on rape probe', *The Age*, 18 March 2004.

248 **Despite the arguments** Jessica Halloran 'Time for codes to unite in protecting women', *The Daily Telegraph*, 23 November 2018.

248 **After four players** 'Greenberg's Warning For Nrl Ban Boys', *The Daily Telegraph*, January 2019.

249 **Worse is the fact** 'Ex-AFL footballer Aaron James allegedly caught with ice in Wangaratta', *The Newcastle Herald*, 3 July 2017.

Chapter 14
253 **I think every woman** 'Interview: Helen Mirren, actress', *The Scotsman*, 6 March 2011.
255 **In 2016 the Australian Press Council** 'New Advisory Guideline on Family And Domestic Violence Reporting', Australian Press Council, 2 March 2016. presscouncil.org.au/media-release-2-march-2016/
255 **Its purpose is** Our Watch, 'Purpose', ourwatch.org.au/Who-We-Are/Our-Purpose
255 **In March 2019** 'Media Resources', Our Watch, ourwatch.org.au/News-media/Reporting-Guidelines
256 **In April 2019 the two** Charlotte Tobitt, 'UK press regulators back feminist group's new guidelines on reporting domestic violence deaths', *Press Gazette*, 16 April 2019.
256 **Similar resources and guidelines** NZ: Reporting Domestic/ Family Violence Guidelines For Journalists, AreYouOK.org.nz; Canada: Resources for Journalists, The Media Hub, https://vaw-mediahub.ca; UN: *UN Women Eastern and Southern Africa Publications Reader Survey Report*, UN Women, 2016, unwomen.org/en/digital-library/publications/2016/10/un-women-eastern-and-southern-africa-publications-reader-survey-report; *WHO: Violence against women*, World Health Organization, 29 November 2017. who.int/news-room/fact-sheets/detail/violence-against-women
257 **If they did respond** Robert Ovadia, 'Margaret River Shootings: Outrage brigade should accept facts as they are', *The West Australian*, 16 May 2018.
257 **ABC's *Media Watch* ran** 'Reporting on murder suicides', *Media Watch*, 21 May 2018.
258 ***The Daily Telegraph*'s front page** Christopher Dore, '"Coward": Coward who killed his children', *The Daily Telegraph*, Christopher Dore, July 7 2018.
259 **Harsh Narde murdered Preethi Reddy** 'Preethi Reddy murder suspect's family wanted to find him an arranged marriage, friend says', ABC News, 10 March 2019.

Acknowledgements

I would never have been able to even start writing this book, let alone finish it, if not for Margaret Simons. You taught me how to see the big picture, have faith in my ability to write and stop overusing commas. Thank you more than I can ever put into words.

Mum, I don't know how to even start to thank you. You dug me out of a hole of my own making too many times and even when you had to watch in frustration and bewilderment as I too often immediately set about digging myself into another one, you never gave up on me. You taught me to read, to think, to argue and to always believe I was good enough and strong enough to find my way. Looks like you were right again.

Lizzi and Adie, the merry clink of bottles and the roars of laughter that kept me sane through all of this will always remind me of you. Thank you and I'm still sorry about the Veuve.

Thank you so much to all the people who subscribed to Fixed It on Patreon. There were many times when that was the only way I was able to pay my rent or buy food. Fixed It was never about money but it did require a lot of time that I wouldn't have had to give without the Patreon subscribers.

Speaking of subscribers, Paddy, one of the first subscribers to *The King's Tribune* from nearly ten years ago, you are still one of my most steadfast supporters and I hope you know how grateful I am. Especially on my birthdays!

Clem, you have been unstinting in your support for my work and I'll never forget that you helped me get my start in mainstream media. You always figured that all I needed was the introduction and I could take it from there. I wasn't so sure about it, but it turned out that you were right. I hope I can do as much for other writers as you've done for me.

Nina, all those hours on the phone talking about our work, our lives and how we manage (and sometimes don't manage) to keep them together. You are always a welcome voice and a wonderful sounding board. Thank you for trusting me with your story.

The online community of women and writers were such a source of strength and encouragement. Sometimes I didn't even need to reach out directly, just watching the conversations scroll by and seeing the strength women can give each other was enough.

The Elwood crew, who are always up for a good time. You are the epitome of 'ladylike is a bullshit term' and I love you for it. Jo, Leeroy, Kristi, Erin, Ana, Di, Bron, Fi, Alex, Pol, Scotty, Janine, Alida, Elissa, Jess, Brendan, Dave, Phil, Greg, Clayton, Ian and everyone else, sláinte to you all!

All the editors at *Daily Life* who had faith in feminist writing and relentlessly pushed back against the idea that it was niche or likely to upset regular subscribers. Thank you for correcting my typos, chasing my deadlines and giving so many of us a place to write and read about the many topics the rest of the mainstream media ignored.

Jacinta and Danielle, you believed in the book before it was a book and I don't know what I would have done without your help to guide me through all the overwhelming decisions a writer has to make that have nothing to do with writing. I was completely unprepared for that and I'd have been lost without you.

Everyone at Penguin Random House who was so lovely and so patient with all the work it took to take a mess of thoughts and turn it into this book, thank you.

After a year of researching, taking notes, three bags of paper scraps covered in illegible scrawl, a mountain of books and research papers, I wrote more than three quarters of this book in a single month (January 2019) when Marguerite and David Shaw allowed me to hire their beach house for a month. I fled my hot, dirty, cramped flat, leaving behind hot, dirty, cramped teenagers, and spent the entire four weeks writing, walking, swimming and sleeping. I wrote 80 000 words that month and I think it was the healthiest and most relaxed I have felt in the last twenty years. Thank you.

To all the survivors who have so bravely shared their stories, I am in awe of your strength, all the more so when you don't see it yourselves. I hope you all understand when I say I wish you had never had to talk to me. More than anyone, this book is for you.